World Book
Discovery Science Encyclopedia

Plants

WORLD
BOOK

a Scott Fetzer company
Chicago
www.worldbook.com

For information about other World Book publications, visit our
website at www.worldbook.com or call
1-800-WORLDBK (967-5325).

For information about sales to schools and libraries, call
1-800-975-3250 (United States); **1-800-837-5365** (Canada).

World Book, Inc.
233 N. Michigan Ave.
Chicago, IL 60601
U.S.A.

Library of Congress Cataloging-in-Publication Data

Encyclopedia of plants.
    p. cm. -- (World Book discovery science encyclopedia)
    Includes index.
    Summary: "An exploration of plants of the world, including such information as
how they grow, their varieties, and their uses. Features include drawings, diagrams,
photographs, and activities"--Provided by publisher.
    ISBN 978-0-7166-7522-8
    1. Botany--Encyclopedias, Juvenile. 2. Plants--Encyclopedias, Juvenile. I. World
Book, Inc. II. Series: World Book discovery science encyclopedia.
    QK49.E53 2013
    580.3--dc23
                                        2012049899
Printed in China by Shenzhen Donnelley
Printing Co., Ltd., Guangdong Province
1st printing July 2013

Front Cover:
© David Norton, Alamy Images; © Shutterstock;
© Florea Paul, Alamy Images; © David
Grossman, Alamy Images

Back Cover:
© Shutterstock; © Shutterstock; © Shutterstock

Staff

Executive Committee

President
Donald D. Keller

**Vice President and Editor
in Chief**
Paul A. Kobasa

**Vice President, Sales and
Marketing**
Sean Lockwood

Vice President, International
Richard Flower

Controller
Anthony Doyle

Director, Human Resources
Bev Ecker

Editorial

**Associate Director,
Annuals and Topical Reference**
Scott Thomas

**Managing Editor,
Annuals and Topical Reference**
Barbara A. Mayes

**Manager, Sciences,
World Book Encyclopedia**
Jeff De La Rosa

**Senior Editor,
Annuals and Topical Reference**
Christine Sullivan

Staff Editors
Michael DuRoss
Daniel Kenis
Nick Kilzer

Senior Researcher
Mike Barr

**Manager, Contracts
& Compliance
(Rights & Permissions)**
Loranne K. Shields

Manager, Indexing Services
David Pofelski

Administrative Assistant
Ethel Matthews

Editorial Administration

Director, Systems and Projects
Tony Tills

**Senior Manager, Publishing
Operations**
Timothy Falk

**Associate Manager, Publishing
Operations**
Audrey Casey

Graphics and Design

Senior Manager
Tom Evans

**Coordinator, Design Development
and Production**
Brenda B. Tropinski

Senior Designers
Matt Carrington
Don Di Sante
Isaiah Sheppard

Contributing Designer
Lucy Lesiak

Media Researcher
Jeff Heimsath

Contributing Photographs Editor
Carol Parden

Manager, Cartography
Wayne K. Pichler

Senior Cartographer
John M. Rejba

Production

**Director, Manufacturing
and Pre-Press**
Carma Fazio

Manufacturing Manager
Barbara Podczerwinski

Production/Technology Manager
Anne Fritzinger

Senior Production Manager
Jan Rossing

Production Specialist
Curley Hunter

Proofreader
Emilie Schrage

How to use World Book Discovery Science Encyclopedia

http://bit.ly/13kOpzd

- Hundreds of illustrations
- Guide words
- Phonetic spellings
- Related article lists
- Experiments and activities
- QR codes

World Book Discovery Science Encyclopedia is filled with information about basic science concepts, tools, and discoveries as well as the world around us. Entries on people who have made important contributions to science are included, too. All entries are written in a way that makes them easy to understand.

Finding entries is easy, too. They are arranged in alphabetical order. There is also an index in each volume. The index lists all the entries, as well as topics that are covered in the volume but that are not themselves entries.

Science experiments and activities are also included in this volume. These and the many other features of *World Book Discovery Science Encyclopedia* make it an encyclopedia that you can use for research as well as reading just for fun.

Easy alphabetical access
Each letter of the alphabet is highlighted to help you locate entries alphabetically.

Ss

Safflower

Safflower *(SAF LOW uhr)* is a plant grown to make oil. The oil comes from its seeds. Most safflower plants have yellow or orange flowers and spiny leaves. Some safflower plants have red or white flowers.

Safflower plants are grown in warm, dry regions. These regions include Australia, India, Mexico, Spain, and the southwestern United States.

Safflower seed oil is popular with health-conscious consumers because it contains low levels of saturated fats, which have been linked to heart disease. Safflower oil also contains high levels of essential fatty acids, which are necessary for good nutrition. The oil is used in cooking and in salad oils, margarine, mayonnaise, and shortening. Safflower oil is also used in paints and varnishes.

Other articles to read include: **Flower; Oil; Seed.**

The safflower has large blossoms and thistlelike leaves and stems. Safflower seeds are used in making nutritious oil and *meal* (ground-up grain).

Saffron

Saffron *(SAF ruhn)* is a valuable spice that is also used as a yellow dye. Saffron comes from the female parts of a flower called the saffron crocus. People must collect these saffron threads by hand. About 60,000 flowers yield only 1 pound (0.45 kilogram) of saffron. Saffron is prized as a food seasoning. It has a sweet odor but tastes bitter. It also is used to color foods and fabrics.

Other articles to read include: **Crocus; Spice.**

Saffron is a valuable spice that comes from the female parts of a flower called the saffron crocus.

Sage

Sage is the name of a large number of herbs and shrubs. One member of this group, called the common sage, is an important herb used for seasoning. The common sage has a strong odor. Its leaves and stems have a bitter taste. Cooks use the leaves to season cheeses, dressings for meat, sauces, and sausages. The leaves are also brewed to make tea. The common sage also may be called garden sage.

The common sage has white, woolly stems. The stems reach 2 feet (61 centimeters) tall. The grayish-green leaves have a rough, pebbled texture. The flowers grow in circular clusters at the tips of the stems. The flowers may be violet-blue, pink, or white. The common sage grows wild in areas around the Mediterranean Sea. It is now raised in many other areas.

Other articles to read include: **Herb; Shrub; Spice; Tea.**

Sage

Sagebrush

Sagebrush is a shrub of the western United States. It grows well in dry soil. Much sagebrush grows in northeastern California, eastern Oregon, Nevada, Utah, Wyoming, and Colorado.

Sagebrush can grow from 2 to 12 feet (0.6 to 3.7 meters) in height. It has a tall, straight stem and small leaves. The leaves grow close together. The plant has tiny yellow or white flowers.

Summer heat and dryness can dry up sagebrush. The plant may look dead. The wind can pull up the plant and blow it around. This is how the seeds are scattered.

Other articles to read include: **Desert; Shrub.**

Sagebrush

Pronunciations
The phonetic spelling for unusual or unfamiliar words is given. A key to the pronunciation is in the front of each volume.

Illustrations
Each volume of *Discovery Science Encyclopedia* contains hundreds of photographs, drawings, maps, and other illustrations. Each illustration is labeled or explained in a caption.

Related references
The references listed at the bottom of many articles tell you which other articles to read to find out more or related information.

Guide words
Guide words at the top of a page help you quickly find the entry you are seeking.

Experiments
Many experiments are found in *Discovery Science Encyclopedia*. These experiments extend or enrich the subject of the article they accompany and are suitable for use at home or in the classroom.

Activities
Many activities are found in *Discovery Science Encyclopedia*. These simple activities, which can be done at home or in the classroom, extend or enrich the subject of the article they accompany.

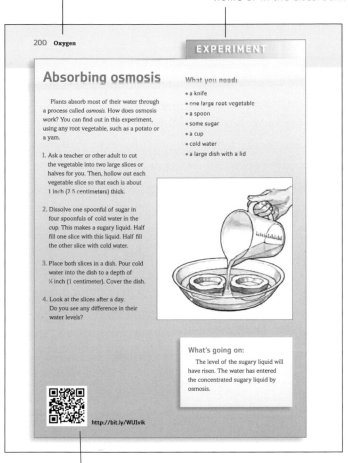

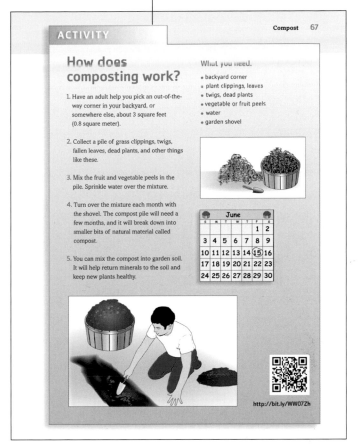

QR codes
This symbol is a QR code. You can find QR codes on all the pages with experiments and activities in the *World Book Discovery Science Encyclopedia*. Simply scan a code with your smartphone or tablet to see a video about the experiment or activity or related information about the subject of the project. (You will need to download a QR code reader to your device if you have not already done so.) If you do not have a mobile device, you can still access the videos linked to experiments and activities by keying in the URL beneath each QR code into a browser on your computer.

You can also find a QR code on the opposite page. This code links to a video explaining how to use the *World Book Discovery Science Encyclopedia*.

A library of the all videos and related information included in the *World Book Discovery Science Encyclopedia* can be found at **http://www.worldbook.com/all/item/1876.**

Key to pronunciation

World Book Discovery Science Encyclopedia provides the pronunciations for many unusual or unfamiliar words. In the pronunciation, the words are divided into syllables and respelled according to the way each syllable sounds. The syllables appear in *italic letters*. For example, here are an article title and the respelled pronunciation for it:

Absorption *(ab SAWRP shuhn)*

The syllable or syllables that get the greatest emphasis when the word is spoken are in capital letters *(SAWRP).*

Adaptation

An adaptation is a feature that helps a living thing to survive. Plants have a variety of adaptations. Many adaptations enable a plant to survive in a particular type of place. For example, cactuses have waxy skin that holds in water. This adaptation helps cactuses to survive in deserts, where water is scarce. The adaptation also gives cactuses an advantage over other plants that try to live in deserts. As a result, cactuses are more common than other plants in many deserts.

Some plants have adaptations that help them to take in more sunlight. Plants use sunlight to make their own food. Trees that can grow tall can take in more sunlight. This adaptation enables them to make more food. It also blocks sunlight from reaching the ground. That is why forests usually have many trees but relatively few plants low to the ground.

Many adaptations help plants to *reproduce* (make a new plant). For example, flowering plants use flowers to attract insects or other animals. The insects feed on a sugary liquid in the flower, called *nectar.* As the insects feed, they become covered in tiny grains called *pollen.* The insects carry the pollen to the next flower. There, the pollen combines with another part of the plant to produce seeds.

Flowering plants also produce fruit. The fruit contains seeds. An animal that eats the fruit carries the seeds in its gut. The animal later passes the seeds with its droppings. That action spreads the plant's seeds to new places. These adaptations have given flowering plants advantages over other plants. As a result, flowering plants are by far the most common type of plant.

Other articles to read include:
Environment; Evolution; Extinction; Natural selection.

The African butterfly has "eyespots" on its wings that startle birds who might try to eat the butterfly. The "eyespots" are an adaptation that helps the butterfly avoid becoming a bird's prey.

The prickly pear can go a long time with little water. This adapatation helps it to survive in the desert.

The woodpecker's chisel-like bill is adapted for drilling into trees to pull out insects.

Agriculture

Agriculture *(AG ruh KUHL chuhr)* is the act of farming. Farmers around the world grow plants or animals to make food, clothing, or other useful things.

The plants that farmers grow are called *crops*. Farmers grow many crops for people to eat. For example, farmers raise wheat and rice. People may eat rice simply by cooking it. Most wheat is used to make bread. Many crops are used to feed animals. For example, much of the corn that farmers raise is fed to cattle and other animals. People then eat the animals.

Farmers also raise crops for other uses. They grow cotton that is turned into fabric. Some of the crops that farmers grow are turned into fuel.

Agriculture first developed more than 10,000 years ago in the Middle East.

Continued on the next page

In modern agriculture, heavy machinery is used to plant and harvest crops, and chemicals are used to fertilize and discourage damaging insects.

For example, much of the sugar cane grown in Brazil is turned into fuel for cars and trucks. Such crops as soybeans may be used in making soap, paint, varnish, and other goods.

Many farmers use such modern machines as powerful tractors and plows. They plant special seeds that grow stronger crops. Many farmers also use such chemicals as *fertilizers* and *pesticides (PEHS tuh sydz)*. Fertilizers help crops grow. Pesticides kill insects and other things that hurt crops. Some farmers do not use artificial fertilizers and pesticides. They use only natural methods to grow crops. The foods they produce are called *organic foods*.

Agriculture began more than 10,000 years ago. Scientists think people first began farming in the Middle East. But people developed agriculture independently in several other areas, including eastern Asia and Central and South America. Before there was agriculture, most people moved from place to place searching for food. Farming enabled people to stay in one place. Eventually, farming communities gave rise to the world's first cities. Civilization could not survive without agriculture.

Other articles to read include: **Agronomy; Botany; Carver, George Washington; Crop; Fertilizer; Horticulture; Pest control; Topsoil;** *and those on individual crops.*

Agronomy

Agronomy is the science of growing crops. Scientists who study agronomy work to improve crops. They study the things plants need to grow and to remain healthy. Scientists who study agronomy are called *agronomists*.

Agronomists work to improve the use of soil. They try to prevent soil from being lost to wind and water. They also study methods to water crops wisely. These methods reduce the amount of water that is wasted.

Many agronomists work to create new crops. Such crops may grow better or produce more food. Other agronomists study ways to keep plants safe from disease. Most agronomists work as teachers or as scientists. They work for governments, universities, and businesses.

Other articles to read include: **Agriculture: Botany; Crop; Horticulture.**

An agronomist evaluates a field of sunflowers in the midwestern United States. Agronomists are scientists who work to improve crops. Protein-rich sunflower seeds are used in make margarine and cooking oil.

Alfalfa is grown chiefly for livestock feed. It is often dried and baled as hay.

Alfalfa

Alfalfa is a valuable crop. It is grown mainly for livestock feed. Farmers also grow alfalfa to provide pasture or for its seeds. In addition, they grow alfalfa to enrich and preserve the soil. Alfalfa is also known as *lucerne*. Important alfalfa-growing regions include North and South America, Australia, eastern Asia, parts of Europe, the Middle East, and South Africa.

The alfalfa plant bears seed pods. Each pod has four to eight seeds. The plant has many slender stems that grow about 3 feet (0.9 meter) high. The stems bear leaves with more than one blade. Each leaf has three blades. New stems grow from buds on the plant's woody base, which is between the stems and the roots. Flowers grow on the stems in clusters.

Most alfalfa roots grow in the upper 1 foot (0.3 meter) of soil. But some roots may extend as deep as 15 feet (4.6 meters) or more. These roots can get water that lies far underground. For this reason, alfalfa can resist *drought* (long periods of dry weather) better than many other crops can. Alfalfa has been farmed since prehistoric times. It was probably first grown in the Middle East.

Other articles to read include: **Agriculture; Crop.**

Algae

Algae *(AL jee)* is a type of living thing that makes its own food using sunlight. Algae are found in oceans, lakes, rivers, ponds, and wet soil. A single living thing of this kind is called an alga *(AL guh)*.

Some algae can be seen only through a microscope. These algae are made up of just one *cell*. A cell is the smallest unit of any living thing. Other algae are large and made up of many cells. Some kinds of algae float or swim in water. Others are connected to stones or weeds. Large water algae are called *seaweeds*.

Algae are important for many reasons. They can help to clean

Continued on the next page

the air and water. They give off oxygen, which animals need to breathe. Algae also serve as food for many animals that live in the water.

Most scientists divide algae into three groups, by color. The three groups are *brown algae, green algae, and red algae.* Another group that is sometimes called algae are blue-green in color. But blue-green algae are actually a type of bacteria.

Brown algae can be seen along many seashores. Kelp is a kind of brown algae.

Green algae live in both fresh and salt water. Most kinds of green algae are too small to be seen without a microscope.

Red algae are found mostly in warm seas, where they sometimes grow with corals. People use a kind of red algae to make rolls of sushi.

Other articles to read include: **Chlorophyll; Kelp; Plankton; Protist; Seaweed.**

All three groups of algae include some forms of seaweed.

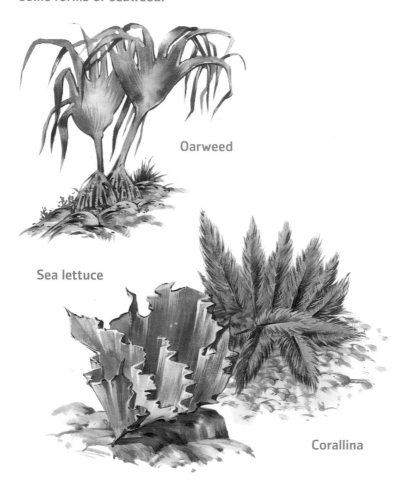

Oarweed

Sea lettuce

Corallina

Kelp is a kind of brown algae.

Almond

Almond trees produce seeds that grow in a thin shell covered in a leathery hull. The trees are grown for these seeds, which are delicious nuts.

The almond *(AHL muhnd)* is a delicious nut. The nut is a seed of the almond tree. Almonds are a popular food. They are usually toasted and salted. Almonds also are added to candies and pastries.

The nut grows in a thin shell. The shell looks somewhat like a peach stone. A green, leathery hull covers the shell. The hull splits open when the almond is ripe.

The almond tree may grow 40 feet (12 meters) high. It has long, pointed leaves that curl. The tree produces showy pink blossoms. The blossoms open early in spring, long before the leaves appear.

The almond tree is native to southwestern Asia. It is widely grown in countries around the Mediterranean Sea. The tree also grows well in California.

Other articles to read include: **Nut.**

Aloe

Aloe *(AL oh)* is a type of fleshy-leaved plant. There are many kinds of aloe. These plants are native to the Middle East, Madagascar, and southern Africa. They are often grown in regions with warm climates.

Aloe plants range in height from a few inches or centimeters to 30 feet (9 meters) or more. The leaves of many kinds become very large. They are sharp-pointed and have jagged edges that end in sharp hooks. The leaves usually grow directly from the ground. They grow in a large, rose-shaped pattern. A flowering stalk ends in a cluster of yellow or reddish tube-shaped flowers.

Aloe vera is a common houseplant. Farmers also raise large quantities of this plant. Aloe vera is also called the *Barbados aloe.* Its leaves contain a bitter juice. Manufacturers heat the juice at low temperatures to produce a powder and a gel. Aloe gel is used to make skin creams, shampoos, suntan lotions, and other products. Research has shown that aloe gel is effective in treating burns and frostbite.

Certain African kinds of aloe have strong fibers in their leaves. These fibers are used to make rope, fishing nets, and cloth. Others have a finer fiber that is used to make lace. Some aloes are used to make violet dye.

Aloe plant

Amazon rain forest

The Amazon rain forest is a tropical rain forest in South America. A tropical rain forest is a type of forest in a part of the world where it is always warm. In a tropical rain forest, it rains nearly every day. The trees in a tropical rain forest are green all year.

The Amazon rain forest is the world's largest tropical rain forest. It covers about 2 million

Continued on the next page

The Amazon rain forest is named for the Amazon River, which flows through it. The forest conains a wider variety of plant life than any other place on Earth.

The Amazon rain forest covers much of northern South America. About two-thirds of the rain forest lies in Brazil. The rain forest also extends into parts of several other countries.

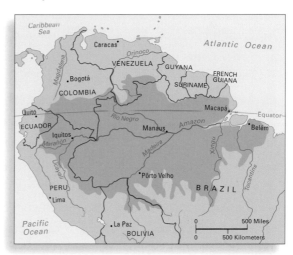

Amazon rain forest *Continued from the previous page*

square miles (5.2 million square kilometers). It is more than seven times as big as Texas.

About two-thirds of the Amazon rain forest is in Brazil. The rest is in eight other countries. The Amazon River flows through the rain forest. There are other rivers in the Amazon rain forest as well.

The Amazon rain forest has many different kinds of plants. Tens of thousands of different kinds of trees and other plants grow there. The tallest trees are more than 165 feet (50 meters) high—or as tall as a 14-story building. Nuts, cocoa, rubber, and other useful products come from the plants.

Colorful poison dart frogs live in many parts of the Amazon rain forest.

The Amazon rain forest also has many kinds of animals. More than 1,000 kinds of birds make their home in the rain forest. Thousands of kinds of fish swim in the rain forest's rivers. There may be millions of kinds of insects there.

The Amazon rain forest is in danger. People are cutting down the trees. They are farming and raising cattle on the cleared land. Many people are working to protect the Amazon rain forest.

Other articles to read include: **Endangered species; Rain forest.**

The squirrel monkey (below) is a small monkey that is native to the Amazon rain forest, which is home to thousands of kinds of animals. Large parts of the Amazon rain forest is subject to seasonal flooding (right).

Amber

Amber is a hard, yellow material. It looks like a yellowish-brown stone. Polished amber lets light pass through like colored glass. Amber is a kind of fossil. It came from trees that died millions of years ago. The trees produced a sticky liquid called resin *(REHZ uhn)*. The dead trees were buried underground or underwater. Resin in the trees slowly hardened into amber.

Many lumps of amber hold the remains of spiders, insects, or other animals. These animals got stuck in the resin. They may be preserved in excellent condition. Scientists study them to learn about prehistoric life.

Most amber comes from northern Europe and Central America. Workers mine amber from a kind of soil called *blue earth*. People use amber to make beads and jewelry.

Other articles to read include: **Resin.**

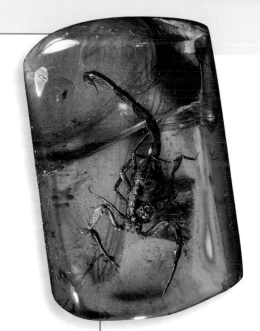

A piece of amber contains the preserved body of an ancient scorpion. Amber often holds bodies of insects and other animals that became stuck in the resin before it hardened.

Anemone

The anemone *(uh NEHM uh nee)* is a type of flower. There are dozens of kinds of anemones. Many grow wild in woodlands and prairies in northern areas with cold winters and warm summers. Anemones bloom in the spring.

The name *anemone* comes from the Greek word for *wind*. Anemones are also called *windflowers*.

One of the best-known anemones is the *wood anemone*. It is a delicate flower about 6 inches (15 centimeters) tall with white blossoms. Other anemones are taller and have blossoms that are pink, purple, or blue.

Other articles to read include: **Flower.**

Anemones grow in woodlands and prairies in northern regions with cold winters and warm summers.

Angiosperm

The flower and fruit of an angiosperm contain the plant's seeds. The flower and fruit of an apple tree are shown here.

Flower

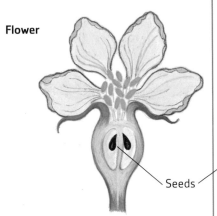

Seeds

Fruit

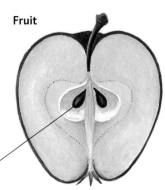

Angiosperms *(AN jee uh sperms)* are plants that produce flowers. Angiosperms are by far the most common kinds of plants on Earth. There are hundreds of thousands of kinds of angiosperms. Most of the plants that grow in meadows and deserts are angiosperms, including grasses and cactuses. So are all *broadleaf trees* (trees with wide, flat leaves) and crop plants.

Angiosperms first appeared more than 130 million years ago.

Angiosperms use flowers to reproduce. The flowers contain both male and female parts. The male parts produce tiny grains of *pollen*. Insects or the wind carries pollen to the female part of another flower to make a seed. The female part then develops into a fruit or a nut. The seed can grow into a new plant.

Other articles to read include: **Flower; Fruit; Pollen; Seed.**

Annuals grow and die in just one season. ▼

Spring

Summer

Autumn

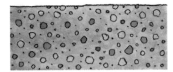

Winter

Annual

An annual is a plant that lives no longer than one year. In that time, it sprouts from a seed, blossoms, produces seeds, and then dies. The time from its sprouting until its death is called the annual's *growing season*.

Petunias, zinnias, and many other garden flowers are annuals. Their seeds must be replanted every year. Many vegetables, weeds, and wild grasses are also annuals. Peas, pumpkins, beans, and squash are examples of annual vegetable plants.

Continued on the next page

Other kinds of plants live longer than annuals. Plants called *biennials* live for two growing seasons. Other plants can keep growing for years. These plants are called *perennials*. Trees, shrubs, and some vines are perennials.

Other articles to read include: **Biennial; Flower; Perennial.**

Many popular summer flowers are annuals, which must be replanted each spring.

Morning-glory   Petunia

Zinnia

Apple

Apples are among the most important fruits that grow on trees. Apples are eaten raw or are cooked. Apples may be baked into pies and other desserts. They can be used to make apple butter, apple juice, apple sauce, jelly, and other products.

There are many varieties of apples. Their color ranges from red to green to yellow. Some apples are *tart* (slightly sour). Tart apples include the Bramley and Rome Beauty *varieties* (kinds). Many apples are sweet. Sweet apples include the Delicious and Gala varieties.

Apples are grown in many places around the world, primarily in places where the winters are not extremely cold.

Continued on the next page

Apples grow on trees and ripen in the late summer or early fall.

There are many *varieties* (kinds) of apples. They differ widely in color, flavor, shape, size, and texture.

Apples *Continued from the previous page*

Delicious

Golden Delicious

Granny Smith

McIntosh

Cortland

Jonathan

The Chinese grow the most apples. They are also grown widely in Italy, Poland, Turkey, and the United States.

Other articles to read include: **Crop; Fruit; Tree.**

People grow artichokes for their flower buds. Parts of the petals are eaten as well as the center, called the heart. ▼

Artichoke

An artichoke is a nutritious vegetable. People eat the flower buds of artichokes. The centers of the buds are called *hearts*. One *variety* (kind), the *globe artichoke,* originated in the Mediterranean region.

Artichoke plants stand 3 to 5 feet (0.9 to 1.5 meters) tall. They may spread over an area 5 to 6 feet (1.5 to 1.8 meters) across. In the spring, the top of the root sprouts stems. These stems are surrounded by large, coarse leaves. Buds develop at the tips of the stems. The buds are immature flowers. They may range from light to dark green. They may have a red or purple tint. The buds are harvested before they are fully grown. Otherwise, they become too tough to eat.

Artichokes thrive in frost-free climates with cool, foggy summers. Artichoke plants may live more than 15 years. Most artichokes are harvested in spring.

Other articles to read include: **Bud; Crop; Vegetable.**

Asexual reproduction

Asexual *(ay SEHK shu uhl)* reproduction is the way that some living things produce offspring. In asexual reproduction, there is only one parent. In sexual reproduction, two parents are needed.

Asexual reproduction occurs in bacteria and other one-celled organisms and with some animals. Sponges, for example, can reproduce when a portion breaks off and gives rise to a new individual. This is called budding.

Some plants also reproduce asexually. A small part of the plant may break away and grow into a new plant. This process is known as *vegetative propagation (PROP uh GAY shuhn)*. People use vegetative propagation to grow certain crops, such as fruit trees.

Other articles to read include:
Reproduction.

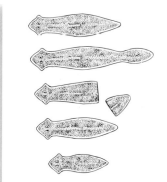

Asexual reproduction by dividing

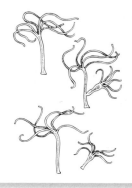

Asexual reproduction by budding

Ash

Ash

Ash is a type of tree that grows in North America, Europe, and Asia. There are many kinds of ash trees. The wood of some kinds is valuable. Also, many people plant ash trees for shade. In the United States, white ash and red ash trees grow in the East and Southeast. Black ash trees grow in the Northeast.

Ash leaves and branches grow in pairs. Each leaf consists of 5 to 11 smaller, pointed leaves called *leaflets.* Small flowers and fruit also grow on the trees.

Ash wood is hard, strong, and stiff. It is used to make baseball bats and handles for shovels, hoes, and rakes. Ash wood is also used for furniture, oars, and skis.

Other articles to read include: **Tree; Wood.**

Asparagus

Asparagus

Asparagus is a nutritious green vegetable. People eat the young stems of the asparagus plant. These stems are called *spears*. Asparagus is an excellent source of protein, vitamins, and minerals. Fresh asparagus should be cooked gently until soft. It should remain a brilliant green color when cooked. This will ensure the best taste and highest nutritional value.

Asparagus plants originated in the Mediterranean region and in Africa. The plant grows best in moderate climates. It requires loose, moist, sandy soil to grow well. Asparagus is a *perennial* plant—that is, it can live for several years without replanting. Plants may produce spears for 15 to 25 years.

The *asparagus fern* is a kind of asparagus used in floral arrangements. It also is a good house plant.

Other articles to read include: **Perennial; Vegetable.**

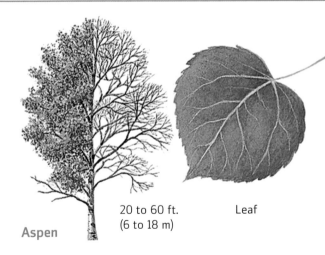

Aspen

20 to 60 ft.
(6 to 18 m)

Leaf

Aspen

The aspen is a type of medium-sized poplar tree. Aspens have smooth, light-colored bark. Their leaves can be round or shaped like a triangle or a heart. They grow in North America, Europe, Asia, and Africa.

The most common kind of aspen in North America is the *quaking aspen*. It is called "quaking" because its leaves shake in even a gentle breeze. It is found across northern North America. It also grows in the western mountains of North America as far south as Mexico.

The *bigtooth aspen* grows in southeastern Canada. It also grows eastward from Minnesota and Iowa in the United States. The edges of its leaves have big, toothlike ridges. The *European aspen* is found in Europe, North Africa, western Asia, and Siberia.

Aspens need sunny places to grow. People use aspen wood to make paper, matchsticks, and boxes.

Other articles to read include: **Poplar; Tree.**

Avocado

The avocado *(AV uh KAH doh)* is a fruit that grows in warm places. The fruit is round, oval, or pear-shaped. Its skin color ranges from green to dark purple. It is raised for the soft pulp inside, which is yellow-green. An avocado fruit has one large seed, which is not eaten.

Avocado trees grow from 30 to 60 feet (9 to 18 meters) tall. Their spreading branches have dark green leaves and small, greenish-white flowers.

Avocados are native to Central America, but they are now grown in many other places. Mexico is the world's leading avocado-producing country.

Avocados are rich in vitamins, minerals, and oil. They are used mainly in dips, salads, and desserts.

Other articles to read include: **Fruit; Tree.**

The avocado has one very large seed.

Azalea

The azalea *(uh ZAYL yuh)* is a flowering shrub. There are many kinds of azalea. Azalea blossoms can be pink, red, white, yellow, or purple. Azaleas grow wild in woodlands, often in swamp areas. They are also valued as a garden plant. Azaleas prefer well-drained soil. They do best in partial shade with filtered sunlight.

Azaleas grow mostly in North America and eastern Asia. Most North American azaleas lose their leaves every autumn. Asian azaleas usually remain green all year. They bloom during May and June. Their long, easily seen *stamens* (stalks that contain pollen) extend beyond the petals. A long, slender capsule covered with spines holds the seeds.

Other articles to read include: **Flower; Shrub.**

Azaleas are shrubs that produce colorful blossoms.

Balance of nature

The term *balance of nature* refers to the relationships among living things in an area. Most places are home to many kinds of plants, animals, and other living things. These living things depend on one another for survival in what scientists call the *web of life*. Any change to one part of the web of life tends to be balanced by a change in other parts. This balance of nature helps to keep the web of life healthy.

An ecosystem is the biological and physical environments of an area. The biological environment is made up of all living things in the area. The physical environment includes air, soil, water, and weather. All these biological and physical factors are interconnected within an ecosystem. For example, rabbits need air and water to breathe and drink. They need plants for food and cover (shelter). On the other hand, rabbits are eaten by foxes and other predators (flesh-eating animals).

Consider an area in which rabbits eat grass and foxes eat rabbits. During one year, good growing conditions might cause the grass to grow well. As a result, the rabbits have more food to eat. The plentiful food may lead to them having more babies.

Continued on the next page

Living things depend on one another for food in a complex web of relationships. The transfer of food energy (arrows) connects many different kinds of animals. Some animals feed on plants. Other animals are meat-eaters. Still others feed on animal and plant remains. A change to any one living thing in area can impact many other parts of the web. The complex ways that living things depend on one another is known as the balance of nature.

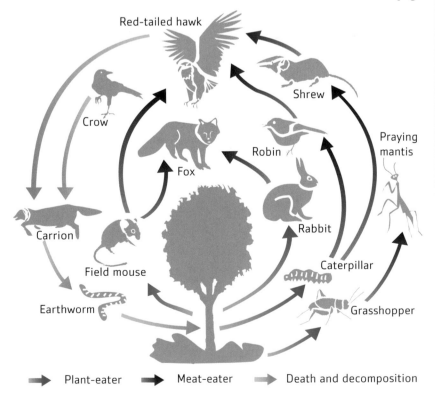

Red-tailed hawk

Crow

Shrew

Praying mantis

Robin

Fox

Rabbit

Carrion

Caterpillar

Field mouse

Grasshopper

Earthworm

➔ Plant-eater ➔ Meat-eater ➔ Death and decomposition

In time, the area may have so many rabbits that the amount of grass falls. There will no longer be enough food for all the rabbits. But the increase in rabbits means more food for foxes. As a result, the number of foxes grows, and these foxes eat many rabbits. Soon, there are not enough rabbits for all the foxes. This example shows how changes to one part of the web of life are balanced by changes in other parts. An increase in rabbits is balanced by an increase in foxes. The number of rabbits thus falls. A drop in the number of foxes soon follows. Thus, the balance of nature tends to prevent any kind of living thing from becoming too numerous.

The balance of nature can be damaged by the activities of human beings. For example, people in the United States have killed nearly all the wolves. These wolves once ate many deer. Since wolves disappeared, the number of deer has increased greatly. These deer overgaze on plants in some areas. Thus, the web of life is thrown out of balance.

Other articles to read include: **Conservation; Ecology; Endangered species; Food chain; Food web.**

When animals feed on prey, it helps keep nature in balance. Without foxes, rabbits would soon become too numerous and damage plants.

Balm

Balm

A balm *(bahm)* is a tall herb with a lemony odor. It is also called *lemon balm*. Balm grows 3 to 4 feet (91 to 122 centimeters) tall. It has wrinkled, egg-shaped leaves and small white flowers. Balm is native to damp and shady woodlands of western Asia. Today, people grow balm as an herb for seasoning. Balm tea, balm wine, and food flavorings are made from the leaves.

Other articles to read include: **Herb; Herbal medicine.**

Bamboo

Bamboo is a kind of giant grass. It grows in warm parts of the world. It can grow very large. Some bamboo grows up to 130 feet (40 meters) high. Such tall bamboo can have stems that are 1 foot (30 centimeters) thick. Bamboo stems are woody and very strong. There are hundreds of kinds of bamboo.

Bamboo has a variety of uses. It can be used to make floors or build entire houses. It is also used to make furniture, baskets, clothing, and many other products. Bamboo has become increasingly important as a building material as it is "ecofriendly." Cutting bamboo does little harm to the *ecosystem* because it is quickly replaced by new growth.

Bamboo is especially common in eastern Asia. The giant panda eats bamboo shoots, stems, and leaves. The smaller red panda eats just the leaves. People also eat tender young bamboo sprouts as vegetables.

Other articles to read include: **Ecology; Grass; Wood.**

Bamboo

Banana

Bananas are long, slender fruits that usually have smooth, yellow skin. The skin is green before the fruit ripens. People all over the world eat bananas. In some countries, bananas with red skin are popular. Bananas grow in hot areas around much of the world.

Bananas are a good source of vitamins and minerals. People usually eat bananas raw. People also eat bananas dried or fried. Dried bananas can be made into flour. Bananas are added to many other foods as flavoring.

The banana plant looks like a palm tree. It grows from 8 to 30 feet (2.4 to 9 meters) tall. However, it is not a tree because it does not have a woody trunk or branches. The leaves of some kinds of banana plants have useful fibers. These fibers can be used to make bags, baskets, and mats. People in tropical countries may use these leaves to make roofs for houses.

Other articles to read include: **Fruit.**

Bananas grow in clusters that curve upward.

Baobab

The baobab *(BAY oh bab)* or *(BAH oh bab)* is a tree with an unusually wide trunk. This trunk can reach 30 to 50 feet (9 to 15 meters) across. The tree can grow to be 80 feet (24 meters) tall. The baobab grows in Asia and Africa.

The baobab tree has white flowers that open at night. Its fruit is called *monkey bread.* The fruit is almost 1 foot (30 centimeters) long. It hangs from the tree like a beanbag on a long rope. People eat the soft center of the fruit.

People sometimes use baobab leaves and bark for making medicines. They use the bark for making cloth, paper, and rope.

Other articles to read include: **Tree.**

30 to 60 ft.
(9 to18 m)

Leaf

Fruit

Baobab

Bark

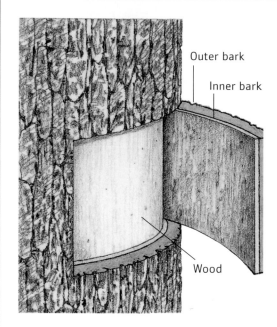

Outer bark

Inner bark

Wood

Bark is the covering on most trees and shrubs. It protects plants from injury, insects, and disease. Bark also helps to keep water inside plants.

Bark has two main parts: the inner bark and the outer bark. The inner bark carries food from the leaves to other parts of the tree. The outer bark is made mostly of a tough, waxy material called *cork*. Cork protects the plant from losing water.

Bark has many uses. The thick outer bark of the cork oak tree is used to make bottle stoppers, flooring, insulation materials, and many other products. Other kinds of bark are used to flavor foods. Burlap and some other fibers are made from certain barks.

Other articles to read include: **Cork; Shrub; Tree**

Barley

Barley is a plant that is grown for food. It is a grain, as are corn, oats, rice, and wheat.

Barley is used to feed livestock. Barley is also dried and ground into a powder called *malt*. Malt is used to make beer and in liquor, malted milk, and flavorings. People also eat barley in soups and stews.

Barley

Barley plants look like wheat. The seeds of the barley plant grow on the tops of long, thin stems. People grow barley in temperate moderate climates around the world.

Barley is one of the world's oldest crops. Barley grains 5,000 to 7,000 years old have been found in Egypt and the Middle East.

Other articles to read include: **Crop; Grain.**

Basil

Basil *(BAZ uhl* or *BAY zuhl)* is an herb used for seasoning food. There are many kinds of basil. Common basil is the most familiar. It also is called *sweet basil.* It has tooth-edged leaves and small, purplish-white flowers. It grows about 1 foot (30 centimeters) tall.

People use basil leaves in soups, salads, and with meats and some pasta dishes. The leaves can be used fresh or dried.

Other articles to read include: **Herb.**

Basil

Bean

Beans are pods and seeds that people eat as vegetables. There are many kinds of bean plants. People eat only the seeds of some bean plants. They eat both the seeds and the pods of other bean plants. Some beans are poisonous.

Farmers around the world grow many kinds of beans. Agriculturally, soybeans are the most important. Soybeans are rich in fat and protein. They can be used in place of meat, eggs, or dairy products. Soybeans are an important ingredient in many processed foods. They also are used to make vegetable oil and to feed livestock.

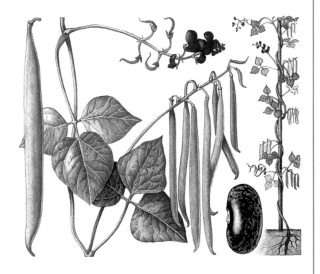

Kidney beans are popular in North America. Kidney beans were first grown by American Indians in South and Central America. There are several kinds of kidney beans. They include red kidney beans, spotted pinto beans, and white navy beans. The lima *(LY muh)* bean is another popular bean. People also eat various kinds of green beans. These beans are picked while they are still young and tender.

Kidney beans grow on plants that bear groups of three leaflets. The flowers develop into seed pods. The seeds are black, white, brown, pink, red, or multicolored.

Bean plants can enrich the soil. Some farmers fertilize their fields by growing bean crops and then plowing them back into the soil.

Some bean plants are low and bushy. Others climb by twining their stalks around poles, strings, or other plants. A favorite climbing bean in gardens is the scarlet runner bean. It has bright red flowers.

Other articles to read include: **Fertilizer; Seed; Soybean; Vegetable.**

Beech

The beech is a tree with thin, papery leaves. The leaves turn gold in the fall. The American beech grows to a height of about 50 to 75 feet (15 to 23 meters). It grows in North America and Europe. The cooper beech is valued as an ornamental tree for its red leaves.

Beech trees have thin twigs with buds at the tips. The buds are shaped like spears. Both male and female flowers grow on beech trees. The male flowers are round, and the female flowers are short and pointed. Beech trees bear nuts that are good to eat.

Leaf

The wood of beech trees is hard and tough. It is used to make furniture and tool handles. The wood is also a good fuel.

Other articles to read include: **Tree; Wood.**

60 to 80 ft.
(18 to 24 m)

Beech tree

Beet

Beet

The beet is a plant grown for food. There are many varieties of beets. The root of the table beet is cooked as a vegetable. The sugar beet is grown for the sugar in its root. Both varieties are important commercial crops. Beets originally grew wild in areas around the Mediterranean Sea. They are now grown around the world.

The thick roots of table beets may be round or pointed. They are dark red, whitish, or golden-yellow. Table beet roots are often canned. They may also be pickled. Fresh roots are often boiled or roasted. Table beet roots are a low-calorie food. They contain iron and calcium. The leaves of young plants may be added to salads. They are an excellent source of calcium, iron, and vitamin A.

The root of the sugar beet is long and pointed. It is creamy-white. Sugar beets provide much of the sugar produced around the world.

Other articles to read include: **Root; Vegetable.**

Begonia

Begonias are popular house and garden plants. There are many kinds of begonia. Most of them have shiny leaves. Some are valued for their brightly colored flowers. Others are admired for their colorful leaves. Most grow best in shade.

The wax begonia is a popular garden plant. It grows small pink, red, or white flowers. Its leaves have a waxy appearance. The rex begonia is another popular garden plant. It is admired for its large, brilliantly colored flowers. The leaves are shades of red, white, or silver.

Other articles to read include: **Flower.**

The rex begonia has richly colored flowers and leaves. It thrives in the shade and is often grown in window boxes or hanging baskets.

Bellflower

The bellflower is a garden flower with bell-shaped blossoms. There are many kinds of bellflower. Some bellflowers grow wild. The blossoms may be blue, pink, purple, or white. Most bellflowers bloom in late spring or summer. Some grow as tall as 6 feet (1.8 meters). Others creep along the ground. Popular bellflowers include Canterbury bells, harebells (or bluebells), and peach bells (or peach-leaved bellflowers). The roots and leaves of one bellflower may be cooked and eaten as a vegetable. Its name is the rampion.

Other articles to read include: **Flower; Vegetable.**

Bellflower is the common name for the Campanula. There are many varieties, but all can be identified by their bell-shaped flowers.

Bergamot

The fruit of the bergamot orange produces an oil that is used to make perfume.

Bergamot *(BUR guh mot)* is a name given to several kinds of plants. The bergamot orange is a citrus tree grown in Italy and southern France. In other parts of the world, it is grown as a decorative tree. The bergamot produces small flowers with a pleasant odor. The fruit is yellow and round or pear-shaped. The skin of the fruit is used to make a liquid called *oil of bergamot*. The oil has a strong, pleasant odor. It is used in making perfume.

Some North American herbs are also called bergamots. Common kinds include the wild bergamot, the purple bergamot, and the prairie bergamot. The wild bergamot is a common garden flower known as bee balm, which is grown across southern Canada and much of the United States.

Other articles to read include: **Flower; Fruit; Herb; Tree.**

Berry

Berries

Watermelon

Orange

Grapes

Berries are a type of fruit. A berry has many small seeds in its center. The seeds are scattered inside the soft part of the fruit. Bananas, blueberries, grapes, green peppers, muskmelons, oranges, tomatoes, and watermelons are all berries.

Most people call any small, fleshy fruit that contains many seeds a berry. For example, many people think that strawberries, blackberries, and raspberries are berries. But even though they have "berry" in their names, they are not true berries.

Botanists (scientists who study plants) put fruits into two main groups. These groups are called simple fruits and compound fruits. Berries are *simple fruits*. Strawberries, blackberries, and raspberries are *compound fruits*.

Some berries, including watermelons, have a hard *rind* (outer covering). Other berries, including oranges, have a leathery rind.

Other articles to read include: **Banana; Fruit; Grape; Melon; Orange; Pepper; Tomato; Watermelon.**

Biennial

A biennial *(by EHN ee uhl)* is a plant that lives for two years or two growing seasons. The plant takes this long to complete its life cycle.

In its first growing season, a biennial plant stores up food. After the growing season, it becomes inactive. In the next growing season, it uses the stored food to flower and make seeds. It then dies.

Flowers such as iceland poppies, hollyhocks, and foxgloves are biennials. Several vegetables are biennials. These include beets, carrots, parsnips, and turnips. The herb parsley is also a biennial. People usually harvest biennials during or soon after the first growing season . At that time, the plants still hold plenty of food.

Other articles to read include: **Annual; Carrot; Foxglove; Hollyhock; Parsley; Parsnip; Perrenial; Poppy; Turnip.**

Foxglove   Iceland poppy

Sweet William

Biennials take two years to complete their life cycle.

Biodiversity

The term biodiversity *(by oh duh VUR suh tee)* is used to describe the variety of plants, animals, and other living things in an area. This word is short for *biological diversity.* The survival of many living things depends on maintaining biodiversity.

All the different kinds of living things in an area are connected in a *web of life.* The web of life describes how living things depend on one another. For example, many animals eat the fruit that plants make. The fruit holds seeds that the plants use to reproduce. An animal that eats fruit carries the seeds in its gut. It later passes the seeds with its droppings. In this way, animals help plants find places to grow. Without plants to make fruit, many animals would starve to death. Without animals to carry their seeds, many plants would not be able to spread. Thus, plants and animals depend on each other.

Biodiversity is important because the web of life is stronger when there are many kinds of living things. One kind of plant might disappear. But there are still many other plants to make

Continued on the next page

Rain forests have the most biodiversity of any place on Earth. A great variety of plants and animals live in rain forests.

Biodiversity *Continued from the previous page*

fruit. Thus, the animals in the area will not suffer greatly. Similarly, one kind of animal might disappear. But there are still many other animals to eat fruit and spread seeds. Thus, the plants in the area will not suffer greatly. In areas with little biodiversity, the web of life can be damaged easily. For example, the disappearance of only one kind of plant might cause many animals to die.

Protecting biodiversity helps human beings in several ways. Biodiversity is important to maintaining a healthy environment. People depend on the environment for air, food, and water. Protecting biodiversity also helps to save plants that might provide food or medicine. In addition, biodiversity contributes to the beauty and wonder of the natural world.

Other articles to read include: **Balance of nature; Conservation; Ecology; Endangered species; Extinction.**

Biology

Biology is the field of science that studies living things. Living things are also called *organisms*. There are millions of different kinds of organisms on Earth. They include everything from tiny bacteria to the largest trees.

Livings things are different from nonliving things. All organisms reproduce to make more of their own kind. Living things also grow. They respond to changes in their surroundings. For example, as winter approaches, many trees shed their leaves. A rock is a nonliving thing. It does not reproduce. It does not grow. It does not respond to changes in its surroundings.

Continued on the next page

The microscope is one of the most important tools used by biologists.

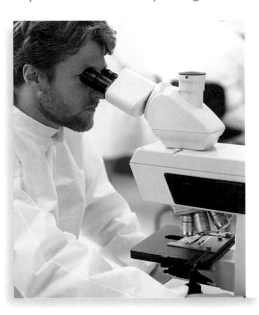

Agronomists are biologists who work to improve crops.

Scientists who study living things are called *biologists*. There are many types of biologists. *Botanists* study plants. They learn how plants grow and reproduce. They study how different kinds of plants are related.

Agronomists study crops and soil. They try to improve agriculture. *Ecologists* study how different kinds of organisms live together in an area. They research how changes to one kind of organism affect the others.

Other kinds of science are sometimes combined with biology. The combination of biology and chemistry is called *biochemistry*. Biochemists study the chemical reactions that take place inside organisms. The combination of biology and astronomy is called *astrobiology*. Astrobiologists search for life on other planets.

Biologists use many different tools and methods. The *microscope* is one of their most important tools. Microscopes help scientists see things that are too small to see with just their eyes.

Many biologists do experiments. In some experiments, the biologist might change something that affects a plant. Then the scientist will see what happens to the plant. For example, a biologist might change the kind of soil a plant grows in to see how this affects its growth.

Biology has made people's lives better. Biologists have learned how to make corn, wheat, and other crops grow bigger and healthier. This work has helped farmers grow better crops, which, in turn, feed more of the world's people.

Other biologists have identified substances in plants that can be made into medicine. This work has helped doctors care for their patients.

Biologists have also learned how to take better care of the Earth and its many living things. They warn if an organism is in danger of dying out. Those warnings help people take steps to protect endangered plants.

Other articles to read include: **Agriculture; Agronomy; Botany; Ecology; Habitat; Life cycle; Plant.**

Many biologists study the effects of pollution on wetlands and other natural areas.

Biomass

Biomass often refers to plants that can be converted into fuel, such as sugar cane.

Biomass (*BY oh MAS*) describes the amount of plant material in an area. Biomass includes both living and dead plant material. It also can describe material from other living things.

Plants make biomass using the energy in sunlight. The biomass of some animals comes from the plants they eat. There is always much more plant biomass in an area than animal biomass.

The term *biomass* also refers to plants and other matter that can be turned into fuel. This biomass includes such wastes as spoiled grain, tree limbs, saw dust, scrap paper, garbage, and manure. Crops are an important source of fuel. Farmers grow corn, sugar cane, and other crops as biomass for fuel.

Biomass is a *renewable* energy source. This means it can be replaced. For example, corn can be replanted after it is harvested. Fuel sources such as petroleum from crude oil cannot be replaced after use.

Other articles to read include: **Compost; Corn.**

Biome

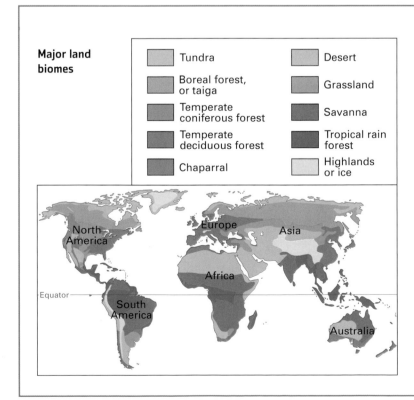

Major land biomes

Tundra	Desert
Boreal forest, or taiga	Grassland
Temperate coniferous forest	Savanna
Temperate deciduous forest	Tropical rain forest
Chaparral	Highlands or ice

A biome *(BY ohm)* is the collection of all the living things in a large area. The boundaries of biomes are usually determined by climate. Each kind of biome has similar plants, animals, and microbes. Thus, the grassland biome in Asia is much like the grassland biome in North America.

The coldest biome is called the tundra *(TUHN druh)*. The tundra is a cold, dry area with no trees. Low shrubs and grasses grow in tundra areas.

Continued on the next page

Forest biomes cover much of Earth. There are many kinds of forest biomes. The largest is the boreal *(BOHR ee uhl)* forest, or taiga *(TY guh)*. It has long, cold winters and short summers. Great forests of evergreen trees grow there.

The desert biome has a hot, dry climate. It is home to cactuses, grasses, and shrubs.

The plants that live in a given biome have features that enable them to survive there. For example, cactuses are common in the desert biome. Cactuses have waxy skin that holds in water. This feature gives cactuses an advantage over other plants in the desert biome.

Continued on the next page

The high mountain tundra is too cold to support large trees.

Grasslands are open areas where grasses are the most plentiful plants.

Biome *Continued from the previous page*

Tropical rain forests grow in regions that have warm, wet weather the year around.

Many kinds of cactus plants grow in the desert biome of the American Southwest. ▼

Other articles to read include: **Chaparral; Desert; Forest; Grassland; Habitat; Rain forest; Savanna; Taiga; Tundra.**

Birch

The birch is a type of tree known for its thin, papery bark. The bark peels off in strips. Birches make a tiny nut. The nut grows in a cone. There are dozens of kinds of birches. Some are shrubs. They grow in North America, Europe, and Asia.

The best-known birch is the *paper birch*. It also is called the *white birch*. It has white bark. The bark is thin and smooth enough to write on. The paper birch grows as tall as 60 to 80 feet (18 to 24 meters). It is found in both North America and Europe. In North America, it grows from far-northern Canada to the southern Appalachian Mountains.

Most kinds of birch trees are used for lumber and wood pulp. The pulp is used to make paper.

Other articles to read include: **Shrub; Tree.**

The paper birch is the best-known birch.

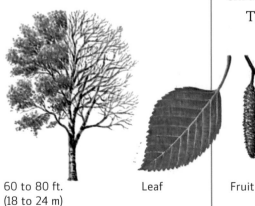

60 to 80 ft.   Leaf   Fruit
(18 to 24 m)

Bladderwort

The bladderwort *(BLAD uhr WURT)* is a type of water plant. Bladderworts get their name from small green or brown bumps. These bumps are called *bladders*. They grow on the leaves and stems. The bladders trap tiny insects and worms, which the plant eats. A plant such as the bladderwort that eats animals is called a carnivorous *(kahr NIHV uhr uhs)* plant.

Most bladderworts grow under water, though some grow in marshes. There are many different kinds of bladderworts. They grow around the world.

Bladderworts have weak stems and no roots. They have yellow or purple flowers. The flowers poke up from beneath the water. The bladders have a small hole on one end with many little hairs inside. When an insect touches the hairs, the bladder snaps open. That creates a sucking action that pulls the insect into the plant.

Other articles to read include: **Carnivorous plant.**

Bladderwort

Bluebell

A bluebell is a plant with blue flowers shaped like bells. There are several different kinds of bluebell.

The bluebell of Scotland is found in Europe, Asia, and North America. It is sometimes called the *hairbell* or *harebell*. It grows in meadows and on mountain slopes.

The Virginia bluebell comes from North America. It is also called the Virginia cowslip. The Virginia bluebell is one of the most beautiful spring wildflowers. Its blossoms grow on leafy stems. The stems are 12 to 15 inches (30 to 38 centimeters) tall. The Virginia bluebell grows near rivers or on moist hillsides.

Bluebells have strong, slender stems, so they can withstand rough winds. The blossoms hang downward, protecting the *pollen* from rain and insects. Pollen is a powdery substance most plants use to reproduce.

Other articles to read include: **Flower.**

Bluebell of Scotland

Kentucky, "the bluegrass state," has many fields of bluegrass on which horses are grazed.

Bluegrass

Bluegrass is a type of grass that grows very thick. For this reason, people plant it on golf courses and lawns. Farmers also plant bluegrass to feed horses, sheep, and cattle. There are many kinds of bluegrass. It grows best in areas with cool weather.

Bluegrass gets its name because some kinds appear greenish-blue. But healthy bluegrass usually looks green. Its blades are flat or folded with tips shaped like the bow of a boat.

Perhaps the best known bluegrass is Kentucky bluegrass. Kentucky is called the *Bluegrass State* because it has many bluegrass fields on which horses are grazed. Early settlers from Europe brought what became known as Kentucky bluegrass to North America.

Other articles to read include: **Grass.**

Decayed plant matter from such bog plants as sedges and rushes may form thick layers of peat.

Bog

A bog is a spongy, swampy area. Bogs are found in cold, wet climates. Bogs are common in northern areas of Asia, Europe, and North America. Bogs are also found in New Zealand.

Bog plants include mosses, grasses, and grasslike sedges and rushes. Small pine trees also grow in bogs. The plants grow slowly because a bog's soil is poor in nutrients. Because the soil is so poor, some bog plants catch insects. These insects provide the nutrients plants need to grow.

Bog plants that die may form thick floating layers of dead material. This material is called *peat*. The peat in a bog can be up to 45 feet (14 meters) deep.

Other articles to read include: **Grass; Moss; Peat; Wetland.**

Trees and shrubs

Sedges and rushes

Moss mat

Peat

Botany

Botany *(BOT uh nee)* is the study of plants. Botany is a part of *biology,* the study of all living things. Scientists who study plants are called *botanists.*

Botanists study all parts of plant biology. They study the different parts of plants, such as the roots, stems, and leaves. They also study how certain plants are alike or different. They try to determine which plants are closely related. Botanists also learn about the substances plants need to grow.

In addition, botanists study the many kinds of places where plants live. They learn why some plants grow best where it is hot and sunny. They learn why other plants grow best where it is cool and shady. A botanist studies how plants live together in one place with animals and other living things.

Some botanists study the many ways that plants are useful to people. They try to discover new ways to use plants. They look for ways to improve crops. They look for plants that can be used to make medicines.

Other articles to read include: **Biology; Plant.**

A botanist examines a flower through a microscope. Botanists study the different parts of plants.

Botanists may grow plants in the lab to study their use of water and other resources.

Breadfruit

Breadfruit

Breadfruit is a type of tropical fruit. It grows on tall trees. Breadfruit trees grow on islands in the Pacific Ocean and Caribbean Sea. The weather on these islands is always warm.

Breadfruit can be round or oval in shape. It is very large. Some breadfruit weighs as much as 5 pounds (2.25 kilograms). Breadfruit has rough, brownish-yellow skin.

Breadfruit got its name from the soft inside of the fruit. Some people think this part tastes and feels like bread. Breadfruit and potatoes can be cooked in the same ways. Both are boiled, broiled, and fried. Breadfruit can also be added to salads and stews. In addition, breadfruit seeds can be cooked and eaten.

Other articles to read include: **Fruit; Tree.**

Broccoli

Broccoli

Broccoli *(BRAHK uh lee)* is a garden vegetable that grows in thick green clusters. These clusters are called heads. The clusters are the flower buds of the plant.

Broccoli is closely related to cabbage and cauliflower. The kind grown most often in North America is called Italian broccoli or sprouting broccoli. It originally came from southern Europe.

People grow broccoli from seeds. The plants grow best in cool weather and in damp, rich soil. Growers pick the heads before they open into yellow flowers. The stems and heads of broccoli are good to eat. They are rich in protein, minerals, and vitamins. People cook broccoli, serve it in salads, or eat it plain as a raw vegetable.

Other articles to read include: **Cabbage; Cauliflower; Vegetable.**

Bromeliad

Bromeliads *(broh MEE lee adz)* are a type of plant that typically grows on other plants. Most bromeliads have leaves shaped like swords. The leaves grow close together. They can hold a lot of water. Bromeliads have brightly colored flowers. Bromeliads are beautiful and easy to grow. Many people keep them as house plants. There are many kinds of bromeliads.

Bromeliads grow in warm areas, mostly in wet forests. Most bromeliads are found in South America. Others grow in Central America and the southern United States.

A plant that grows on other plants is called an epiphyte *(EHP uh fyt)*. Like other epiphytes, bromeliads do not take food from the plants on which they grow. The other plants simply provide a place for the bromeliad to live. Not all bromeliads grow on other plants. The pineapple is a bromeliad that grows on the ground.

Other articles to read include: **Epiphyte; Pineapple.**

Bromeliads are plants that grow on other plants, such as trees.

Brussels sprouts

Brussels sprouts are a vegetable with a flavor like that of mild cabbage. They are closely related to cabbage and cauliflower. The plant sends up a tall stalk. Sprouts grow along the stalk at the base of the leaves. The earliest sprouts form near the ground. Later in the season, others appear farther up the stalk. Each sprout looks like a tiny head of cabbage.

Farmers gather the sprouts by snapping or twisting them off the stalk. Several harvests can be made in each year from one plant. The plants do best where the growing season is long and cool.

Brussels sprouts are a good source of vitamins A, B, and C. The sprouts have the same food value as cabbage.

Other articles to read include: **Cabbage; Cauliflower; Vegetable.**

Brussels sprouts

Bryophyte

A bryophyte *(BRY uh fyt)* is a type of small green plant that does not produce seeds or flowers. Mosses, liverworts, and hornworts have traditionally been considered bryophytes. However, many scientists consider mosses to be the only true bryophytes.

Some bryophytes have simple stems and leaves. Others appear flat and ribbonlike. Tiny hairs called *rhizoids (RY zoydz)* act as roots. Bryophytes reproduce by spores rather than by seeds. If part of a bryophyte breaks off, it can grow into a new plant.

A bryophyte cannot carry food and water through its body. Instead, all parts of the plant absorb water and nutrients directly from its surroundings. Most bryophytes live in moist places. They may live near streams and ponds or in areas of high rainfall. But some live in near desert conditions. Except in very wet areas, bryophytes usually are less than 2 inches (5 centimeters) tall.

Bryophytes may have been the first land plants. Scientists have found fossils of bryophytes from about 470 million years ago.

Other articles to read include: **Moss; Spore.**

Polytrichum moss

Bryophytes lack true leaves, stems, and roots

Peat moss

Liverwort

Leafy liverwort

Bud

A bud is a group of developing leaves on a plant. The leaves surround a growing point on the plant. The growing point contains cells that divide to form new leaves. They also form flowers and stems. The buds of most woody plants are covered by tight leaves. They keep water inside the bud.

The buds of many woody plants do not grow in winter. New leaves and flowers form again in the spring. More new leaves form later during the growing season. These become the next year's buds.

Continued on the next page

1. Leaves form inside a bud.

2. The bud opens in spring as warmth and moisture cause the bud scales to fall off.

3. The young leaves unfold. As they turn darker green, they begin to make food.

4. A twig develops with many young leaves several weeks after the bud has opened.

The buds on woody plants may form just leaves or just flowers. But some grow into both. Leaf buds and flower buds have different shapes and sizes. Individual flowers also are called buds before they bloom.

Other articles to read include: **Bulb; Flower; Leaf.**

A bulb stores food for plant growth in layers of fleshy leaves. The central bud will produce a stem, leaves, and flowers above the ground. The lateral buds will grow into separate buds. ▼

Bulb

A bulb is an underground plant structure that can grow into a plant. It is usually round in shape. It is made up of a stem surrounded by thick, fleshy leaves. Roots grow from the bulb's bottom.

Bulbs store up food during the plant's growing season. The parts of the plant that are above ground eventually die. But the bulb remains alive underground. When the next growing season comes, the stem inside the bulb sends out a shoot. The food stored in the bulb helps the shoot to grow. Eventually the shoot grows above the ground. It then produces a stem, leaves, and flowers.

Some flowers grow from bulbs. These include tulips, daffodils, and narcissuses. Onions and garlic are bulbs you can eat.

Other articles to read include: **Bud; Daffodil; Flower; Garlic; Narcissus; Onion; Stem; Tulip.**

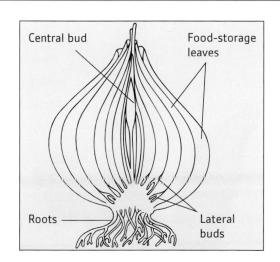

Central bud

Food-storage leaves

Roots

Lateral buds

Bulrush

Bulrush

The bulrush is a green plant. It looks like grass. Bulrushes grow in shallow water and near lakes and rivers. They belong to a family of plants called *sedges*.

Bulrushes have hard stems. They can grow up to 12 feet (3.7 meters) tall. Some bulrushes have leaves, but others do not. Bulrush flowers and seeds grow at the tops of the stems in brown bunches.

Bulrushes are important to people and animals. Fish lay their eggs among bulrushes. Ducks and other birds eat bulrush seeds for food. Such animals as muskrats eat bulrush roots. People can use dried bulrushes to make mats and baskets.

Other articles to read include: **Cattail.**

Burdock

Burdock is a large green weed. It has wide, heart-shaped leaves. It grows from 4 to 9 feet (1.2 to 2.7 meters) tall. Burdock grows in many places, including pastures and fields.

Burdock lives for two growing seasons. During its first growing season, the plant's stem and leaves grow. In the second season, the plant grows purple flowers. The flowers produce sharp, sticky seeds. These seeds stick to clothing or to the hair of animals that brush against the plant.

A new burdock plant may grow where the seeds fall. Most farmers do not like burdock growing in their pastures. The seeds tangle the hair of cows, sheep, and horses. Burdocks can be destroyed by cutting off the flowers before seeds form.

Other articles to read include: **Biennial; Weed.**

Burdocks are coarse, hairy weeds.

Buttercup

The buttercup is a type of bright yellow wild-flower. There are many kinds of buttercups. They grow in areas of the world that never get extremely hot or terribly cold. They grow best in damp places and in fields, forests, and along roads. Buttercups bloom mostly in the spring.

The plant's name comes from its flowers. They often have five petals and are shaped like a cup. The buttercup's leaves are divided into three main parts. Some people think the leaves look like birds' feet. For that reason, the buttercup is also called the *crowfoot.*

Farmers think of buttercups as troublesome weeds. Cattle will not eat buttercups because they have a bad taste.

Other articles to read include: **Flower; Weed.**

Creeping buttercups have stems that spread along the ground and send down roots that grow into new plants.

Butterwort

The butterwort is a type of plant that traps insects for food. Butterworts grow in grassy fields and in wet areas called *bogs.* These places often have poor soils. Butterworts cannot get everything they need from such soil. This is why they must catch insects.

The butterwort has flat, sticky leaves. When an insect lands or walks on a leaf, it gets stuck. The edges of the leaf curl over, trapping the insect. The insect dies inside the leaf. The plant slowly digests the insect. A plant that eats animals is called a carnivorous *(kahr NIHV uhr uhs)* plant.

Butterworts grow in several parts of United States and Canada. They also grow in Asia and Europe. Most butterwort plants have purple flowers on long, thin stems.

Other articles to read include: **Carnivorous plant.**

Butterworts trap insects for food.

Cc

Cabbage

Cabbage is a leafy vegetable. The leaves of cabbages grow close together to form a hard, round head. Cabbage first grew in England and northwestern France. Today, people around much of the world grow cabbage. It is a nutritious food. People eat it raw in salads or cooked as a hot vegetable. People also use cabbage to make a popular food called sauerkraut *(SOW uhr krowt)*.

White cabbage has smooth, pale green leaves.

Cabbage is closely related to cauliflower, Brussels sprouts, broccoli, and turnips. It grows from small seeds. Most farmers grow cabbage by planting seeds. Home gardeners often plant young, small cabbage plants in their gardens. The young plants grow into adult cabbages.

Other articles to read include: **Broccoli; Brussels sprouts; Cauliflower; Turnip; Vegetable.**

Cacao

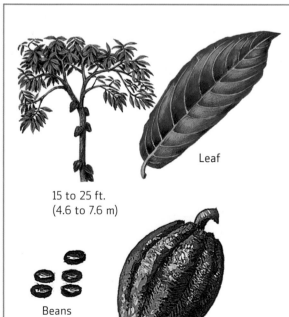

15 to 25 ft. (4.6 to 7.6 m)

Leaf

Beans

Pod

Cacao *(kuh KAY oh)* is an evergreen tree whose seeds are used to make chocolate. The seeds also supply cocoa and cocoa butter, a thick oil used to make candy. Cacao seeds grow inside a melon-shaped pod that may reach 12 inches (30 centimeters) long. The seeds are about the size of lima beans. Their color ranges from light brown to purple.

People grow cacao trees in Central and South America, the Caribbean Islands, Southeast Asia, and West Africa. These cacao trees are kept at a height of about 25 feet (7.6 meters). In the wild, they grow taller. The people of Mexico and Central America once used cacao beans as money.

Other articles to read include: **Bean; Seed; Tree.**

Cactus

Cactuses are plants that typically grow in hot, dry places. Cactuses have waxy skin. They are protected by sharp spines. Cactuses are native to North and South America. There are many kinds of cactus.

Cactuses come in many shapes and sizes. For example, the giant saguaro *(suh GWAH roh)* can grow taller than a house. Other cactuses are less than 1 inch (2.5 centimeters) high. Some small cactuses look like pincushions, starfish, or even blades of grass.

Cactuses have parts that help them live in dry places. Most cactuses have thick, fleshy stems. These thick stems hold water. The stems are covered by waxy skin that keeps water from escaping. Cactuses also have long roots. The roots grow close to the top of the ground and spread wide around the plant. When it rains, the roots can collect as much water as possible.

The spines of a cactus may be long or short. They may have straight or hooked tips. They protect the plant from being eaten by animals. All cactuses grow flowers. They may be white or brightly colored.

Cactuses are important to animals and people. Animals such as insects and birds eat the stems and flowers of cactuses. Many birds build nests in cactus stems. After the spines are removed, people can eat cactus stems, fruits, and seeds.

Other articles to read include: **Desert; Saguaro.**

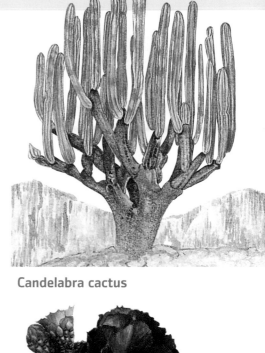

Candelabra cactus

Beaver-tail cactus

The saguaro cactus is a tree that has spine clusters instead of leaves. It can grow up to 60 feet (18 meters) tall. It has a thick, woody stem and bears sweet fruit.

Spine cluster

Fruit

Canola oil

Canola oil is a kind of vegetable oil. It comes from the seeds of the canola plant. Canola oil is used in cooking and food processing. The oil is pale yellow and has almost no flavor.

Canola seeds are about 45 percent oil. To get the oil, producers squeeze the seeds with a machine. Then they soak the seeds in a liquid. The liquid draws out the remaining oil. The material that is left is called *canola meal*. It is fed to animals. Plant breeders first developed the canola plant in 1974. It is a variety of the *rapeplant*. But canola oil has little of a certain fatty substance found in rapeseed oil. That substance is thought to contribute to heart disease.

Other articles to read include: **Rape; Seed.**

Canola oil comes from the seeds of the canola plant.

Capillary action

Capillary *(KAP uh LEHR ee)* action is the rising of water in a narrow tube. Capillary action helps raise water from a plant's roots up to its leaves. For example, tree trunks and branches have many tiny tubes, called *capillaries.* Water in a capillary rises higher and higher.

Water is made up of tiny particles called *molecules.* The sides of the capillary pull the water molecules to them. They pull more strongly than gravity pulls the molecules down. As a result, the water molecules climb the sides of the capillary.

Other articles to read include: **Leaf; Root.**

Capillary action explains how water can rise in a narrow tube. Glass tubes of different widths are placed in a bowl of water (near right) and mercury (far right). Water rises highest in the narrowest tube because water molecules are attracted to the walls of the tube and pulled upward against the force of gravity. But mercury molecules are slightly *repelled* (pushed away) by the walls of the tubes, lowering the mercury levels more in the narrower tubes. So the mercury level is highest in the widest tube.

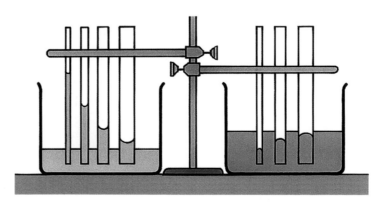

Carnation

The carnation is a plant with colorful blossoms and a unique, pleasant scent. The blossoms may be blue, pink, purple, red, white, or yellow. Carnations may bloom throughout the year. The plants grow from 1 to 3 feet (30 to 90 centimeters) high. They require a rich, loamy soil.

Carnations originally came from southern Europe. They are now grown around the world.

Gardeners have raised carnations since ancient times. The blossom is often used in bouquets. It also is used as a lapel flower. Carnations are one of the special flowers of January. The scarlet carnation is the state flower of Ohio.

Other articles to read include: **Flower.**

Carnations

Carnivorous plant

A carnivorous *(kahr NIHV uhr uhs)* plant is any plant that traps insects for food. The word *carnivorous* comes from carnivore *(KAHR nuh vawr),* a word that means *meat-eater.*

Carnivorous plants do not feed on insects for energy. Like other plants, they use the energy in sunlight to make their own food. But carnivorous plants grow in places with poor soil. This soil does not have enough of the chemical nitrogen. Plants need nitrogen to grow. Carnivorous plants get nitrogen by breaking down the bodies of insects they trap.

One carnivorous plant, the pitcher plant, has tube-shaped leaves that hold rain water in which the insects drown. Another carnivorous plant, the Venus's-flytrap, has leaves that look like jaws. If an insect goes inside these jaws, the leaves snap shut.

Other articles to read include: **Bladderwort; Butterwort; Pitcher plant; Venus's-flytrap.**

Pitcher plant

Venus's-flytrap

Carrot

People eat mainly the long orange roots of carrots. The plant also grows stems, leaves, and blossoms.

A carrot is a plant with a long orange root. This root is eaten as a vegetable. The root contains many minerals and vitamins. Carrots can be eaten raw. Raw carrots are often added to salads. People also cook carrots. They boil them in soups and stews. In some parts of the world, people use carrots to make a drink like coffee. They roast and grind up carrots instead of coffee beans. The plant's thick, lacy leaves and long stems can also be eaten.

Carrots are grown all over the world. Their tiny seeds are planted in rows about ½ inch (1.3 centimeters) deep. A crop takes about 100 days to grow.

Other articles to read include: **Crop; Root; Vegetable.**

Carver, George Washington

George Washington Carver (1864?-1943) was an African American scientist. He became famous around the world for his research on soil and crops.

Carver was best known for his work with peanuts. He made more than 300 products from peanuts. These products include face powder, printer's ink, and soap.

Carver was born into slavery on a farm in Missouri. When he was a baby, his father was killed in an accident. His mother was kidnapped. Carver was raised by his owners, Moses and Susan Carver, until 1865, when slavery became illegal in the United States. The Carvers taught young George to read and write. When he was 11, he went to a school for African American children in Missouri.

Carver went to college at Iowa State Agricultural College (now Iowa State University). He then moved to Alabama to teach at the Tuskegee Institute (now Tuskegee University).

Continued on the next page

At Tuskegee, he studied soil and found ways for farmers to get more from their crops. He also taught Southern farmers, especially black farmers, how to use modern farming methods.

In 1910, Carver began his study of peanuts. He traveled around the United States to talk about the value of peanuts. He also worked to improve relations between black people and white people. Throughout his career, Carver received many awards for his work.

Other articles to read include: **Farm and farming; Peanut; Soil.**

George Washington Carver (center) won worldwide fame for agricultural research. He taught at Tuskegee Institute in Alabama.

Catnip

Catnip is an herb with a strong aroma. It grows to a height of 2 to 3 feet (60 to 90 centimeters). Catnip bears little clusters of whitish flowers with small purple dots. The downy, heart-shaped leaves are green on top and whitish below. Catnip is grown in many parts of the world. It is a common weed in North America and Europe.

Catnip has been grown for centuries. It may be used in home remedies. For example, it may be used to treat colds. Catnip provides a seasoning for cooking. It also is used as an herbal tea. Catnip gets its name from the effect it has on cats. Cats typically become excited or playful around catnip.

Other articles to read include: **Herb; Weed.**

Catnip

Cattail

Cattail

The cattail is a grasslike plant that grows in swamps, marshes, and other wetlands. Cattails grow a brown, sausage-shaped spike at the end of the stem. This spike is said to resemble a cat's tail. There are many different kinds of cattails. They grow in most parts of the world.

Some cattails can reach about 13 feet (4 meters) tall. Most cattails are shorter. The brown spikes are made up of tiny flowers. They develop into thousands of tiny seeds.

Cattails provide shelter and food for many wild animals. People also use cattails in many ways. The roots of cattails can be eaten for starch. Cattail pollen can be used like flour. A silky down surrounds the seeds of cattails. It can be used to stuff life jackets and mattresses. The leaves of cattails can be woven into mats and chair seats. But thick growths of cattails can block drainage ditches.

Other articles to read include: **Bulrush; Wetland.**

The cauliflower plant has large leaves that surround the cauliflower head. People eat the plant's clustered white flower buds.

Cauliflower

Cauliflower is a vegetable with a large, white head. This head is made up of thick clusters of undeveloped flower buds. The buds fuse together. People eat the head. Cauliflower can be eaten cooked, raw, or pickled. Most people eat it cooked. Cauliflower has many minerals and vitamins. The plant also grows large green leaves that surround the head. Cauliflower grows best in cool, moist weather. If the weather is too hot, the heads will not form. If the weather is too cold, the heads will be too small. Cauliflower is closely related to broccoli, Brussels sprouts, and cabbage.

Other articles to read include: **Broccoli; Brussels sprouts; Cabbage; Vegetable.**

Cedar

A cedar is any of a variety of large evergreen trees. They grow in many parts of the world. There are two major groups of cedars. These groups are the *scale-leaved cedars* and the *needle-leaved cedars*.

Scale-leaved cedars have small, scalelike leaves. The leaves grow flattened against the branches. Scale-leaved cedars have small cones. Many clothing chests and closets are lined with this type of cedar. Its pleasant odor seems to keep moths away.

Needle-leaved cedars have tufts of needlelike leaves. Their cones grow straight up on the branches. The cedar of Lebanon is the best-known kind. It has attractive, fragrant wood. The people of early Middle Eastern civilizations used it for building palaces, ships, temples, and tombs.

Other articles to read include: **Evergreen; Tree.**

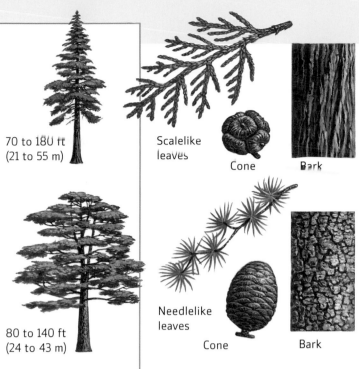

70 to 180 ft
(21 to 55 m)

80 to 140 ft
(24 to 43 m)

Scalelike leaves

Cone   Bark

Needlelike leaves

Cone   Bark

The main types of cedars, scale-leaved and needle-leaved cedars, differ in structure. Scale-leaved species include the Port-Orford-cedar (top). The cedar of Lebanon (above) is a needle-leaved cedar.

Celery

Celery is a crunchy green vegetable. It is related to carrots and parsley. People eat raw celery in salads or with dips. They also eat celery in soups.

The celery plant has several long stalks with feathery leaves on top. The stalks grow from a short base. The stalks can measure up to 14 inches (36 centimeters) long. They are the part of the plant people eat.

Celery grows best in a cool climate. It needs a long growing season and moist, fertile soil. Growers often plant celery in greenhouses. Inside a greenhouse, the plants are protected from extreme cold. After the plants reach a certain height, they are taken out and replanted in a field. People usually harvest celery after one year and then replant.

Other articles to read include: **Carrot; Parsley; Vegetable.**

Celery

Cell

Cells are tiny building blocks of life. All living things are made of cells. Some living things are made of only one cell. Most plants are made of many millions of cells. A large tree contains trillions of cells.

Cells are so small that they typically can be seen only with a microscope. Tens of thousands of cells could fit into this letter *O.*

There are many different kinds of cells. They may be shaped like coils, corkscrews, cubes, rods, saucers, or blobs of jelly. Most plant cells are shaped like cubes. Cells have different jobs. Some plant cells form the roots. Others carry water throughout the plant. Still others use the energy in sunlight to make food.

Cells have different parts. The outside of a plant cell has a tough covering called the *cell wall.* The cell wall protects the rest of the cell. It helps to provide structure and support for the plant. Animal cells do not have cell walls. Inside the cell wall is a thin layer called the cell membrane *(MEHM brayn).* It controls what passes in or out of the cell. Inside the cell membrane are two main parts called the nucleus *(NOO klee uhs)* and the cytoplasm *(SY tuh plaz uhm).*

The nucleus is in the middle of the cell. The nucleus contains the cell's *genetic program,* the master plan that controls almost

Continued on the next page

Plant cells differ from animal cells by being enclosed by rigid cell walls.

Plant cell

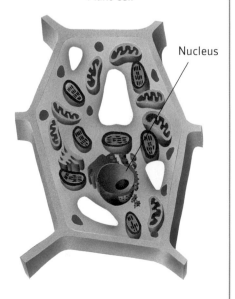

Nucleus

Magnified plant cells

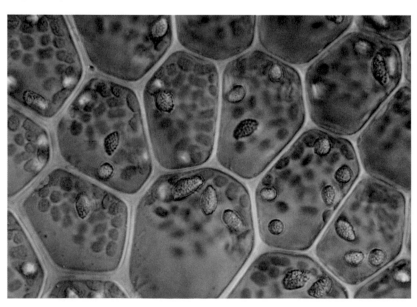

everything the cell does. The genetic program is "written" in the structure of a chemical substance called *DNA (deoxyribo-nucleic acid)*. Genes are units of DNA. The genetic program carried in DNA makes every living thing different from all others. This program makes a rose different from a dog, and a dandelion different from an oak tree.

The cytoplasm is all the material between the nucleus and the cell membrane. The cytoplasm contains many smaller parts, each of which has a special job to do. Green parts called *chloroplasts (KLAWR uh plasts)* use energy from sunlight to turn water and the gas carbon dioxide into sugar. The plant uses this sugar to live and grow. Most of the food that animals eat can be traced to the sugar made by chloro-plasts in plant cells. Plant and animal cells have parts called *mito-chondria (MY tuh KON dree uh)*. Mitochondria are the "power plants" of the cell. They convert food into a form of energy the cell can use to grow and do work.

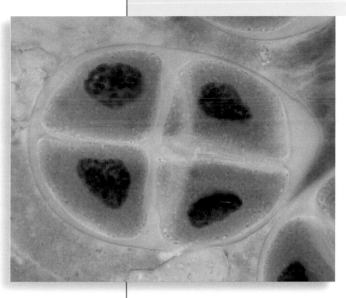

This photo shows lily pollen—a sex cell—splitting apart in a process called meiosis.

Cells reproduce, or make copies of themselves. One cell becomes two cells by dividing in half. Then, these two cells divide again to make four cells. The cells keep dividing to make more and more cells. This is how a plant grows and how it replaces cells that die. This process is called *mitosis (mih TOH sihs)*. Special *sex cells* are often involved in making new plants. Sex cells have only a part of the genetic program. They must combine with a sex cell from another plant. The combined cell has a complete genetic program for making a new plant. The process that produces sex cells is called *meiosis (my OH sihs)*.

Most plant diseases are caused by different kinds of microbes that attack plant cells. For example, mosaic *(moh ZAY ihk)* diseases affect many plants, including such crops as beans, soybeans, and potatoes. These diseases are caused by tiny viruses. Viruses enter cells in the plant and take them over. They force the cells to make more viruses. These viruses then go into other cells and do the same thing. Fungi cause a variety of plant diseases. Some take food from living plant cells. Others kill plant cells and feed on the remains.

Other articles to read include: **Chloroplast; Gene; Life; Reproduction.**

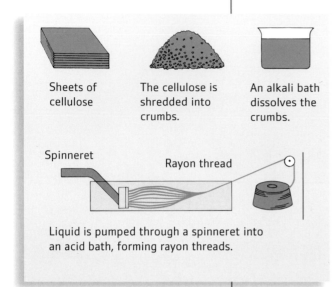

Sheets of cellulose

The cellulose is shredded into crumbs.

An alkali bath dissolves the crumbs.

Spinneret

Rayon thread

Liquid is pumped through a spinneret into an acid bath, forming rayon threads.

The man-made fabric rayon is made from the cellulose fibers of wood pulp or cotton. The cellulose fibers are formed into sheets and treated with chemicals. The cellulose is then shredded into crumbs, treated with carbon disulfide, and dissolved in an alkali bath. Next, pumps force the liquid through the tiny holes of a device called a *spinneret* and into an acid bath to form rayon threads.

Cellulose

Cellulose is a material found in the *cells* of plants. Cells are the tiny building blocks that make up all living things. Fruits, vegetables, trees, and grasses contain cellulose. Cellulose helps make roots, stems, and leaves strong.

Cellulose is an important part of many products that we use every day. Wood contains cellulose. Wood is used to build houses and make furniture. Cotton that we use for clothes is mostly cellulose. Paper is almost all cellulose.

Cellulose can also be mixed with chemicals to make plastics. These plastics are used to make many products, such as suitcases and steering wheels for cars. Sometimes cellulose and other chemicals are added to paint to make it thicker.

Other articles to read include: **Cell; Wood.**

Ready-to-eat cereal

Cereal

Cereal is a food made from such grains as wheat, oats, corn, rice, barley, and buckwheat. These plants, also called *cereals,* are descended from wild grasses. Cereal grains are made from their seeds. Many people eat cereal for breakfast with milk or cream.

The two main types of breakfast cereal are ready-to-eat cereals and hot cereals. Both types are usually made in factories.

Manufacturers of ready-to-eat cereals use a variety of processes, including grinding and rolling, to form the grains into flakes, puffs, and other shapes. Sugar or another sweetener may be added. Manufacturers *fortify* (strengthen) many ready-to-eat cereals with iron, protein, and vitamins.

Most hot cereals are precooked. They must be heated with water in a pan on the stove or in a microwave oven before they can be eaten. To make instant hot cereal, you just add hot water and stir.

Other articles to read include: **Barley; Corn; Grain; Oats; Rice; Seed; Wheat.**

Chaparral

The chaparral *(CHAP uh RAL)* is a region of shrubs and small trees. Chaparrals are found in areas with mild, moist winters and hot, dry summers. They are found in the Mediterranean region, in southern California, and in parts of Mexico, Chile, southern Australia, and South Africa. The chaparral is a type of *biome (BY ohm)*. A biome is a community of plants and animals.

Plants of the North American chaparral include the manzanita, mountain mahogany, scrub oak, and especially the *chamiso (shuh MEE soh)* shrub. Most chaparral plants have tough, crooked branches. Their thick, leathery leaves do not fall off in winter. Few of the plants grow more than 10 feet (3 meters) tall. In some areas, plants grow so close together that people cannot walk through them. Animals of the North American chaparral include coyotes, mule deer, and lizards.

Fires often break out during long, hot summers on the chaparral. Many chaparral shrubs have thick juices in their leaves, called *essential oils*. This helps them catch fire easily. The fires are a natural part of life in the chaparral. They help clear overgrown areas. They also expose the ground to the sun and make way for new plant growth.

Other articles to read include: **Biome; Shrub; Sage; Tree.**

1. Sugarbush
2. California buckwheat
3. White sage
4. Chamiso
5. Black sage
6. Coyote brush
7. California scrub oak
8. Deerweed

Shrubs and small trees grow well in the hot, dry summers and cool, wet winters of the chaparral. Fires frequently occur during the summer and help start new plant growth.

Cherries

Cherry

Cherries are small, round fruits that grow on trees. Ripe cherries are yellow, red, or nearly black. The small fruit has a hard core called a *pit*. The fruit is eaten raw. It also is cooked in pies and other desserts.

Sweet cherry trees reach up to 40 feet (12 meters) high. The trunk may be more than 1 foot (30 centimeters) across. They grow best in areas with mild weather. Sour cherry trees are smaller than sweet cherry trees. They can handle colder and drier weather.

Some kinds of cherry trees are admired for their beautiful flowers. They grow many pinkish blossoms in the spring.

Other articles to read include: **Fruit; Tree.**

Chickpea

Chickpeas are plants raised for their large, tasty seeds. They also are called *garbanzos (gar BAHN zohz)*. The seeds are usually called *chickpeas* or *garbanzo beans*. People grow chickpeas around much of the world.

Chickpea plants produce large, tasty seeds inside long pods.

Chickpea plants grow up to 2 feet (60 centimeters) tall. The plants produce many pods. Each pod contains one or two chickpeas. The chickpeas may be white, yellow, red, brown, or nearly black. Dried chickpeas are usually pale brown or reddish.

One of the most popular uses of chickpeas is in *hummus*. Hummus is a creamy food used as a sauce, spread, or dip. It traditionally consists of cooked chickpeas mashed with lemon juice, olive oil, garlic, and sesame paste. Chickpeas are also made into small fried cakes called *felafel*. In India, cooks use chickpeas to make a variety of dishes, including a dish called *chana masala*.

Other articles to read include: **Bean; Seed.**

Chlorophyll

Chlorophyll *(KLAWR uh fihl)* is the green coloring found in plants. It is also found in simple living things called *algae (AL jee)* and in some bacteria.

Plants and other living things use chlorophyll to make their own food. Plants take a gas called carbon dioxide from the air. They take water from the soil. Chlorophyll enables plants to combine these ingredients using the energy in sunlight. This process is called *photosynthesis (FOH tuh SIHN thuh sihs)*. The chemicals that result from photosynthesis become the sugars plants need to live. Oxygen is also released during this process.

Most plants cannot make chlorophyll without light. That is why plants kept away from light are yellow or white instead of green.

Other articles to read include: **Algae; Chloroplast; Leaf; Photosynthesis.**

Chlorophyll causes plants to be green.

A green substance in plants called chlorophyll takes energy from sunlight. The energy is used to combine water and carbon dioxide to make sugar. Oxygen is given off as a waste product.

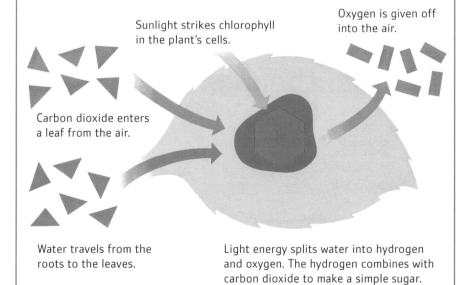

Sunlight strikes chlorophyll in the plant's cells.

Oxygen is given off into the air.

Carbon dioxide enters a leaf from the air.

Water travels from the roots to the leaves.

Light energy splits water into hydrogen and oxygen. The hydrogen combines with carbon dioxide to make a simple sugar.

Chloroplast

A chloroplast *(KLAWR uh plast)* is a tiny working part of a plant cell. Inside the chloroplast, *photosynthesis (FOH tuh SIHN thuh sihs)* takes place. Photosynthesis is the process by which green plants make their own food.

Continued on the next page

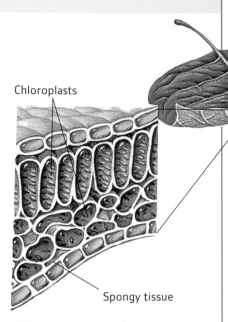

Chloroplasts

Section of the leaf enlarged at left

Spongy tissue

Chloroplasts are the tiny, green parts of plant cells where photosynthesis occurs.

Chloroplast *Continued from the previous page*

Chloroplasts contain a substance called *chlorophyll (KLAWR uh fihl)*. Chlorophyll is a green pigment coloring material. It is what makes a plant's leaves look green. Chloroplasts use sunlight, carbon dioxide, and water to make food for the plant. The chloroplasts of most plants are shaped like disks or lenses.

Chloroplasts are one of several types of special plant-cell structures called *plastids (PLAS tihdz)*. Other plastids contain yellow, orange, or red pigments. They provide the colors of many flowers and fruits. Plastids also store oil, protein, and starch.

Other articles to read include: **Cell; Chlorophyll; Photosynthesis.**

Chrysanthemum

The chrysanthemum *(kruh SAN thuh muhm)* is a strong-scented plant with beautiful blossoms. The blossoms may be white, yellow, pink, or red. Many individual flowers make up each blossom. The name *chrysanthemum* comes from two Greek words meaning *golden flower.* There are many kinds of chrysanthemum.

Chrysanthemums are easy to grow. They grow from cuttings or root divisions. Most are perennial.

The chrysanthemum has been called the *flower of the East.* People in Asian countries have grown chrysanthemums for over 2,000 years. In China during the 400's, Tao Yuanming became a famous grower of these plants. After his death, his native city was named Juxian. This name means *city of chrysanthemums.* Chrysanthemums also grow well in Japan. In 797, the ruler of Japan made this flower his personal symbol. He ordered that it could be used only by royalty. In October, the Japanese celebrate the Feast of the Chrysanthemums. Today, chrysanthemums are grown in many places with mild climates.

Other articles to read include: **Flower; Perennial.**

Chrysanthemums

Class

A class is one of the groups used by scientists to classify living things. The basic system in scientific classification is made up of eight groups. The primary groups are (1) domain, (2) kingdom, (3) phylum or division, (4) class, (5) order, (6) family, (7) genus, and (8) species. Domain ranks as the highest level and largest group. Species is the lowest and smallest. Every plant has a place in each group.

A class ranks below a *phylum (FY luhm)* and above an *order* in this system. A phylum is a larger group used by scientists to classify living things. Usually there are several classes in a phylum.

Living things in the same class will have many similarities. For example, flowering plants make up a *division* (major group) of plants called Anthophyta. This division is split up into two major classes: (1) eudicotyledons, also called eudicots, and (2) monocotyledons, also known as monocots. The pollen of eudicots has a structure that is different from that of other flowering plants. Also, the seeds of eudicots and other flowering plants have two tiny leaves. The seeds of monocots have only one tiny leaf. The petals and other flower parts of most monocots usually grow in threes or in multiples of three. The flower parts of eudicots typically grow in fours or fives or in multiples of four or five. There are many more species of eudicots than monocots.

Other articles to read include:
Classification, Scientific; Monocotyledon; Order; Phylum.

Wild geraniums are members of the class eudicots. The flower parts typically grow in fours or fives.

Irises are members of the class monocotyledons. The petals and other flower parts usually grow in threes.

Classification, Scientific

Scientific classification is the way scientists arrange plants, animals, and other living things into different groups. To *classify* means to place into groups. All the living things in a group are alike in certain ways. For example, plants are placed in one group because they have many features in common. One important similarity is that most plants can make their own food using sunlight. They are similar because they are all related to one another. Classifying living things into groups is also called *taxonomy (tak SON uh mee).*

Scientists look at many features to decide how to classify a plant. They look at how the plant reproduces. They may study the shape of the plant's seeds. They may examine the flowers, the leaves, and the bark. Today, one of the most important methods scientists use to classify plants is to examine *genes.* Genes are the tiny structures inside cells that tell a plant how to grow. Closely related plants share many genes.

Each specific kind of living thing has a scientific name made up of two parts. Each part is a word, generally in the languages of Latin or Greek. The scientific name for common wheat is *Triticum aestivum,* for example. The first part tells which *genus (JEE nuhs)* the plant belongs to. The second part tells the plant's *species.* There are often two or more different species in one genus. For example, durum wheat is used mainly to make pasta. It is closely related to common wheat and belongs to the same genus. Durum wheat's scientific name is *Triticum durum.*

Scientists all over the world use the same scientific name for a particular plant. People who are not scientists often call the same plant by different names. For example, common daisy, English daisy, and lawn daisy are different names used for the same plant. But scientists always call this plant *Bellis perennis.* Similarly, many other plants are called daisies. But each has its own scientific name.

The scientific classification system is made up of seven main groups. These groups are called *kingdom, phylum, class, order, family, genus,* and *species.* They are listed here from the largest group to the smallest group. Each group is made up of the

Continued on the next page

smaller groups that come after it. For example, a class can be made up of many different orders. An order can be made up of many different families. The smaller the group, the more closely related are the organisms in it.

Plants make up the kingdom Plantae. This kingdom contains many *phyla (FY luh)*. *Phyla* is the plural of *phylum*. Among plants, phyla are often called *divisions*. The plant kingdom is made up of several divisions. For example, mosses make up the division Bryophyta. Flowering plants make up the division Anthophyta. Each of these divisions can be further divided into classes, orders, families, and individual species.

Other articles to read include: **Algae; Class; Family; Fungi; Gene; Genus; Kingdom; Linnaeus, Carolus; Order; Plant; Species.**

The highest level of scientific classification is kingdom. The common buttercup *(Ranunculus acris)* is in the kingdom Plantae, which includes all plants. The lowest level of classification is species. It includes only the buttercup. Plants at higher levels of classification are less closely related than those that share lower levels of classification.

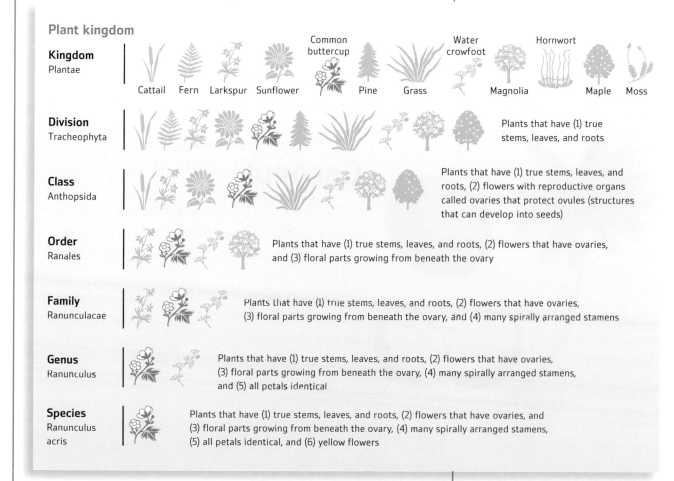

Plant kingdom

Clover

Clover

Clover is a valuable crop that is used to feed farm animals. Clover provides such nourishing substances as proteins and minerals. Pastured animals may graze on clover. Farmers also turn clover into hay. Growing clover and then plowing it under also adds nutrients to the soil. These nutrients are used to fertilize other crops.

There are many kinds of clover. Red, white, strawberry, and crimson clovers rank among the most common. The various clovers differ in how they grow. Some live for only one growing season. Others live for more than one season. Clovers also differ in appearance. They range from 6 inches to 3 feet (15 to 91 centimeters) tall. They have leaves with three to six leaflets. Four-leaf clovers are rare. Clover produces clusters of tiny flowers. The flowers are white, yellow, or red. The number of flowers in each cluster ranges from 5 to 200.

Clover probably first grew in southwestern Asia. Today, clover is grown around the world.

Other articles to read include: **Farm and farming; Crop.**

Seed

Tree

Meat inside seed

The coconut seed is a ball of sweet-tasting coconut meat. It is covered by a tough, brown skin.

Coconut

The coconut is a large, round fruit. It comes from coconut palm trees, which grow in warm places. The coconut fruits grow together in groups among the leaves.

Coconuts that you can buy are often covered with a brown, woody shell. Two layers outside the shell are usually removed before coconuts are sold. These layers are called the *rind* and *husk*. The coconut seed lies inside the shell. The coconut seed measures 8 to 12 inches (20 to 30 centimeters) long and 6 to 12 inches (15 to 25 centimeters) across. The coconut seed is shaped like a ball and is made of coconut meat. Coconut meat is a white, sweet-tasting food. To get the meat, you break open the shell.

Continued on the next page

Many people like to eat coconut meat when it is fresh and juicy. It is also good dried and shredded. The shredded pieces are used in many kinds of foods, such as candy bars. People may drink the juice inside the coconut. This juice is called *coconut water*. Liquid also comes from the coconut meat itself. The meat is squeezed to produce *coconut milk*. Coconut milk is an ingredient in many dishes. It is especially common in the foods of Southeast Asia. Coconut husks are used to make mats, ropes, and brooms.

Coconut palm trees probably first grew in Southeast Asia and the islands of Melanesia in the Pacific Ocean. Today, they grow in many parts of the world. The wood is used to build houses, and the leaves are used to make hats and baskets.

Other articles to read include: **Fruit; Palm; Tree.**

Coffee

Coffee is a drink made from the dried and ground beans of the coffee plant. It is the favorite hot drink in almost every country in the world.

Coffee is very important to the incomes of many countries. The plant is grown in Southeast Asia, India, Arabia, equatorial Africa, Hawaii, Mexico, Central and South America, and the Caribbean Islands. Brazil is the leading grower of coffee.

Each coffee berry typically contains two coffee beans.

The coffee plant has shiny leaves and white flowers. Its fruit is called a berry. Most berries are picked by hand and then washed. Each berry has two beans, or seeds. At first, the beans are soft and bluish-green. Later, they become hard and pale yellow. The beans are left to dry out for many weeks. Then the outer skins of the beans are taken off. The beans are then shipped in cloth bags to be roasted. After they are roasted, the beans are stored until they are ready to be ground into tiny pieces. The ground coffee is then packaged for sale.

Coffee contains caffeine *(kaf EEN)*, a substance that may keep people awake and alert. Some people like to drink coffee from which the caffeine has been removed. Such coffee is called *decaffeinated coffee*.

Other articles to read include: **Bean; Berry.**

Collards

Collards

Collards *(KAHL uhrdz)* are the leaves of the collard plant. People eat the cooked leaves as a vegetable. The collard plant is closely related to cabbage and kale. But unlike cabbage leaves, collards are loose and curly. Collard leaves greatly resemble kale. But collards can grow in warmer climates.

The collard plant is grown in many parts of the world. In the United States, it is usually grown in the South. The plant may grow 2 to 4 feet (61 to 120 centimeters) tall. Cooked collards are a good source of vitamins.

Other articles to read include: **Cabbage; Vegetable.**

Compost

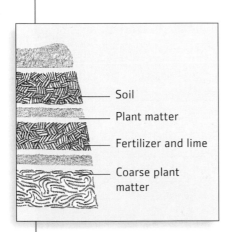

- Soil
- Plant matter
- Fertilizer and lime
- Coarse plant matter

A compost pile (above and below right) consists of alternate layers of plant matter, soil, and fertilizer and lime. The compost is allowed to decay for several months and then used as a fertilizer or mulch.

Compost is a material used by gardeners. It is made from dead plant material. It is mixed with soil to help plants grow.

To make compost, gardeners place dead plant material in a pile. The materials most commonly used are grass and garden clippings, leaves, and coffee grounds. But any plant material is suitable.

The plant material is left to *decay,* or break down. It is packed in layers about 6 inches (15 centimeters) deep. A thin layer of *manure* (animal waste) or soil is usually spread between layers. This speeds decay. Watering the mixture also speeds decay. If the compost is in a

container, its walls should allow some air to enter. The compost should decay for five to seven months before being used.

Gardeners mix compost with the soil to loosen the soil. Most compost also enriches the soil. Compost may also be used as a *mulch.* Mulch is a material spread on top of the soil to keep moisture in.

Other articles to read include: **Decay; Fertilizer; Soil.**

How does composting work?

What you need:

- backyard corner
- plant clippings, leaves
- twigs, dead plants
- vegetable or fruit peels
- water
- garden shovel

1. Have an adult help you pick an out-of-the-way corner in your backyard, or somewhere else, about 3 square feet (0.8 square meter).

2. Collect a pile of grass clippings, twigs, fallen leaves, dead plants, and other things like these.

3. Mix the fruit and vegetable peels in the pile. Sprinkle water over the mixture.

4. Turn over the mixture each month with the shovel. The compost pile will need a few months, and it will break down into smaller bits of natural material called compost.

5. You can mix the compost into garden soil. It will help return minerals to the soil and keep new plants healthy.

http://bit.ly/WW07Zh

Conifer

A conifer *(KOH nuh fuhr* or *KON uh fuhr),* is a tree or shrub that has its seeds in cones. Most conifers grow in cool places, such as on mountains. There are many kinds of conifers, including cedars, firs, spruces, hemlocks, larches, balsams, pines, redwoods, and sequoias. Conifers belong to a group of seed plants called *gymnosperms (JIHM nuh spurmz).*

Most conifers are also called *evergreens* because they have green leaves all year long. This makes them different from such trees as oaks, elms, and maples, which drop their leaves every fall. Those kinds of trees are called *deciduous (dih SIHJ u uhs).* However, a few kinds of conifers, like tamarack and baldcypress, do lose their leaves every year. The leaves on conifers are long and skinny. They are called *needles.* The cones on conifers are different shapes and sizes, depending on the type of tree. Some cones are less than 0.5 inch (1.3 centimeters) long. Others are more than 2 feet (61 centimeters) long. Cones may be male or female. These cones differ in appearance and where they grow on the tree.

Norway spruce

Life of a cone

1. The small male cones are produced in groups at the ends of twigs. These cones produce large amounts of yellow pollen grains.
2. The young female cones are produced upright and singly at the ends of the shoots. At first they are pink, but later they become green and turn downward.
3. The wind carries pollen grains from male cones to female cones, where they are caught between the scales of young female cones. The pollen fertilizes eggs inside the female cones.
4. Seeds inside the female cone mature in one to two years.

5. The cones usually open their scales to let the seeds out. Some types of cones fall apart to release their seeds.
6. The seeds have small wings and are easily carried away by the wind.
7. In dry weather, the scales of a cone open and the seeds blow away. When it rains, the scales close up again. Rain will wash the seeds down onto the ground.

Conifers are some of the largest and oldest living things on Earth. For example, the redwood tree of the western United States is a conifer that can stand more than 360 feet (110 meters) high. Some bristlecone pines, which are also found in the western United States, are more than 4,600 years old.

People use conifers for many things. For example, much of the wood used in houses and other buildings comes from pine trees. Most of the wood that paper and cardboard is made from also comes from conifers. Telephone poles are often made from tall, skinny conifers.

Other articles to read include: **Cedar; Cycad; Cypress; Deciduous tree; Evergreen; Fir; Gymnosperm; Hemlock; Juniper; Pine; Redwood; Sequoia; Shrub; Spruce; Tree.**

There are many kinds of conifers, including balsams, cedars, firs, hemlocks, larches, pines, redwoods, sequoias, and spruces.

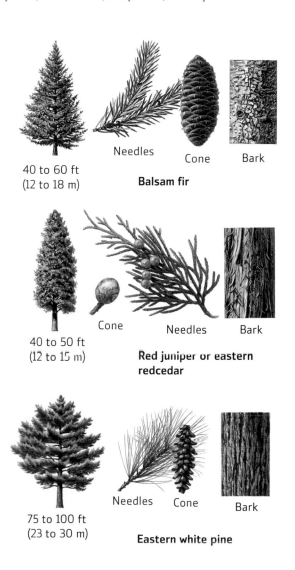

Needles   Cone   Bark

40 to 60 ft
(12 to 18 m)

Balsam fir

Cone   Needles   Bark

40 to 50 ft
(12 to 15 m)

Red juniper or eastern redcedar

Needles   Cone   Bark

75 to 100 ft
(23 to 30 m)

Eastern white pine

Student volunteers plant a tree at their school. Conservation includes such individual efforts to preserve natural resources.

Conservation

Conservation is the protection and careful use of natural resources. Natural resources include all the things that help support life. Sunlight, water, soil, and minerals are natural resources. Plants, animals, and other living things are also natural resources.

Earth has only a certain amount of natural resources. But the number of people in the world keeps increasing. As a result, people use more and more of those resources. Also, as people's lives improve, they have more things. They use more of Earth's resources to make these things. Conservationists work to ensure that the environment can continue to provide for human needs. Without conservation, most of Earth's resources would be wasted, damaged, or destroyed.

Experts called *conservationists* usually identify four kinds of resources. Some resources will never be used up. For example, there will always be plenty of sunshine. Other resources can be used and then replaced. For instance, a field of corn can be harvested and soon regrown. Still other resources cannot be replaced after they are used. There is only so much oil in the ground. After it is used up, it cannot be replaced. Some resources

Continued on the next page

Contour plowing is practiced on sloping land. Farmers plow around features such as hills and valleys, instead of plowing straight across the land and back. Contour-plowed soil forms ridges across the slope. The ridges help slow the flow of rain water, conserving the soil.

can be recycled. For example, the aluminum in soda cans can be used to make new soda cans. Recycling helps to conserve natural resources.

Conservation is important because it involves the wise use of natural resources. People will not be able to meet their needs without conservation, especially as Earth's population grows. Conservation also works to save threatened wildlife. Plants and animals are vital to maintaining healthy natural environments. People depend on such environments in a variety of ways. For example, much of the oxygen that people breathe is made by plants in forests. Nature also provides great beauty. Many people believe nature is valuable in its own right, apart from whether it is useful to people.

There are many kinds of conservation. Each kind faces different challenges. These challenges are met in different ways.

Soil conservation is important to keep plants healthy. *Erosion (ih ROH zhuhn)* happens when wind or water carries soil away. Planting the same crops year after year also can hurt the soil. Too much watering can cause salt to build up in the soil. Plants do not grow well in soil with too much salt.

Water conservation preserves the supply of fresh, clean water. People need clean water to drink, cook, and bathe. Factories and farms also use water. Many kinds of wildlife depend on fresh water. But some areas of the world do not have enough water. People waste huge amounts of water in many areas. Some areas have problems with water pollution *(puh LOO shuhn),* harmful substances that dirty the water.

Forest conservation makes sure that forests are preserved. It also works to replant trees in areas where forests were cut down. Forests are the homes of many plants, animals, and other living things. Trees keep water from running off the land. They help to prevent erosion.

The conservation of grazing *(GRAYZ ihng)* land is important in areas with grasslands. Cattle and other animals feed on the plants. If too many animals graze, the plants die and the soil *erodes* (wears away).

Continued on the next page

Recycling is an important conservation activity. Workers at a waste transfer station remove plastics and other recyclable materials from household trash. Industries then reuse the materials.

Prescribed burns clear the forest floor of debris that could fuel a major forest fire.

Conservation *Continued from the previous page*

Wildlife conservation protects habitats for wild plants and animals. People damage many natural areas to use the land for farms, homes, and factories. Wildlife conservation works to preserve natural areas. Pollution also kills wildlife. Conservationists try to discover sources of pollution and reduce the damage it does to nature.

Energy conservation works to waste less power. Modern civilization depends on fuel for transportation, heat, and electric power. But much fuel is wasted. Someday, the supply of such fuels as natural gas and oil will be used up. Also, these fuels cause much pollution. People are working to develop new kinds of fuels. Many of these fuels are based on plants. These fuels cause less pollution, and they can be replaced after they are used.

In prehistoric times, there were far fewer people on Earth. Those few used little of Earth's resources. Even then, people may have hunted too many animals in some areas. Some scientists believe such giant animals as mammoths died out in part because of hunting. More problems arose when people began to raise animals. In many areas, herds were allowed to graze until the plants died. Then the soil eroded, and the land turned to desert.

Some early people practiced conservation. Some early farmers in the Middle East dug flat fields called *terrace*s on hillsides. Terraces prevent the soil from washing away. More than 2,000 years ago, the Greeks learned to *rotate* (switch) the crops in their fields to keep the soil rich. Later, the Romans invented ways to bring water to many of their lands.

Continued on the next page

Land overgrazed by livestock (below left) is in sharp contrast to grazing land properly conserved (below right). Such improper management of pasture land as short-term overgrazing destroys the vegetation on the land over the long run.

Cranes feed in the Lower Klamath National Wildlife Refuge in California. Wildlife conservation requires setting aside such areas where animal habitats will remain undisturbed.

During the 1700's and 1800's, industries grew rapidly in Europe and the United States. Smoke, soot, and waste from factories and homes caused pollution. The number of people in the world also increased. As people moved into new lands, forests and wildlife were destroyed.

In the United States, the growing population caused many problems. People cut down huge forests. They destroyed the plants that lived in grasslands and replaced them with crops. Farms damaged the soil and caused it to erode. People also trapped and killed many animals. During the late 1800's, people began to see the harm they had done. The world's first national park, Yellowstone, was established in 1872. It was set up to help protect wildlife. It became the first of many national parks.

Today, conservation is important worldwide. Conservationists try to save wild areas from being destroyed by farming, building, and industry. They try to replant trees, grasses, and other plants. Some nations are working together on worldwide programs. They make agreements to cut water and air pollution and pass laws to protect endangered wildlife.

Other articles to read include: **Balance of nature; Ecology; Endangered species; Environment; Extinction; Farm and farming; Habitat; Irrigation; Soil.**

Coral tree

Coral tree

Coral trees are tropical plants people grow for shade and decoration. They are also known as *coral bean*. There are many kinds. They grow around much of the world.

Coral trees have compound leaves made up of three leaflets. Most coral trees lose their leaves and grow new ones each year. Many have thorns along the branches. They also may have thorns on the stems of the leaves. Most coral trees bear large, showy flowers that are red or orange. Birds pollinate the flowers. In the Americas, coral trees are chiefly pollinated by hummingbirds.

Most coral trees have either red or black seeds. The seeds are sometimes used for necklaces and other jewelry. However, the seeds often contain poisons that are harmful if eaten.

Other articles to read include: **Tree.**

The seeds of the coriander plant are used as a food seasoning. The stems and leaves provide another seasoning called cilantro.

Coriander

Coriander *(KAWR ee AN duhr)* is an herb that produces a food seasoning. The seasoning is made from the herb's seeds. The seeds have a pleasant odor when ripe. They taste sweet after they have been dried out. The seeds are often ground and used as a spice in curries, sauces, and liqueurs. They are also used to make small round candies. Coriander-seed oil is used to flavor food and as a medicine. The coriander plant reaches about 3 feet (91 centimeters) high. It has small white flowers. It is native to countries around the Mediterranean Sea. It is now grown in many places around the world. The leaves and stems of coriander plants are used as a seasoning called cilantro. Cilantro is especially important in Latin American cooking.

Other articles to read include: **Herb; Seed.**

Cork

Cork is a lightweight, spongy material that comes from the bark of the cork oak tree. Cork is often used to make stoppers. Stoppers keep liquid from spilling out of bottles. They are often used in wine bottles. These stoppers are usually called corks. Ground cork can be used to make something soundproof. It also can keep something warm or cold.

Most cork comes from Spain and Portugal, where many cork oaks grow. Cork oaks have a thick outer layer of dead bark. Under that, there is a layer of growing, live bark. After the tree is about 20 years old, the bark can be stripped every 8 to 10 years without hurting the tree. Workers cut long pieces of bark from the lower branches to the ground. After that, the bark is boiled, scraped clean, and dried.

Other articles to read include: **Oak; Tree.**

Cork comes from the bark of the cork oak tree, which is native to southern Europe.

Corn

Corn is one of the world's most important crops. It is also called *maize* (mayz). Corn is related to wheat, rice, oats, and barley. It is rich in fats, proteins, and other things people need to stay healthy.

Corn is planted from seed, or *kernels (KUR nuhlz)*. It takes about 9 to 11 weeks to reach full size. Corn plants have branching roots, a stem called a stalk, and long, broad leaves.

At the top of the cornstalk, clusters of small flowers form a tassel. One or more ears grow farther down. Each ear consists of a long, round cob covered by rows of kernels. Threads of silk grow from the kernels out through the end of the ear. Leaves called husks cover each ear.

People often eat corn by itself. They also use corn in foods such as cooking oil, flour, cereal, margarine, and syrup. Food for farm animals and pets often contains corn. Industries use corn in making cloth, drugs, paints, and other products. Corn also is used to make fuel for cars and trucks.

The United States grows more corn than any other country. China grows the second largest amount of corn. Other leading producers of corn include Argentina, Brazil, France, India, Indonesia, and Mexico.

Other articles to read include: **Barley; Cereal; Crop; Grain; Oats; Rice; Seed; Wheat**

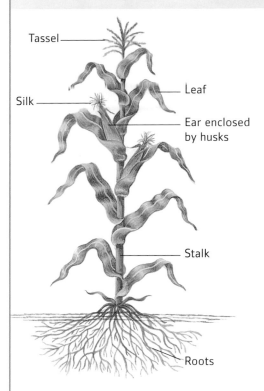

A corn plant consists of the roots, stalk, leaves, ears, and tassel. Special leaves called *husks* enclose the ears. Long, threadlike *silks* extend beyond the tips of the husks.

Cotton

Cotton is a plant that produces *fibers (FY buhrs)* used mainly to make cloth. Cotton cloth is widely used in clothing.

Every part of the cotton plant is useful. The long cotton fibers are made into cloth. The short fibers are used in making paper and other products. Cotton seeds are used for oil and for such foods as margarine. The hulls, or outer covering, of cotton seeds are used to make food for farm animals. And farmers plow cotton stalks and leaves into the soil as fertilizers. Fertilizers help soils produce better crops.

Continued on the next page

Cotton fibers come from the seed pods of cotton plants. An open flower stays on the cotton plant for about three days before the petals fall. After the petals fall, the seed pod turns into a *boll.* When the boll opens, the cotton is ready to harvest.

Cotton *Continued from the previous page*

There are dozens of kinds of cotton, but farmers raise only four kinds. The most common kinds are pima and upland cotton. They are used to make many kinds of cloth and other goods.

China, India, and the United States are the biggest cotton growers. Many countries in Asia, Africa, South America, and Central America also produce cotton. In Europe, Greece and Spain grow cotton. Australia also produces a large crop.

Early in spring, growers plow the soil. Then cotton seeds are planted by machines or by hand.

Most cotton plants grow 2 to 5 feet (0.6 to 1.5 meters) tall. Flower buds called squares begin forming about three weeks after the plants appear.

After the flowers blossom, the *bolls (bohlz),* or seed pods, develop. When they dry and split open, the cotton is harvested.

First, the fibers in the bolls are separated from the seeds. The fibers are cleaned and dried. Then they are combed straight and spun into yarn. Some yarn is colored before it is woven. The rest is woven into cloth. Then it is treated, bleached, and colored.

People learned to grow cotton in Asia more than 5,000 years ago. Native Americans in Central America learned how to grow cotton around the same time. People of European descent began growing cotton in the American Colonies in the 1600's. In the late 1700's and early 1800's, people invented machines that made it easier to process cotton and weave cotton cloth. Machines invented later made it much easier to plant and harvest cotton.

In the 1960's, *synthetic (sihn THEHT ik)* cloth became popular. Synthetic cloth, such as nylon, is made in factories. For a while, less cotton was sold. But since the late 1970's, people have used more cotton.

Other articles to read include: **Crop; Seed.**

Nearly all cotton is now harvested using farm machinery, eliminating what was once backbreaking work.

Crab apple

A crab apple is a small tree that produces apples less than 2 inches (5 centimeters) across. There are many kinds. Many crab apple trees are used as landscape trees. They are especially

popular in urban areas. Some are raised for their edible fruits. Crab apples are mostly used for making jellies.

Most crab apple trees measure less than 30 feet (9 meters) high. The trees produce white to deep pink flowers in the spring. Some bear red or yellow fruits that remain colorful through autumn and early winter.

Other articles to read include: **Apple; Tree.**

Crab apple trees yield small fruits but are primarily planted as an ornamental that produces beautiful flowers in spring.

Cranberry

The cranberry is a sour red fruit that grows on a vine. Cranberries can be eaten fresh or dried. But most cranberries are made into juice or sauce. Cranberry sauce is a traditional food for Thanksgiving in the United States.

The cranberry vine is native to North America. It grows low to the ground. The plant has oval-shaped leaves and white or pink flowers. It is supported by woody stems. The plant grows best in cool, swampy areas.

People grow cranberries in specially made swampy areas called bogs. When the berries are ready to be harvested, growers flood the bog. They knock the berries off the vines. The fallen berries float to the surface of the water. Workers collect them and process them for juice or sauce.

Other articles to read include: **Berry; Bog; Fruit; Vine.**

Cranberries

Crocus

Crocus blossoms

Crocus *(KROH kuhs)* is a popular garden flower. It is grown from a bulb. Its blossom may be white, yellow, or purplish. The blossom consists of six parts of nearly equal size. The crocus's leaves look like large blades of grass. Most crocuses grow about 3 to 4 inches (8 to 10 centimeters) tall. There are many kinds of crocus. Some crocuses are among the earliest of spring flowers. Others bloom in the autumn.

The saffron crocus provides the flavoring called saffron. It is an important ingredient in both Mediterranean and Indian dishes. Saffron is prepared by hand harvesting and drying the threadlike female parts of the flower, which makes it very expensive. About 60,000 flowers yield just one pound (0.45 kilogram). Saffron also is used as a dye.

Crocuses are native to southern Europe and Asia. They are now grown around the world.

Other articles to read include: **Flower.**

Crop

Corn, which is harvested in the fall, is both a food and feed crop. Besides being fed to livestock, it is used to make oil and syrup as well as for fuel.

A crop is a plant grown for human use. Crops grown to feed people are called food crops. Most crops are food crops. Crops eaten by animals are called feed crops. Some crops are grown because they produce threadlike pieces of material called fiber. Plant fiber is used in clothing and many other products. These crops are called fiber crops. Other crops are grown for the beauty they add to our surroundings.

Food crops include fruits, vegetables, and grains. Animal feed crops include such crops as alfalfa, corn, and soybeans. Cotton, flax, and hemp plants provide fiber. Crops grown for their beauty include flowers, lawn grasses, shrubs, and decorative trees.

Other articles to read include: **Agriculture; Farm and farming; Flower; Fruit; Grain; Vegetable.**

Cucumber

The cucumber is a garden vegetable. It is covered by a thin green skin that is either smooth or prickly. The inside of a cucumber is white or yellowish. Most cucumbers have many seeds inside them, but some kinds have no seeds at all.

Cucumbers are often eaten raw. Many times, they are added to salads. They are also made into pickles. Cucumbers are a good source of iron, calcium, and some vitamins.

The cucumber plant is a hairy-stemmed vine. The leaves of the plant are shaped like triangles. It has yellow or whitish flowers. Cucumbers grow from the flowers. They may grow from 1 to 36 inches (2.5 to 91 centimeters) long. Cucumbers are grown in many parts of the world.

Other articles to read include: **Vegetable; Vine.**

Cucumbers grow from the flowers of the cucumber vine.

Cyanobacteria

Cyanobacteria *(SY uh noh bak TIHR ee uh)* are tiny living things that make their own food using sunlight. Cyanobacteria typically live in water, though some live in soil. They are sometimes called *blue-green algae (AL jee).* But cyanobacteria are not true algae. Instead, they are a type of bacteria. Their color may be blue-green, black, brown, or pinkish. Most cyanobacteria can be seen only with a microscope.

Many kinds of cyanobacteria live as individual cells. Others live as long strings of cells. Cyanobacteria are especially common in ocean water. They sometimes form colorful areas of growth called *blooms.* The blooms provide food for many other living things. Some cyanobacteria form slippery, dark coatings on rocks along the shores of rivers, lakes, and oceans.

Cyanobacteria are bacteria that make their own food using the energy in sunlight.

Cyanobacteria make their own food through a process called *photosynthesis (foh tuh SIHN thuh sihs).* This process requires water and the gas carbon dioxide. Photosynthesis uses these ingredients and the energy in sunlight to make sugar. It gives off the gas oxygen. In fact, cyanobacteria provide much of the oxygen that animals breathe.

Other articles to read include: **Algae; Photosynthesis.**

Cycad

Cycads *(SY kadz)* are large seed plants that look much like palm trees. Their leaves resemble fern leaves. But cycads are not closely related to palm trees or ferns. Instead, cycads belong to a group of seed plants called *gymnosperms (JIHM nuh spurmz).* This group is made up of cone-bearing trees, such as pine and spruce trees. There are many kinds of cycads.

Cycads live in warm, moist regions. Some are the size of shrubs. Others can grow up to 60 feet (18 meters) tall. Cycad leaves grow in a circle at the end of the stem. New leaves grow every year. Cycads bear a heavy cone. The cone may grow 3 feet (90 centimeters) long. The cone holds the plant's seeds. Cycad bark is rough.

Some cycads have stems without branches. Others have an underground stem, called a *tuber (TOO buhr),* that looks like a potato.

Cycads covered large areas of land when dinosaurs roamed Earth. In fact, many dinosaurs likely fed on cycads. Today, cycads grow in only a few small areas. Many cycads have become endangered.

Other articles to read include: **Conifer; Fern; Gymnosperm; Palm; Tuber.**

The cycad plant bears its seeds in cones.

Up to 60 ft (18 m)   Leaf   Cone   Bark

Cypress trees

Cypress

The cypress *(SY pruhs)* is an evergreen tree. People often plant cypresses for their beauty. Cypress trees may live for thousands of years. Cypresses grow in warm climates in Asia, Europe, and North America. The cypress tree has small, scalelike leaves. The leaves grow in dense, fan-shaped sprays. The cypress has globe-shaped cones. The cones are covered by woody scales that look like small shields. The cypress's light brown wood has a strong, cedarlike odor.

There are several kinds of cypresses. The Monterey cypress is named for the Monterey Peninsula of California, its native region. The trunk is rarely more than 20 inches (50 centimeters) across. The tree has long, heavy branches that spread and grow in unusual shapes. The tree often grows near the ocean shore. There, its branches are twisted and bent by strong ocean winds.

Other articles to read include: **Conifer; Evergreen; Tree.**

Dd

Daffodil

A daffodil *(DAF uh dihl)* is a type of flower that blooms in the spring. It has a cup-shaped center with petals around it. Most daffodils are white or yellow. Some are orange, pink, or cream. Some daffodils are also called *jonquils (JONG kwuhls).*

Daffodils first grew in Europe and northern Africa. Now, people grow daffodils in gardens around the world.

Growers have created thousands of different kinds of daffodils. The best known is the trumpet narcissus, or trumpet daffodil. Each stem of this daffodil has one flower. The flower has a long, cup-shaped center. Most other daffodils have more than one flower on each stem.

Daffodils grow from round underground parts called *bulbs.* People plant daffodil bulbs in the fall.

Other articles to read include: **Bulb; Flower; Narcissus.**

Daffodil

Dahlia

The dahlia *(DAL yuh)* is a garden flower grown for its beautiful blossoms. There are many kinds of dahlia. Dahlia blossoms come in different shapes and sizes. Some are ball-shaped. Others have long, flat petals. A dahlia called the *cactus dahlia* has twisted petals. Some are so large that they are called *dinner plate dahlias.*

Dahlias grow from *tuberous* (thick, fleshy) roots. The roots should be planted in a sunny spot in late spring, after the last chance of frost has passed. The flowers will bloom in late summer into fall. After the first frost of winter, the roots must be be dug up and stored in a cool, dry place until the next spring.

Dahlias are native to Central America. Today, they are grown around the world. Dahlias were named for the Swedish scientist Anders Dahl.

Other articles to read include: **Flower.**

Dahlia

Daisy

Daisy is the name of many different kinds of flowers. The name comes from the Old English words for *day's eye*. The flower closes at night and opens in the morning, like people's eyes.

Some kinds of daisy belong to a group of flowers called *chrysanthemums (kruh SAN thuh muhmz)*. Such daisies have a yellow center with white or yellow petals all around. One of them is called the *oxeye daisy* or *white daisy*. It grows up to 3 feet (1 meter) tall. Its blossoms are up to 2 inches (5 centimeters) across. Oxeye daisies grow wild in fields and roadsides in North America.

Another type of daisy is called the *English daisy*. English daisies have a yellow center with white, pink, red, or purplish petals all around. They grow only about 6 inches (1.5 centimeters) tall.

Other articles to read include: **Chrysanthemum; Flower.**

Daisy

Dandelion

A dandelion (*DAN duh LY uhn*) is a type of yellow wildflower. It grows throughout the world in lawns and meadows. Most gardeners think of the dandelion as a weed. As a weed, it is hard to control.

Dandelion leaves have notches that look like teeth. The dandelion has a straight, hollow stem. The stem contains a white, milky juice. The golden-yellow head is actually a bunch of tiny flowers. After blooming, the flowers form cottony seeds. The wind carries the seeds far and wide. Wherever they land, new dandelions may grow.

To get rid of dandelions, gardeners must cut the roots as deeply as possible. Dandelion roots can grow as long as 3 feet (91 centimeters) underground. People can also use special chemicals to kill dandelions without hurting the grass.

Young dandelion leaves can be used in salads or eaten cooked. People sometimes make wine from dandelion flowers.

Other articles to read include: **Flower; Weed.**

Dandelion

Darwin, Charles Robert

Charles Robert Darwin (1809-1882) was a British scientist. He became famous for his theory of *evolution (ehv uh LOO shuhn)*, the way living things develop on Earth. Darwin argued that all of Earth's different kinds of plants and animals developed over many millions of years from a single life form.

Charles Robert Darwin

Darwin suggested that evolution works mainly through a process called *natural selection*. According to natural selection, individuals are born with different *traits* (characteristics). Certain traits help individuals to survive and to have offspring. Successful individuals pass their traits on to their offspring. In this way, the traits that aid in survival become more common. Over time, differences in traits cause the development of new kinds of plants and animals.

Darwin wrote about his ideas in his 1859 book *On the Origin of Species by Means of Natural Selection*. Darwin's ideas were shocking to many of the people of his day. Many believed that each type of living thing had been created by an act of God. Nearly all scientists now accept Darwin's theory. But some people do not accept it because it does not agree with their religious beliefs.

Darwin was born in Shrewsbury, England. From 1831 to 1836, he worked as a scientist aboard a ship named the *Beagle*. The ship traveled to places throughout the world. Darwin studied the plants and animals everywhere the ship went. On the Galapagos Islands in the Pacific Ocean, he noticed many variations among plants and animals of the same general type as those in South America. Studies of these variations helped Darwin form his ideas about evolution.

Other articles to read include: **Adaptation; Evolution; Natural selection; Naturalist; Species.**

Darwin sailed aboard the H.M.S. *Beagle,* studying plants and animals around the world.

Death

Death is the end of life. Every living thing eventually dies. Plants sometimes die after being attacked by insects and other pests. They may be infected by microbes that cause disease. Plants also die if they do not get enough water and sunlight. Plants can even die of old age.

Plants that die lose their green color. They usually turn brown. Trees that die lose their leaves. Soon, a variety of living things break down the plant. Termites eat wood. Fungi slowly break down dead plant matter. Microbes also feed on dead plants. These living things help to return the nourishing substances in a dead plant to the soil. That enriches the soil for new plants to grow.

Other articles to read include: **Decay; Life; Soil.**

A dead tree continues to stand, but weathering, insects, and decay slowly break down the branches and trunk.

Decay

Decay is the breaking down of dead plant or animal material. Decay is also called *decomposition*. Bacteria and fungi cause most decay. They use chemicals called *enzymes* to make things decompose. Enzymes speed up chemical changes.

Decay plays an important role in enriching the soil. Dead plants and animals hold valuable nourishing substances called *nutrients*. Plants need nutrients to grow. Without decay, many nutrients would remain locked inside dead plants and animals. Decay returns these nutrients to the soil. Plants then take up these nutrients through their roots. Animals take in the nutrients by eating plants. In this way, decay is important for the survival of all living things.

Other articles to read include: **Compost; Death; Life; Soil.**

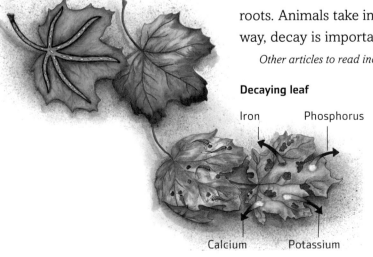

Decaying leaf

Iron   Phosphorus

Calcium   Potassium

Dead leaves fall from trees and decay. Decayed leaves make the soil rich in iron and other minerals.

Deciduous tree

A deciduous *(dih SIHJ u uhs)* tree is any tree that loses its leaves at a certain time of year and later grows new ones. Most deciduous trees lose their leaves in autumn and grow new leaves in the spring. Beech, birch, elm, hickory, maple, and oak are examples of deciduous trees.

The leaves of most deciduous trees are broad and green. Such trees are also called *broadleaf trees.* Broadleaf trees that grow in tropical rain forests are not deciduous. They keep their leaves the year around. Deciduous trees are different from *coniferous (kuh NIHF uhr uhs)* trees. These trees have needlelike leaves that stay on the tree all year long.

Deciduous trees grow on every continent except Antarctica. They grow best in places that have warm weather and plenty of rainfall for at least part of the year. Some deciduous trees grow well in colder places. These trees include birch and aspen.

Deciduous trees lose their leaves to help them survive the winter. Trees lose large amounts of water through their leaves. That is usually not a problem in the summer, because the tree's roots keep it supplied with water. But it can be difficult for trees to take in water during the winter. Snow that remains frozen does not soak into the ground. Also, roots cannot take in water when

Continued on the next page

In a temperate deciduous forest, the dominant trees occupy the top level, or *story,* with smaller trees forming the second level, or *shade.* Shrubs form a level of their own, below which is another level of plants.

Top level
Dominant trees

Second level
Smaller trees

Third level
Shrubs

Bottom level

Autumn   Winter   Spring

The leaves of some deciduous trees turn bright colors before falling off in autumn. After having bare branches in winter, deciduous trees grow new leaves in the spring.

Deciduous *Continued from the previous page*

the ground is frozen. Dropping the leaves helps a tree conserve its water.

In the past, forests of deciduous trees covered large areas of the eastern United States and Europe. People cut down much of these forests to make room for farms and houses and to get lumber and firewood. Today, smaller forests of deciduous trees grow in these areas.

Other articles to read include: **Beech; Forest; Leaf; Maple; Oak; Tree; Wood.**

Deforestation

Deforestation *(dee fawr uh STAY shuhn)* is the destruction or damage of a forest. It usually occurs when people clear away trees to build farms or cities. Large areas of forest are also cut for lumber and fuel. Diseases that kill trees are also a major cause of deforestation.

Natural forests once covered much of the world. About half of these native forests have been destroyed. Much of the forest that remains has been damaged. Many forests have been *fragmented* (divided) into smaller patches separated by farmland, roads, or cities.

Many areas have lost at least 90 percent of their native forests. Such areas include much of Europe, eastern North America, and eastern and southern Asia. Many islands have been deforested. For instance, most native forests have vanished from the islands of Japan, Madagascar, and New Zealand.

Continued on the next page

Deforestation is especially severe in the tropics. As many as 40 million acres (16 million hectares) of tropical forests are destroyed each year—the equivalent of 50 football fields a minute. Tropical forests provide a home for a great variety of plants and animals. These living things are at risk of becoming extinct as the forest is destroyed.

The loss of forests causes many problems. The roots of trees hold rain water. This anchors the soil. Thus, deforestation causes loss of soil through *erosion* and flooding. Trees also release large amounts of the gas oxygen. People and other animals need oxygen to breathe. Trees also remove carbon dioxide from the air. Increases in carbon dioxide are a major cause of global warming, an increase in the average temperature at Earth's surface.

During the past 100 years, people have tried to protect more of the world's forests. In many areas, they have set up national parks and other protected areas to reduce deforestation.

Other articles to read include: **Conservation; Endangered species; Extinction; Forest; Rain forest.**

The burning of rain forest in Brazil to make room for ranches contributes to global warming. Cutting the trees means there is less oxygen released into the air and less carbon dioxide removed.

Desert

A desert is an area where little rain falls. Most deserts are also extremely hot. Relatively few plants and animals can survive in these difficult conditions. However, some plants thrive in deserts. These include a variety of cactuses and the mesquite *(mehs KEET)* tree. Some animals also can live in deserts.

Deserts receive less than 10 inches (25 centimeters) of rain a year. Sometimes it does not rain for several years. In the summer, the temperature in some deserts can reach 100 °F (38 °C) during the day. At night, the temperature may drop to 45 °F (7 °C). However, some deserts can have freezing temperatures or even snow during the winter. *Continued on the next page*

The plants in Organ Pipe Cactus National Monument in southern Arizona, in the United States, thrive on dry, hot conditions.

The Gobi is a windswept, nearly treeless desert that stretches across part of southern Mongolia and northern China. It is very cold in winter and hot in summer.

Desert *Continued from the previous page*

Plants have special ways of getting water in deserts. Some plants have strong roots that grow deep into the ground in search of water. Plants also may send roots far into the surrounding area. This enables the plant to take in as much water as possible when it does rain. Cactuses have features that help them to store water. They are covered with waxy skin that holds water in. They also lack ordinary leaves, through which they would lose water. Many desert plants can store water in their leaves, roots, or stems. For example, the stem of a plant called the *barrel cactus* swells up with water after a rainfall. The stem shrinks as the plant uses the water.

Many plants may grow around an *oasis (oh AY sihs)*. An oasis is an area of land where underground water comes close enough to the surface to be easily reached by roots. Streams of water can be found in some parts of deserts. The water in these streams begins in mountains that lie outside deserts.

About ⅕ of Earth is covered by deserts. Deserts exist on every continent. The largest desert in the world is the Sahara in northern Africa. The Sahara covers about 3 ½ million square miles (9 million square kilometers) of land. That is about the same size as the entire United States.

Deserts cover about 500,000 square miles (1.3 million square kilometers) of land in North America. Deserts in the United States include the Painted and Sonoran deserts in Arizona and the Mojave and Colorado deserts in California.

Not all deserts are hot. For example, some areas near the North and South poles are deserts. Most of Antarctica is a frozen desert. The land is covered in ice, but little snow falls.

Other articles to read include: **Cactus; Irrigation; Mesquite; Oasis.**

Much of Antarctica is a frozen desert. It is quite cold, but little snow or other precipitation falls.

Dill

Dill is a plant used to flavor foods. The leaves, called *dill weed,* are often used to flavor pickles. Dill also is used to flavor fish, sour cream, and other foods. Dill is also grown for its seeds. The seeds have a strong, bitter taste. A flavoring oil is also produced from the plant.

Other articles to read include: **Herb; Seed.**

Dill is an herb that is used to flavor foods.

Dogwood

The dogwood is a small tree or shrub. The best-known dogwood in North America is the flowering dogwood. It rarely grows more than 40 feet (12 meters) tall or 18 inches (46 centimeters) across. Its wood is hard and heavy.

Flowering dogwood grows small, greenish-white flowers. Most of the bright red fruits have two seeds. The leaves have veins that curve upward. The unusual pattern of the bark and the gray flower buds make the dogwood an attractive winter tree.

Flowering dogwood is the state flower of North Carolina. It is also the state tree of Missouri and the state flower and tree of Virginia. The Pacific dogwood is the provincial flower of British Columbia.

There are about six kinds of dogwood shrubs. The most common is the red twig dogwood. The berries attract birds.

Other articles to read include: **Flower; Shrub; Tree.**

Dogwood trees produce beautiful white blossoms in the spring.

Corn is especially subject to damage by drought. Severe drought can destroy an entire crop.

Drought

A drought *(drowt)* is an unusually long period without rain. Droughts can cause crops to wither and die. Droughts sometimes cause famine. A famine is a shortage of food that results in widespread hunger and death.

Higher-than-normal temperatures often occur during periods of drought. These high temperatures add to the crop damage. Forest and grass fires also happen more often and spread quickly. These fires may destroy valuable land used for timber and grazing. Houses and other buildings may be lost to the flames.

Soil that is dried out by drought may be blown away by strong winds that create dust storms. Streams, ponds, and wells often dry up during a drought. Animals suffer and may even die because of the lack of water. Government officials may limit the amount of water people can use during a drought.

The Great Plains region of the United States suffered one of the worst droughts in its history from 1931 to 1938. Few food crops could be grown, and food became scarce, driving up food prices. The area struck by this drought became known as the Dust Bowl.

Other articles to read include: **Crop; Desert; Farm and farming; Great Plains; Irrigation; Soil.**

The common duckweed is the smallest flowering plant known.

Duckweed

Duckweed is a tiny water plant. It floats on the surface of small lakes, ponds, and slow-moving rivers. Duckweed is found around much of the world, except in extremely cold places. It can spread quickly. Small ponds often have thousands of duckweeds. The duckweeds cover the water's surface like a green carpet.

Duckweeds are flat and green. They usually have one root, which looks like a hair. Duckweeds do not have a stem or leaves.

One type of duckweed is called the *common duckweed*. It measures only $\frac{1}{16}$ to $\frac{3}{16}$ inch (1.6 to 4.8 millimeters) long. It is the smallest flowering plant in the world.

Duckweeds help keep the water clean. They remove small bits of dirt from lakes and rivers. Ducks and fish eat duckweed.

Other articles to read include: **Wetland.**

Ebony

Ebony *(EHB uh nee)* is a hard black wood. It can be polished so that it shines almost as bright as metal. Ebony trees grow around much of the world.

Only the inner wood of the ebony tree is dark in color. The outer wood is a lighter color. The wood contains a hard material called *gum.* This gum makes ebony easy to carve. Ebony wood is used mainly to make black piano keys, musical instruments, handles for knives and brushes, and fancy carvings.

Other articles to read include: **Gum; Tree; Wood.**

Wood carvers prize the dark, inner wood of the ebony tree, which can be polished.

Ecology

Ecology *(ee KAHL uh jee)* is the study of how living things relate to one another and to the world around them. Scientists who study ecology are called *ecologists (ee KAHL uh jists).*

Every living thing depends on other living things and on non-living things in its *environment* (surroundings). For example, a moose eats certain plants for food. If the plants in its surround-ings were destroyed, the moose would have to move to another area. Otherwise, it could starve to death. Plants also depend on animals. Wastes from animals provide many of the nourishing substances that plants need to live. These nourishing substances are called *nutrients.*

The living and nonliving things in an environment make up an *ecosystem.* Ecologists divide most ecosystems into six parts: (1) the sun, (2) nonliving things, (3) primary producers, (4) primary consumers, (5) secondary consumers, and (6) decomposers. The sun provides all the energy in nearly every ecosystem. Plants and certain other living things use the energy in sunlight to make their own food. These living things are *primary producers.* Plants also need such nonliving things as nutrients and water. Plants are eaten by many kinds of animals, including grasshoppers, rabbits,

Continued on the next page

Ecology *Continued from the previous page*

and deer. The animals that feed on plants are *primary consumers*. Animals that feed on primary consumers include foxes, hawks, and snakes. These animals are called *secondary consumers*. Secondary consumers may also feed on other secondary consumers. *Decomposers* break down dead plants and animals into simple nutrients. The nutrients go back into the soil and are used again by plants. Decomposers include fungi and microbes.

Energy passes through an ecosystem in a set of stages called a *food chain*. In one simple food chain, grass is the primary producer. A rabbit is the primary consumer that eats the grass. A fox is the secondary consumer that eats the rabbit. This example shows how energy flows in a chain from the grass, to the rabbit, to the fox.

Ecologists study the natural world on three levels: *populations, communities,* **and** *ecosystems.* **An ecosystem is a scientific name for all the living and nonliving things in an area and the relationship among them. One type of ecosystem is shown below. Each main part is shown in a different color.**

Most ecosystems have a variety of producers, consumers, and decomposers. For example, grass, shrubs, and trees might grow in an area. Tree leaves might be eaten by insects. Insects are eaten by birds, and birds may be eaten by larger birds.

In this way, different food chains overlap. These overlapping food chains make up a *food web*.

Most living things use only a small part of the energy available to them to grow. Plants can change no more than 1 percent

Continued on the next page

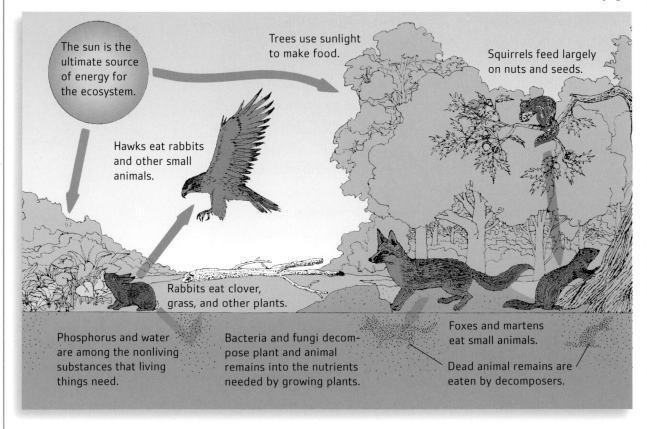

The sun is the ultimate source of energy for the ecosystem.

Trees use sunlight to make food.

Squirrels feed largely on nuts and seeds.

Hawks eat rabbits and other small animals.

Rabbits eat clover, grass, and other plants.

Phosphorus and water are among the nonliving substances that living things need.

Bacteria and fungi decompose plant and animal remains into the nutrients needed by growing plants.

Foxes and martens eat small animals.

Dead animal remains are eaten by decomposers.

of the sunlight that reaches them into food. Plants use most of this food to live. Similarly, animals that feed on plants use only 10 to 20 percent of the energy in the plants to grow. They use the rest to live. Animals that feed on animals also use only 10 to 20 percent of the food they eat to grow. In this way, less and less energy is available at each stage of a food chain. Thus, all ecosystems develop an *energy pyramid*. Plants form the base of the pyramid. The animals that eat plants form the next level. It is smaller than the level below, because there is less energy. Animals that feed on animals form the next level. It is smaller than the level below it.

Animals that feed on plants are called *herbivores (HUR buh vawrz)*. Animals that feed on other animals are called *carnivores (KAHR nuh vawrz)*. Animals that eat both plants and animals are known as *omnivores (OM nuh vawrz)*. Most carnivores hunt for their food. Hunting animals are known as *predators*. Some carnivores are *scavengers* that feed on dead animals.

Many ecologists try to find ways to protect the environment. They work to protect Earth's natural resources, including forests, soil, and water. Others try to solve environmental problems that hurt plant and animal life.

Other articles to read include: **Adaptation; Balance of nature; Conservation; Decay; Environment; Food chain; Food web; Habitat**

In an ecological restoration area in Australia, ecologists attempt to restore plants to the area. Ecologists work to protect the environment and restore damaged ecosystems.

Eggplant

Eggplant is a plant that bears large, egg-shaped fruit. The fruit also is called *eggplant, garden egg*, or *aubergine (oh behr ZHEEN)*. It sometimes grows nearly as large as a football. Eggplant is eaten as a vegetable. It is often fried or baked.

Eggplant may be white, brown, yellow, purple, or striped. The fruit grows on a bush that stands from 2 to 6 feet (60 to 180 centimeters) tall. It grows only in warm weather and takes 115 to 120 days to ripen. The first eggplant probably grew in northern India. The plant later spread to other areas of the world. The purple variety has been a popular vegetable in the United States since about 1860, even though it contains low levels of vitamins.

Other articles to read include: **Fruit; Vegetable.**

Eggplant

Elm

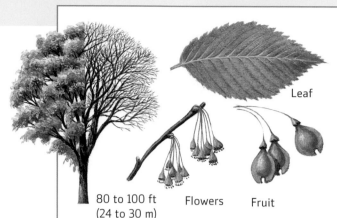

Leaf

80 to 100 ft
(24 to 30 m)

Flowers

Fruit

Bark

The American elm tree has gray bark and oval leaves with saw-toothed edges. The nutlike fruits have flat wings around them.

The elm is a large, beautiful tree. Elms grow in North America, Europe, and some parts of Asia. Elms are grown for shade and lumber. Elm wood is tough and hard. It is used to make many things, including boats and furniture.

There are several kinds of elms. The *American elm* is the most common elm in North America. It is also called the *white elm*.

An elm can grow to a height of 100 feet (30 meters). It can live for up to 150 years.

Many American elms have been killed by Dutch elm disease. The disease is caused by a kind of fungus. The fungus is spread by beetles. Other kinds of elm trees can resist Dutch elm disease. Many of them have been planted to replace trees killed by the disease.

Other articles to read include: **Tree; Wood.**

Embryo

Pine seed embryo

Embryo

An embryo *(EHM bree oh)* is a plant or other living thing in an early stage of growth. An embryo is created when sex cells combine. A *sperm* is the male sex cell. An *egg* is the female sex cell. Their combination is called *fertilization*. The fertilized egg divides over and over to form a clump of connected cells. This group of cells is the embryo.

Among flowering plants, eggs are housed within the *ovary* of a flower. Tiny grains of pollen carry sperm from one flower to another. Each grain of pollen holds two sperm cells. One sperm fertilizes the egg. The other sperm fertilizes tissue that will provide food for the developing embryo. Together, the embryo and its food supply form a seed. The ovary housing the seed soon develops into a fruit. Animals that eat the fruit pass the seed with their body waste. The seed may then develop into a new plant. Many fruits house more than one seed.

Other articles to read include: **Fertilization; Flower; Fruit; Pollen; Reproduction; Seed.**

Endangered species

Endangered species are living things that are in danger of dying out and disappearing forever. Thousands of plant species are endangered. In fact, scientists think that about one out of every five plant species is now threatened.

Endangered plants include the running buffalo clover, Santa Cruz cypress, snakeroot, and many kinds of cactus. Many plants on islands are endangered. For example, many plants native to Hawaii have become endangered. These plants include yellow hibiscus, the state flower. Many plants in tropical rain forests are endangered. The giant rafflesia of Southeast Asia grows the largest flowers of any plant. These flowers can grow more than 3 feet (90 centimeters) wide. Giant rafflesia has become endangered because the forests where it lives are being destroyed.

Scientists call a species *endangered* if they expect it to die off in less than 20 years unless it receives special protection. Some species are small in numbers but not endangered because their population is not dropping. The loss of a species is called *extinction*.

Extinction is a normal part of nature. A change in climate or competition with other plants might cause a plant to become extinct. However, extinction was ordinarily rare, and most species were not endangered. Today, the number of endangered species is much higher. Many more species are also becoming extinct. This increase in endangered and extinct species has been caused by people. There are several main reasons why so many plants are endangered.

Habitat destruction is the most serious problem for species in the wild. Habitat is the place where a plant lives. Most plants can live only in a certain habitat. If their habitat is destroyed, the species cannot survive.

People destroy plant habitats in many ways. They cut down forests to build houses or make room for farmland. They graze their livestock in grasslands. The livestock eats too much grass, and the grass does not have a chance to grow back. Wetlands and swamps are being drained or filled in so people can build new housing on them.

Continued on the next page

Yellow hibiscus, the state flower of Hawaii, has become endangered in the wild. Many plants native to the Hawaiian islands are threatened by loss of habitat.

The titan arum is an unusual plant of Southeast Asia. It has become endangered because people are destroying the forests where it grows.

Endangered species *Continued from the previous page*

Tropical rain forests have more species of plants than any other area on Earth. But the rain forests are being destroyed faster than any other wild habitat. The loss of rain forests also causes countless animal species to become extinct. Rain forests are being destroyed faster than scientists can identify new species of plants and animals. Thus, species are likely disappearing before they have been counted and named.

Poaching is another problem. Poaching is the illegal collection of wildlife. People sometimes remove wildflowers or other rare plants from wild areas. Some of these plants are used as medicines. Others are prized for their beauty. For example, people have illegally removed many orchids from wild areas. Many of these orchids are endangered.

Competition with or destruction by introduced species is another problem, especially on many islands. People have introduced such animals as rats and pigs to some areas. These animals may eat seeds or otherwise harm native plants. People also have introduced foreign plants to many areas. For example, kudzu is an Asian vine that grows quickly. People brought kudzu to the southern United States to provide food for livestock. The vine soon grew out of control and has spread throughout much of the country. Kudzu grows in thick stands that can crowd out native plants. It threatens a number of rare wildflowers and other native plants.

Loss of animals threatens plants that depend on animals for pollination or spreading seeds. Many flowering plants rely on insects or other animals to spread pollen from one flower to another. This pollen fertilizes the plant's seeds. If an animal becomes endangered, the plants that depend on it may also become endangered. Many plants also rely on animals to spread their seeds. For example, many flowering plants house their seeds in fruit. Animals that eat this fruit pass the seeds with their waste. That helps plants reach new locations to grow. The loss of animals that eat fruit may also cause plants to become endangered.

There are many reasons to protect endangered species. Many people believe that all living things have a right to exist. Also,

Continued on the next page

every species is part of the beauty and wonder of nature. Preserving such beauty enriches the lives of people.

Plants are valuable in other ways. Plants are the source of nearly all our food. They also produce much of the oxygen we breathe. Some plants provide building material. Other plants provide medicines. Scientists worry that valuable medicines are being lost because plants are disappearing from rain forests before they can be studied.

In recent years, people have done many things to help protect endangered species. But these efforts may not be enough to save many plants.

Many countries have passed laws to protect endangered species. In the United States, the Endangered Species Act protects endangered wildlife against anything that harms them or their habitats. Also, many wild species are protected by CITES. *CITES* stands for the *C*onvention on *I*nternational *Tr*ade in *E*ndangered *Sp*ecies of Wild Fauna and Flora. *Fauna* means *animals,* and *flora* means *plants.* This agreement forbids people to buy and sell endangered living things or their parts.

Some laws protect plants from poaching. For example, it is illegal in many countries to remove protected wildflowers from their habitats.

Rare plants also may be saved by being grown in large gardens called botanical gardens. The seeds of many plants are being stored in special seed banks. These seeds can be used for future planting if the plants become extinct in the wild.

Other articles to read include: **Conservation; Deforestation; Extinction; Habitat; Invasive species; Rain forest; Seed; Species.**

Scientists have stored vast numbers of seeds in special seed banks. These seeds may later be used to grow plants that are extinct in the wild.

The environment includes living things such as flowers and trees. It also includes nonliving things such as temperature and sunlight.

Environment

An environment is everything that makes up the surroundings of a living thing. A plant's environment may be made up of soil, sunlight, and animals that eat the plant.

Nonliving things include temperature and sunlight. They make up what is called the *abiotic (AY by AHT ihk)* environment. The word *abiotic* means "not living." Living things, or things that were once alive, such as fallen trees, make up the biotic environment. Together, the abiotic and biotic environments make up the total environment of living and nonliving things.

The study of the relationships between living things and their environment is called ecology. People who study ecology are called ecologists.

Other articles to read include: **Biome; Ecology; Habitat.**

Ferns grow on the branches of live oak trees in the southern United States. Such ferns are epiphytes, a plant that grows on another plant.

Epiphyte

An epiphyte *(EHP uh fyt)* is a plant that grows on another plant. Epiphytes do not take food from the other plant. Instead, they make their own food. Most epiphytes live in warm parts of the world. But others grow in cool or cold areas.

Epiphytes are sometimes called "air plants." Most regular plants use their roots to dig into soil. This is how they get water and nourishing substances called *nutrients.* An epiphyte is different. Its roots are exposed to the air. It gets nutrients from the air or from nearby plant wastes. It takes in water through its roots or through leaves.

An epiphyte usually does not harm the plant that it is growing on. But an epiphyte can hurt the other plant if it grows too big. A large epiphyte may block the plant's sunlight.

Other articles to read include: **Bromeliad; Fern; Moss; Orchid.**

Eucalyptus

The eucalyptus *(YOO kuh LIHP tuhs)* is a type of tree that is native to Australia. People also grow eucalyptus in many other areas of the world with warm climates. There are hundreds of kinds.

Eucalyptus trees grow quickly and can reach a gigantic size. They have long, narrow, leathery leaves. Their flowers are filled with nectar.

People use eucalyptus trees for their wood, oil, and a sticky liquid called *gum.* Eucalyptus wood is used in ships, railroad ties, telephone poles, and fences. Eucalyptus bark contains *tannin,* a substance used to make ink, dye, leather, and medicine. Eucalyptus leaves contain a valuable oil. It is used for cleaning and for masking unpleasant smells. The oil prevents most kinds of animals from eating the leaves. Koalas are among the few animals that can eat eucalyptus leaves.

In Australia, people grow a kind of eucalyptus called *jarrah* for its wood. The most common kind of eucalyptus in the United States is called the *blue gum.* In California, people plant the trees around orange and lemon groves to protect them from wind.

Other articles to read include: **Gum; Nectar; Tree; Wood.**

Koalas are among the few animals that eat eucalyptus leaves. The leaves contain an oil that most animals avoid.

Euglena

Euglenas *(yoo GLEE nuhz)* are tiny one-celled *organisms* (living things). There are about 150 *species* (kinds) of euglenas. They live in fresh water. Most euglenas multiply during warm weather. Euglenas may form a green scum on the surfaces of ponds or drainage ditches.

Euglenas can only be seen with a microscope. They range in length from $\frac{1}{1,000}$ to $\frac{1}{100}$ of an inch (0.025 to 0.25 millimeter).

Euglena

Most euglenas are green. They contain *chlorophyll (KLAWR uh fihl),* a green coloring material found in plants and other organisms. Like plants, green euglenas get energy from sunlight. Some euglenas eat tiny bits of food in the water.

A euglena's body is shaped like a tiny rod. It has a whiplike part called a *flagellum (fluh JEHL uhm).* It uses the flagellum to move through water.

Other articles to read include: **Chlorophyll; Flagellum.**

Evergreens stay green throughout the year.

The evergreen Monterey cypress often grows near the ocean. Its branches are gnarled and bent by strong winds.

Evergreen

An evergreen is a plant that stays green throughout the year. It does not shed leaves in the fall. Many evergreens are trees. But there are also smaller evergreens.

The best-known evergreen trees in North America include the cedar, cypress, fir, hemlock, pine, and spruce. Most Christmas trees are fir or spruce trees. Smaller evergreen plants include holly, ivy, and myrtle.

Many evergreens live on mountains or in other areas where it is cold much of the year. Such evergreens include pine and spruce trees. But other evergreens grow in the *tropics,* the warm areas near Earth's equator. Many tropical evergreens are called *broadleaf* evergreens because they have wide leaves. Evergreens that grow in colder climates often have needle-shaped leaves.

Other articles to read include: **Cedar; Conifer; Cypress; Fir; Hemlock; Pine; Spruce; Tree.**

Evolution

Evolution is the scientific theory that life changes, or *evolves,* usually over long periods of time. This change is called evolution. The different kinds of living things that evolve are called *species.* The theory of evolution explains why there is such a great variety of living things. It describes how species change over time. It also explains how living things adapt to their surroundings.

Much evolutionary change happens through *natural selection.* In natural selection, members of a species are born with different *traits* (features). Certain traits help individuals to survive and have offspring. They pass these traits on to their offspring. Individuals without these traits are less likely to survive and have offspring. In this way, the traits that aid in survival become more common over time.

Continued on the next page

Consider how trees compete with one another for sunlight. They use the energy in sunlight to make food. Trees that grow taller lift their leaves into the light. They may block sunlight from reaching shorter trees. Thus, taller trees are able to make more food and produce more seeds. They are more likely to survive and have offspring. Over time, taller trees will become more common than shorter trees.

Individuals are born with different traits partly because of changes in *genes*. Genes are chemical instructions inside cells. They direct how a living thing grows. Plants pass down their genes to their offspring. However, genes sometimes change. These changes are called *mutations*. Mutations can cause new traits. Natural selection determines whether these new traits become common.

Evolution also causes new species to appear. In fact, the theory of evolution suggests that all species evolved from a single form of life. Scientists believe that the first living thing appeared more than 3 ½ billion years ago. It is the common ancestor of all the millions of species on Earth today. Thus, all living things are related. Closely related species share a relatively recent common ancestor. For example, wheat and bamboo are closely related. Scientists have determined that they evolved from a common ancestor that lived between 30 million and 40 million years ago. Wheat and mosses are distantly related. Scientists have determined that they evolved from a common ancestor that lived more than 400 million years ago.

New species arise in a variety of ways. One way occurs when members of a species are separated by some barrier. For example, plants sometimes reach an island far out in the ocean. These plants will no longer have contact with those of their species that live on the mainland. Natural selection may favor different traits among plants

Moss grows on a hillside in a pine forest in Norway. Mosses often grow in moist environments and are more abundant in old forests than in young ones.

Continued on the next page

Cabbage trees are among the many plants found only on the islands of New Zealand. New species often evolve on islands.

The image of an ancient cycad leaf is preserved as a fossil. Cycads were among the most common plants 200 million years ago, but most became extinct.

Evolution *Continued from the previous page*

living on the island. Over time, these plants may become quite different from plants on the mainland. The plants on the island have become a new species.

The British scientist Charles Darwin described evolution by natural selection in a book he wrote in 1859. This book was called *On the Origin of Species by Means of Natural Selection*. Today, nearly all scientists believe that evolution is true. However, some people do not accept evolution for religious reasons.

Other articles to read include: **Adaptation; Darwin, Robert Charles; Extinction; Fossil; Gene; Natural selection; Species.**

Extinction

Extinction is when a kind of living thing dies out completely. All types of life may become extinct, including plants, animals, and *microbes* (microscopic organisms).

Extinction is a normal part of life. Most of the living things that once existed are now extinct. When a living thing becomes extinct, a new living thing may take its place. For example, cone-bearing plants called cycads were among the most common plants about 200 million years ago, in the time of the dinosaurs. Since then, most cycads have become extinct. Many of the remaining cycads are in danger of extinction. Today, flowering plants have taken the place of cycads.

Human beings have caused many hundreds of extinctions. Extinct plants include Cuban holly, the St. Helena olive, and the Kerala legume tree. Many plants that have become extinct were found only on islands. Others lived in forests that people destroyed. The greatest threat to plants is the destruction of the places where they live.

Many people try to save living things that are in danger of extinction. For example, it is illegal in many countries to collect plants that are in danger of extinction.

Other articles to read include: **Adaptation; Cycad; Deforestation; Endangered species; Evolution; Fossil; Habitat.**

Ff

Family

A family, in biology, is a group of closely related living things. Biologists classify each living thing according to seven major groups. These groups are *kingdom, phylum* (sometimes called *division*), *class, order, family, genus,* and *species.* Each group is made up of the smaller groups that come after it. For example, a family is made up of genuses, and a genus is made up of species.

The smaller the group, the more alike all its members are. Members of a particular family are more closely related to one another than are members of a particular order. But they are less closely related than are members of a particular genus.

There are many different families. Roses belong to the family Rosaceae. True grasses make up the family Poaceae.

Other articles to read include: **Class; Classification, Scientific; Genus; Kingdom; Order; Phylum; Species.**

Roses belong to the family Rosaceae.

Farm and farming

Farming is one of the most important jobs in the world. Nearly all the food we eat comes from plants grown on farms. We get most of our meat from animals that were fed farm plants. Many materials used to make clothes, such as cotton and flax, come from farm plants.

For thousands of years, farming was a way of life for most people in nearly every country. In the 1700's and early 1800's, for example, most American families lived on small farms. They grew corn, wheat, hay, fruits, and garden vegetables. They also raised livestock. Everyone in the family worked long and hard. But most families produced only enough food for themselves.

Continued on the next page

Soybeans and corn are the primary crops on farms across much of the midwestern United States.

Fern *Continued from the previous page*

Ferns have stems, roots, and leaves. The stem stores food for the plant. Stems may live for 100 years or more. The roots may also live a long time. They anchor the stem to the ground and soak up water and other nutrients the plant needs to make food. Food is made in the leaves. The leaves live only one or two years.

Nearly all plants reproduce by making seeds. But ferns release tiny particles called *spores*. Some spores enter the ground and start to grow into small, heart-shaped plants. These plants produce sperm and eggs. Eggs that are fertilized by sperm develop into new ferns.

Ferns are among the oldest kinds of plants that live on land. Scientists believe that ferns appeared from 400 million to 350 million years ago. Ferns were common in the great forests that covered Earth long before the dinosaurs appeared. Plant matter from these forests built up in vast swamps. This plant matter later formed large coal deposits.

Other articles to read include: **Forest; Spore.**

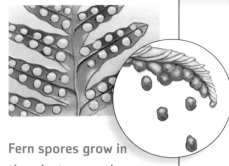

Fern spores grow in tiny clusters on the underside of the plant's leaves. These clusters are made up of tiny podlike parts called *sporangia*. Each sporangium splits open and releases the spores, which then fall to the ground below.

Insects pick up pollen from flowers, which they carry to other flowers, fertilizing them.

Fertilization

Fertilization *(fur tuh luh ZAY shuhn)* takes place when male and female sex cells unite to form a new individual. It is the most important step in *sexual reproduction*. In sexual reproduction, two parents produce offspring. The male sex cell is called a *sperm*. The female sex cell is called an *egg*. A sperm fertilizes the egg. The fertilized egg can develop into a new individual.

Among flowering plants, sperm are carried by tiny grains called *pollen*. Pollen is produced by the male parts of a flower. Each grain of pollen holds two sperm. Pollen is carried from male flower parts to female flower parts by animals or wind. Pollen that reaches female flower parts produces a *pollen tube*. The sperm swim down this tube. One sperm fertilizes the egg. The other sperm fertilizes tissue that provides food for the fertilized egg. The fertilized egg and its food supply form a seed. Seeds may develop into new plants.

Other articles to read include: **Flower; Pollen; Reproduction.**

Fertilizer

Fertilizer is a material that helps plants grow. Farmers add fertilizer to the soil to grow crops. People also use fertilizer in their gardens and on their lawns.

Fertilizers contain *nutrients,* nourishing substances that plants need to grow. Some fertilizers are *organic fertilizers.* They are made from materials produced by living things. Organic fertilizers include such things as dead plant matter and manure. Manure is solid animal waste. Other fertilizers are made in factories from chemicals. They are called *inorganic fertilizers.*

People must be careful when using fertilizer. Fertilizer is often washed away by rain. It can pollute rivers, lakes, and underground water supplies.

Other articles to read include: **Compost; Crop; Farm and farming; Soil.**

Small planes called *crop dusters* spray farm crops with liquid fertilizer.

Fir

The fir is a handsome evergreen tree. Firs are related to pine trees. There are several kinds. Firs are found around much of the world.

Firs typically grow in mountain areas. The largest fir tree is called the noble fir. It can grow to a height of 250 feet (75 meters).

The tops of fir trees are shaped like narrow pyramids. The trees have needle-shaped leaves. The needles are not hard and sharp like pine tree needles. They are soft and rounded and have a pleasant smell.

Many fir trees are cut down for lumber or to make paper. Some people use firs as Christmas trees.

Other articles to read include: **Conifer; Evergreen; Pine; Tree.**

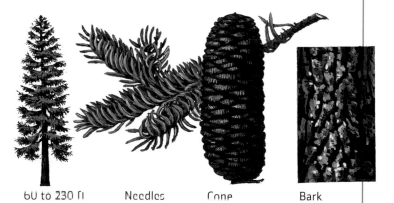

60 to 230 ft (18 to 70 m)   Needles   Cone   Bark

The California red fir grows in the mountains of California and southern Oregon.

Flagellum

A flagellum *(fluh JEHL uhm)* is a whiplike part on some living cells that is used to move. The plural of flagellum is *flagella*. Many kinds of tiny living things called *protozoans* have flagella. Protozoans with a flagellum are called *flagellates (FLAJ uh layts)*. A flagellate may have one or more flagella. The flagella whip about rapidly to move the flagellate through liquid.

Among plants, male sex cells move using a flagellum. These sex cells are called *sperm*. Sperm must swim to reach female sex cells, called *eggs*.

Other articles to read include: **Algae; Cell; Euglena.**

Flora

Flora is the name given to the plant life of a certain place or time. It is often used together with the word *fauna. Fauna* refers to the animal life of a certain place or time. For example, scientists might refer to the flora and fauna of rain forests of South America. The scientists are referring to the plants and animals that live there. Scientists often discuss the flora and fauna of a past period in Earth's history.

Other articles to read include: **Habitat; Plant.**

Flora of the Florida Everglades include a wide variety of plants that thrive in water.

Flower

A flower is a blossom. Plants use flowers to reproduce, or make new plants. Most plants have flowers. Sometimes whole plants are called flowers. Most flowers make pollen and seeds.

Flowers may be big or small, brightly colored or plain. Many flowers have a pleasant smell. Some kinds of plants produce only one flower. Others grow many large bunches of flowers. Still others, such as dandelions and daisies, have flower heads made up of many tiny flowers.

There are hundreds of thousands of kinds of flowering plants. Some trees, such as horse chestnuts and catalpas, have beautiful flowers. But the trees themselves are never called flowers. Only garden flowers and wildflowers are called flowers.

People enjoy flowers for their beautiful shapes, colors, and scents. Many people use blossoms to decorate their homes and workplaces. Some people give flowers as gifts to express their feelings. They place flowers on graves to show that they remember a loved one. Flowers are symbols of love, faithfulness, and long life. They are

Continued on the next page

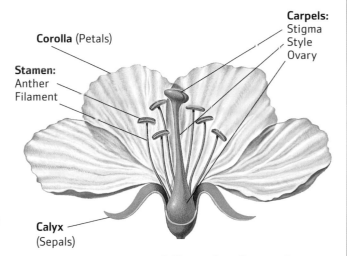

Corolla (Petals)

Stamen:
Anther
Filament

Carpels:
Stigma
Style
Ovary

Calyx
(Sepals)

A flower has four main parts. They are (1) the *calyx,* (2) the *corolla,* (3) the *stamens,* and (4) the *carpels.* The calyx forms the outermost part and is made up of leaflike sepals. The corolla consists of the petals. The stamens and carpels make up a flower's reproductive parts.

Garden annuals include sunflowers (left) and snapdragons (right).

Garden perennials include chrysanthemums (left) and lily of the valley (right).

Garden biennials include canterbury bells (left) and hollyhocks (right).

Flower *Continued from the previous page*

part of many ceremonies and celebrations, including weddings and parades. Certain flowers have a religious meaning. For example, the white Easter lily stands for purity in the Christian church. Buddhists and Hindus regard the lotus as sacred, perhaps because its lovely flower rises above the mud in which it grows.

All flowers were once wildflowers. The first flowering plants appeared about 130 million years ago. The evolution of flowering plants made possible the appearance of thousands of new species of animals, particularly insects. Great forests of flowering plants came to cover much of Earth beginning about 65 million years ago. In time, people learned to grow flowering plants from seeds. By 3000 B.C., the Egyptians and other peoples of the ancient Middle East had begun to grow a variety of garden flowers, including jasmines, poppies, and water lilies. Today, flowers are raised in every country. Breeders have developed many new kinds of flowers that are not found in the wild. Thousands of kinds of flowering plants still grow in the wild throughout the world. But many of them are becoming rare as people destroy wilderness areas to make room for farms and cities.

Wildflowers grow in cold places, warm places, and hot places. Some live in deserts, where it is very dry. Others live in such wet places as ponds or tropical jungles. Each flower is adapted to its environment. For example, flowering desert plants can live many months without rain. Some of these plants

Thousands of wildflowers bloom all at once in an Alpine meadow. When conditions are right, wildflowers grow almost everywhere.

The greatest variety of wildflowers grows in the warm, humid tropics and rain forests.

have many roots to gather as much water as they can when it rains. Others store water in their thick, spongy stems. Flowering plants that live in the far northern parts of the world can survive many months of freezing cold. They bloom only during the short summer.

Garden flowers are kinds of flowers that were once wild but are now raised in gardens. Garden flowers are grown in home gardens, on farms, and in nurseries and greenhouses. Some kinds of garden flowers make good house plants.

There are three main kinds of garden flowers: (1) annuals, (2) biennials, and (3) perennials. Annuals grow and have flowers during just one growing season and then die. *Biennials (by EHN ee uhls)* live for two growing seasons. They bloom during the second growing season. *Perennials (puh REHN ee uhls)* live for at least three growing seasons. They usually bloom every growing season. Most garden flowers are annuals or perennials.

Hardy flowers such as lupines come to life during a brief frost-free period in the Alpine tundra.

Flowers develop from buds at the tip of a flower stalk. Most flowers have four main parts: (1) the calyx, (2) the corolla, (3) the stamens, and (4) the carpels. The carpels are often called *pistils*. The flower parts are attached to the stem.

The *calyx (KAY lihks)* is made up of small, leafy parts called *sepals (SEE puhls)*. The sepals protect the bud before the flower opens. Afterward, they may look like leaves on the underpart of the flower. Inside the calyx are the petals. The petals are the largest, most colorful part of most flowers. They make up the *corolla (kuh ROL uh)*. The *stamens (STAY muhns)* and the carpels take part in reproduction. The stamens are the male parts, and the *carpels* are the female parts. Some flowers have both stamens and carpels. Others have only the stamens or the carpels. Each stamen has a long, narrow stalk with a fat tip. The tip is called an *anther*. The anther makes the flower's pollen. Some flowers have only one carpel. But most flowers have two or more. When these carpels are fused together, they are called a *pistil*. The carpels are like tubes. The tubes have a sticky top called a *stigma* and a round bottom. This bottom part is called an *ovary*. The flower seeds grow in the ovary.

Pollination (pol uh NAY shuhn) takes place when pollen reaches the stigma. The wind pollinates many flowers, especially those with small, plain blossoms. In some flowering plants, the flower gets pollen from its own anthers. Many flowers get pollen that is carried by insects or other animals. Each grain of pollen holds two male sex cells called *sperm*. These sperm swim down a tube produced by the pollen. One sperm fertilizes a female sex cell called the *egg*. The other sperm fertilizes tissue that will provide food for the fertilized egg.

Continued on the next page

Flower *Continued from the previous page*

After pollination, the ovary develops into fruit. The rest of the flower gradually dies as the fruit grows.

Many insects depend on flowers for food. Bees eat pollen and nectar, a sweet liquid found in some flowers. Honey bees also use nectar to make honey, which they eat in winter. Butterflies and moths also eat nectar. Certain beetles and flies eat both nectar and pollen. When an insect travels from flower to flower in search of food, pollen sticks to its body. Some of this pollen brushes off onto the sticky stigma of the flowers.

Flowers attract insects with their bright colors or scents. Bees are especially drawn to yellow and blue blossoms with a sweet fragrance. Butterflies and moths prefer flowers with a lot of nectar. They suck up the nectar with their long, tubelike mouthparts.

Many moths search for flowers at night. Many of the flowers that moths visit open up and give off scent only at night and close during the day. Most of these flowers are pale-colored or white. They are easier to see at night than dark blossoms. Such flowers include evening primroses and honeysuckles.

Some flowers depend on flies or beetles to spread their pollen. Many of these flowers give off a smell similar to that of rotting meat. Such flowers include rafflesia and the titan arum, the largest of all flowers. The blossoms of rafflesia can grow more than 3 feet (90 centimeters) wide. The titan arum grows many tiny flowers on a long stalk. This stalk can reach more than 10 feet (3 meters) long.

Birds and bats that eat nectar help spread pollen, too. Hummingbirds are especially drawn to red, orange, and yellow flowers, including columbines, fuchsias, and Indian paintbrushes.

Other articles to read include: **Annual; Biennial; Bud; Bulb; Fertilization; Nectar; Perennial; Pollen; Reproduction; Weed;** *and those on individual plants.*

Flowers attract insects with their bright colors and scents. The insects feed on nectar and transport pollen.

Many woodland flowers, such as rhododendrons, bloom in early spring before the trees develop leaves.

Food chain

A food chain is a figure showing the feeding relationships among living things. Each living thing in a food chain feeds on the living thing below it. For example, birds eat insects, so birds are higher in a food chain. Insects eat plants, so insects are higher than plants.

Plants are below animals on a food chain. Plants are known as *producers* because they make their own food. Plants provide all the energy in food chains on land. Animals are known as *consumers* because they eat plants or other animals for food.

The arrows in a food chain show the movement of energy. This energy moves from plants, to animals, and then on to larger animals.

Animals that eat only plants are called *herbivores (HUR buh vawrz).* Herbivores include rabbits, mice, cows, and chickens. Animals that eat other animals are called *carnivores (KAHR nuh vawrz).* Carnivores include wolves, lions, foxes, and hawks. In the food chain, carnivores rank above herbivores.

There are many different kinds of food chains. Every living thing is in at least one food chain. But many living things are in more than one food chain. For example, grass may be eaten by grasshoppers, sheep, or cattle. Grass is at the bottom of each of these food chains. A group of overlapping food chains is called a *food web.*

Other articles to read include: **Balance of nature; Ecology; Food web.**

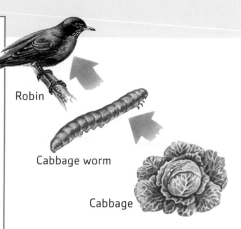

Robin

Cabbage worm

Cabbage

In this food chain, the cabbage worm gets its food energy from the cabbage. The robin gets its food energy by eating cabbage worms.

Food web

A food web describes a feeding relationship among living things in an area. A food web is made up of overlapping *food chains.* In a food chain, each living thing feeds on the living thing below it. For example, rabbits eat grass, so rabbits are higher in the food chain than grass. However, many living things are in more than one food chain. For example, grass may be eaten by grasshoppers, sheep, and cattle. Grass is at the bottom of each of these food chains. Thus, the food chains overlap. These overlapping food chains make up a food web.

Nearly all the energy in food webs on land comes from plants. Plants make their own food using the energy in sunlight. They also use water and the gas carbon dioxide. The food that plants make provides energy for the rest of the food web.

There are many food webs in the world. Some of the largest ones are in tropical rain forests and the oceans.

Other articles to read include: **Balance of nature; Ecology; Food chain.**

Forest

Canopy

Understory

Shrub layer

Herb layer

Forest floor

Every forest has several layers of plants. The five basic layers, from highest to lowest, are (1) the canopy, (2) the understory, (3) the shrub layer, (4) the herb layer, and (5) the forest floor. This illustration shows the layers as they might appear in a temperate deciduous forest.

A forest is a large area of land covered with trees. But a forest is much more than trees. Other kinds of plants also live in forests. These include mosses, shrubs, and wildflowers. Many birds, insects, and other animals also make their home in forests.

People depend on forests for many things. Forests supply such important products as wood for lumber and paper. Forests prevent floods by soaking up water. The natural beauty and peace of the forest bring great enjoyment to people. Forests also provide much of the oxygen that people and animals breathe.

Forests once covered much more of the land than they do today. Many forests have been cut down for their lumber and to make room for farmland and cities.

Tropical rain forests grow near the equator, where the climate is warm and wet all the year around. The largest tropical rain forests are in the Amazon River Basin of South America and in the Congo River Basin of Africa. A river basin is an area of land drained by a river. Rain forests also cover much of Southeast Asia.

Tropical seasonal forests grow where the climate is a little cooler. They also grow where there is a wet season and a dry season. They are found in Central America, central South America, southern Africa, India, eastern China, northern Australia, and islands in the Pacific Ocean.

Temperate deciduous forests grow where the summers are warm and the winters are cold. *Deciduous (dih SIHJ u uhs)* is a term for trees that shed their leaves before the winter. Deciduous forests are found in eastern North America, western Europe, and eastern Asia.

Temperate evergreen forests grow along coastal areas with mild winters and heavy rainfall. These forests grow along the northwest coast of North America, the south coast of Chile, the west coast of New Zealand, and the southeast coast of Australia.

Continued on the next page

Temperate deciduous forests grow in cooler parts of the world.

Boreal forests are found where the winters are extremely cold. Boreal forests also are known as the *taiga (TY guh)*. Boreal forests stretch across northern Asia, Europe, and North America.

Savannas are areas where the trees are far apart and the ground is covered by grasses. Tropical savannas can be found in Central America, Brazil, Africa, India, Southeast Asia, and Australia. Temperate savannas are also called *woodlands*. The United States, Canada, Mexico, and Cuba have temperate savannas.

Other articles to read include: **Amazon rain forest; Conifer; Deciduous tree; Deforestation; Evergreen; Forestry; Rain forest; Savanna; Taiga; Tree;** *and those on individual trees.*

When a forest overtakes grasslands, such fast-growing trees as pines and poplars may grow first. Slowly, this turns into a deciduous forest, made up of trees that lose their leaves in the fall. The canopy of a mature deciduous forest consists of such slow-growing, long-lived trees as oaks and maples.

A grassy meadow grows first. Small pine trees sprout among the grass.

An evergreen forest slowly forms. The evergreens grow taller. Deciduous trees grow underneath.

More deciduous trees grow as the older pines die.

A deciduous forest takes over.

Boreal forests grow in cold, northern areas with a short growing season, such as Russia.

Tropical rain forests grow in the warmest parts of Earth, on or near the equator.

A forester measures new growth on a tree at a nursery for a paper company.

A forester gauges the growth of a mature Douglas fir tree.

Forestry

Forestry is the science of using forests wisely. People who work in forestry are called *foresters*.

Forests are important in many ways. The plants in a forest give off oxygen that people and other animals breathe. Wood comes from trees that are harvested from forests. Water that people use may also come from forests. Forests provide food and shelter for many kinds of wildlife and grazing for livestock. People also enjoy forests for camping, hiking, and picnicking.

Foresters work to keep forests healthy. They plant trees so forests have many trees at different stages of growth. They also study and try to control insects and diseases that can kill trees. In many forests, foresters help in planning the wise harvesting of trees.

Foresters are also involved in the management of forest animals. They help to maintain a balance between the number

Continued on the next page

of animals in a forest and the supply of food, water, and shelter. Some foresters plan the building of forest campgrounds. They help people to enjoy the forests without damaging them.

Forest fires can move quickly if many trees are old and dry. In some forests, foresters watch out for fires from lookout towers and aircraft. They can then warn people who might be in danger from the fire. Foresters fight wild-fires that endanger lives or property. But they permit certain types of fires to burn. Such fires clear trees and other vegetation that can prevent the growth of new trees.

Other articles to read include: **Conservation; Deforestation; Forest; Wood.**

Foresters sometimes set fires to clear the forest floor of debris that could fuel a major forest fire.

How timber is harvested

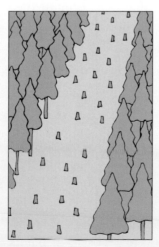

Clearcutting removes all the trees in a large area. It provides full sunlight in which new seedlings can develop.

Shelterwood cutting, which is used for trees that require shade to develop, removes trees in several stages.

Seed tree cutting leaves a few scattered trees in the area to provide a source of seeds for a new crop.

Selection cutting involves harvesting small patches of mature trees to make room for new and younger trees.

A fossil of an ancient fern (above top) was made by an impression in mud slowly pressed into stone. Petrified wood (above) is a kind of plant fossil in which minerals carried by water eventually turn wood into stone. Plant fossils give scientists clues about early plants.

Fossil

A fossil is the remains of a living thing that died long ago. A fossil can be thousands or millions of years old. Fossils help scientists learn about plants and animals that lived in the past. Most of those living things became *extinct*—that is, they died off completely—long ago. Fossils are one of the main ways that scientists learn about prehistoric life.

Some fossils are wood that was preserved because it was turned to stone. Fossils form in this way when stony substances called *minerals* are carried into the wood by water. The minerals slowly replace the wood. Large areas of fossilized trees are known as *petrified forests*. Stony fossils can survive for many millions of years. Some petrified forests are more than 200 million years old. Fossils of animal bones form in a similar way.

Other fossils are marks called *impressions*. These fossils preserve the outline of a living thing. Impressions form after a living thing dies in mud and is covered. Over millions of years, the mud gets pressed down and turns into rock. A flattened print of the living thing remains in the rock. Most fossils of plants and of animals without bones formed in this way.

Plants may also form fossils called *molds* after being buried in mud. Instead of being flattened, these plants kept their shape when the mud turned to stone. Later, water washed away the plant's remains. This process leaves a space with the plant's shape. Sometimes minerals filled the space. That created a fossil called a *cast*. A cast is like a sculpture made of stone.

There are other kinds of fossils. A hardened sap called *amber* can preserve pollen and other plant matter. Plants may be preserved in tar pits. Fossils of plants are also preserved in permanently frozen ground. Scientists have even found plant matter in the guts of frozen mammoths that became extinct thousands of years ago.

Other articles to read include: **Amber; Extinction.**

ACTIVITY

How are fossils made?

1. Spread a layer of clay in the pie plate, about ½ inch (1.25 centimeters) thick.

2. Press your "fossil form" into the clay. Make sure you get a good print in the clay, and take the form out.

3. Mix the plaster of Paris and water in the mixing can. Stir it with the stick until it looks like thick cream.

4. Pour the mixture into a layer about 1 inch (2.5 centimeters) thick over the clay. Wait about 3 hours for the plaster to harden.

5. When the plaster is hard, pop it out of the pie plate. Peel the clay off to find your instant "fossil." Many real fossils formed in mud or sand. Over thousands of years, more layers of mud or sand pressed down on the lower layers and hardened them into rock.

What you need:

- modeling clay or "play dough" clay
- small foil pie plate
- fossil form (leaf, twig, or shell, for example)
- 1 cup plaster of Paris (from a craft or hardware store)
- ½ cup water
- can for mixing
- stirring stick

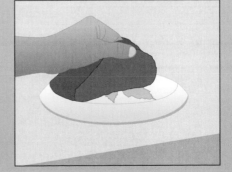

http://bit.ly/TUXDxq

Foxglove

Foxglove

Foxgloves are flowering plants with bell-shaped blossoms. The flowers grow in groups along one side of the plant's stem. They look somewhat like the fingers of a glove. The blossoms can be purple, pink, lilac, yellow, or white. There are several kinds of foxglove. They grow in Europe, northern Africa, and western and central Asia.

Foxgloves grow from 2 to 5 feet (60 to 150 centimeters) tall. They have rounded leaves that grow along the stem. Some foxgloves have poisonous leaves. The poison can be made into a medicine called *digitalis*. Doctors still use digitalis to help people with a weak or uneven heartbeat. The drug makes the heart beat more strongly or evenly.

Other articles to read include: **Flower; Poisonous plant.**

Fruit

Fruit is part of a flowering plant. The fruit holds the plant's seeds. Fruits develop from a part of the flower called the *ovary*. The ovary holds female sex cells called *eggs*. Male sex cells called *sperm* fertilize the eggs, that is, the sperm combine with the eggs. After fertilization, the ovary develops into a fruit.

Many plants rely on animals to eat their fruit. Animals that eat fruit carry the seeds inside their guts. The seeds are later passed with the animal's waste. This process enables the offspring of plants to spread to new locations.

There are two main types of fruit. They are *simple fruits* and *compound fruits*. Simple fruits develop from a single ovary. Compound fruits develop from two or more ovaries.

Simple fruits make up the largest group of fruits by far. There are three main kinds of fleshy simple fruits: (1) true berries, (2) *drupes* (*droopz*) , and (3) *pomes* (*pohmz*).

True berries include bananas, blueberries, grapes, oranges, and watermelons. Berries are made up almost entirely of fleshy fruit. They have many seeds. But many fruits that have the word

Continued on the next page

Simple fruits are classified into two main groups, depending on whether their tissue is fleshy or dry. Fleshy simple fruits are divided into three main types: (1) berries, (2) drupes, and (3) pomes.

Orange **Grapes** **Watermelon**

Berries consist entirely of fleshy tissue, and most species have many seeds. The seeds are embedded in the flesh. This group includes only a few of the fruits that we usually call berries.

Peach **Cherries** **Plum**

Drupes are fleshy fruits that have a hard inner stone or pit and a single seed. The pit encloses the seed.

Pear **Apple**

Pomes have a fleshy outer layer, a paperlike core, and more than one seed. The seeds are enclosed in the core.

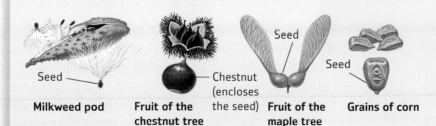

Milkweed pod **Fruit of the chestnut tree** **Fruit of the maple tree** **Grains of corn**

Dry simple fruits are produced by many kinds of trees, shrubs, garden plants, and weeds. The seed-bearing structures of nearly all members of the grass family, including corn and wheat, belong to this group.

Continued on the next page

Fruit *Continued from the previous page*

Strawberry   Blackberry   Raspberry

Compound fruits develop from two or more ovaries.

berry in their name are not true berries. They include blackberries, raspberries, and strawberries. They are actually compound fruits.

Drupes include apricots, cherries, olives, peaches, and plums. They are fleshy fruits that have a hard inner stone or *pit*. Drupes hold only one seed, inside the pit.

Pomes include apples and pears. They have a fleshy outer layer. Their core is paperlike and usually holds from 5 to 10 seeds.

Compound fruits grow from a cluster of ovaries. Some develop from single flowers, each of which has many ovaries. This type of compound fruit includes blackberries, raspberries, and strawberries. Others develop from a cluster of flowers on a single stem. This type of fruit includes figs, mulberries, and pineapples.

Other articles to read include: **Berry; Reproduction; Seed;** *and those on individual fruits.*

Fungi

Many kinds of fungi produce mushrooms, such as the toadstool, to spread their spores. Unlike many mushrooms, the toadstool can not be eaten.

Fungi *(FUHN jy)* are living things that absorb food from their surroundings. Like plants, fungi cannot move around. Like animals, fungi cannot make their own food and must eat to survive. But fungi are neither animals nor plants. Instead, they make up one of the major groups of living things, called *kingdoms*. The singular of fungi is *fungus*. There are many thousands of kinds of fungi. The most familiar fungi are mushrooms. Molds and yeasts are other types of fungi. Some fungi, such as yeasts, have only one cell. They are too tiny to see without a microscope, unless in a large group. Fungi with many cells, such as mushrooms, can be seen easily.

Fungi live almost everywhere on land. Some live in water. Fungi generally feed on the rotting parts of dead plants and

Continued on the next page

animals. Other fungi feed on living plants and animals. Fungi put chemicals called enzymes *(EIIN zyms)* into what they eat. The enzymes break down the material into little bits the fungi can absorb.

Mushrooms are actually the *fruiting body* of a fungus. The mushroom enables the fungus to reproduce by making cells called *spores*. These spores are typically released from the underside of the mushroom. Each spore can develop into a new fungus. The body of the fungus is found beneath the mushroom, usually just beneath the surface of the soil. It is made up of thousands of threadlike cells. These cells sometimes form a tangled mass. They feed on plant and animal matter in the soil.

Fungi are an important part of nature. By breaking down plant and animal matter, fungi enrich the soil for plant growth.

People use fungi to make a variety of foods. Molds are added to many cheeses to make them ripe and tasty. Yeast makes bread rise before it is baked. Yeast also is used to make such alcoholic beverages as beer and wine. Many people like to eat certain mushrooms. Some molds make important drugs called *antibiotics*. Penicillin was the first antibiotic discovered by scientists. It is made by a mold to protect the fungus from bacteria. Doctors use penicillin to treat people who are infected by bacteria.

Some fungi can cause problems, however. Certain fungi harm crops and other plants. Other fungi cause disease in animals and people. Molds can spoil food. Molds also can build up in houses and make people sick. These molds can be difficult to remove.

Other articles to read include: **Mold; Mushroom; Spore; Yeast.**

Mildew (left) is a type of fungus that attacks plants.

Rust is a type of fungus that attacks plants, including wheat and apples.

Mold grows on rotting tomatoes and other plant remains.

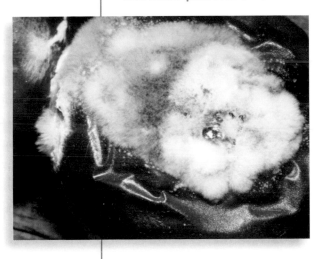

Gg

Gall

Galls are typically rounded swellings on plants caused by insects or by infection by bacteria or fungi.

A gall is an unusual growth on a plant. It often appears as a rounded swelling. Galls can grow on roots, stems, leaves, flowers, and seed pods. Some galls are small. Others are very large.

Most galls are caused by *parasites* (organisms that live on and feed on the plants). Some galls are caused by viruses or bacteria. Others are caused by fungi *(FUHN jy),* worms, or certain wasp young. These parasites produce special chemicals that make plant cells multiply quickly. The cells grow into galls.

Some galls and the parasites that cause them can seriously damage plants. Other galls benefit plants. For example, galls formed by *Rhizobium* bacteria on the roots of *legumes* (plants in the pea family) help supply life-giving nitrogen. *Rhizobium* converts nitrogen gas from the air to nitrogen compounds the plant can use.

Other articles to read include: **Fungi; Parasite.**

Garlic

Garlic

Garlic is a plant grown for its sharp-tasting bulb. The bulb is used to season foods. Garlic is related to onion, which also has a strong flavor. The garlic bulb has several parts called *cloves.* People eat the cloves.

Farmers plant garlic in the form of cloves in late fall or early winter. The cloves grow to their full size as bulbs in the summer. Farmers then dry the bulbs. They remove the stems and leaves and send the bulbs to market. Garlic bulbs may be sold whole, dried, or ground into powder. The juice from the bulbs is also sold as a flavoring.

The garlic plant is originally from central Asia. It has been an important crop since ancient times. Today, countries around the world grow the plant.

Other articles to read include: **Bulb; Onion.**

Gene

Genes are chemical instructions inside cells. They direct how a living thing grows. Genes determine what shape a plant will be. They tell a plant how to make roots, leaves, and flowers. They also direct how plants function.

Living things get genes from their parents. Most get half of their genes from one parent and half from the other.

Every plant cell has tens of thousands of genes. These genes lie on tiny, threadlike structures called *chromosomes (KROH muh sohmz)*. Genes are located in a specific place on a certain chromosome. The chromosomes are in a part of the cell called the *nucleus*.

Genes are made of a chemical called *DNA*. The letters *DNA* stand for *deoxyribonucleic acid*. DNA is shaped like a long, twisted ladder. The "rungs" of the ladder are made of chemicals called *bases*. A pair of bases forms each rung. Most genes consist of several thousand base pairs.

Scientists can change certain genes in some living things. For example, they may add genes to crop plants. The genes make the plants stronger, disease resistant, or higher in food value. Changing genes in this way is called *genetic engineering*.

Other articles to read include: **Cell; Crop; Heredity; Life; Mendel, Gregor Johann.**

A plant's genes lie on tiny, threadlike structures called chomosomes. Genes are made of a chemical called DNA, which is shaped like a twisted ladder.

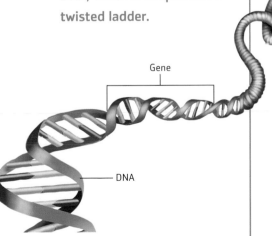

Chromosome

Gene

DNA

Genetically modified food

Genetically modified food is food made from living things that have been *altered* (changed) through *genetic engineering*. Genetic engineering involves efforts to alter *genes*. Genes are chemical instructions inside cells. They largely determine how living things grow and function. Genetically modified food is often abbreviated as *GM* food. To create GM foods, scientists alter the genes of crops to introduce new *traits* (features). These traits are usually meant to benefit farmers, consumers, or the environment. For example, a GM crop may have a greater ability to fight certain diseases. In addition to plant crops, scientists can also alter the genes of livestock. For instance, GM livestock might grow more quickly.

New strains of genetically modified corn are grown in an experimental field station to allow scientists to evaluate it. Most corn grown in the United States has been genetically modified.

Virtually all foods people consume today have had their genetic makeup gradually modified through thousands of years of selective breeding. Selective breeding involves carefully breeding certain plants or animals to produce offspring with desirable traits. Scientists first directly altered crop genes through genetic engineering in the 1980's. The first widely available GM foods reached the market in the mid-1990's. Today, some GM crops have largely replaced traditional crops. For example, most of the corn, cotton, and soybeans planted in the United States are genetically modified.

Most scientific organizations have found that genetically modified foods are safe to grow and eat. But some people worry that genetically modified foods might be dangerous for people to eat. They argue that GM foods are still relatively new and that experts may not have enough information about their safety. Some people also worry about the long-term consequences of releasing GM crops into the environment. Some countries have banned planting GM crops and selling GM foods. In other countries, government agencies must review any GM food for safety before it can be sold. Nearly all GM foods have been found to be safe.

Other articles to read include: **Agriculture; Crop; Gene.**

Genus

A genus is a group of closely related living things. Biologists classify each living thing according to seven major groups. These groups are *kingdom, phylum* (sometimes called *division*), *class, order, family, genus,* and *species.* Each group is made up in turn of the smaller groups that come after it. For example, an order is made up of families, a family is made up of *genera* (the plural of genus), and so on. The smaller the group, the more alike are all its members. Each living thing belongs to a species, the most basic of the seven major groups. A genus is a group of related species.

For example, the genus *Triticum* includes the different kinds of wheat. The common wheat generally used to make bread has the scientific name *Triticum aestivum.* The durum wheat often used to make pasta is *Triticum durum.*

Genera are arranged into larger groups called families. For example, wheat is in the family of true grasses, called Poaceae. Rices make up the genus *Oryza.* Oats make up the genus *Avena.* Both of these genera are also in the family Poaceae.

Other articles to read include: **Class; Classification, Scientific; Species.**

All the different kinds of wheat belong to the same genus, *Triticum.*

Geranium

The geranium is a popular garden flower in the United States and Canada. Geraniums are native to temperate regions throughout the world. Wild geraniums may be called *crane's bill* or *heron's bill.* There are many kinds of geraniums.

Geranium plants differ in their size, their leaves, and the color of their flowers. The common geranium has fragrant red, pink, or white flowers. Cooks may use the leaves of another variety, the rose geranium, to flavor jellies.

Other articles to read include: **Flower.**

The geranium has clusters of fragrant blossoms. Geraniums are often grown in gardens and in window boxes.

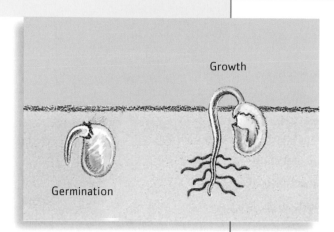

Growth

Germination

A seed begins to sprout and grow through germination. First, a tiny root pushes down into the ground in search of water. A tiny stem pushes up through the soil in search of sunlight. The plant soon pokes up above the ground.

Germination

Germination *(jur muh NAY shuhn)* is the process by which seeds sprout and grow. Seeds only germinate when conditions are good for growth. Seeds typically need water and warmth to germinate.

The seeds of most plants in warm parts of the world germinate soon after they fall to the ground. That is because there is plenty of water and warmth for the seeds. The seeds of most plants in cooler places do not germinate during the winter months. They germinate in the spring when the weather gets warmer and it starts to rain.

A germinating seed takes in large amounts of water from the ground. The water causes the seed to swell. The tiny plant then breaks through the covering of the seed, called a *seed coat*. A tiny root grows downward, and tiny leaves grow upward through the soil surface.

Other articles to read include: **Reproduction; Seed; Stem.**

Ginger

Ginger is a tangy spice. It is used in baking and cooking. It is also used to flavor beverages.

Ginger comes from the underground stem of the ginger plant. It grows across much of the world.

Ginger spice comes in many varieties. Dried ginger, black ginger, and white ginger are all sold dried. Black ginger is scalded in water before drying. In white ginger, the outer layers of the stem have been peeled off. *Preserved ginger* has been peeled and boiled in syrup.

Ginger

Fresh ginger root is used in cooking. It is used especially in recipes from East Asia and India.

Other articles to read include: **Spice.**

Ginkgo

Ginkgo *(GIHNG koh)* is a tree that produces seeds covered in orange, foul-smelling flesh. It also is called the *maidenhair tree*. The ginkgo is the last surviving member of a group of trees that were common many millions of years ago. Dinosaurs ate ginkgo during the Mesozoic Era, which lasted from 251 million to 65 million years ago.

Ginkgo trees can grow from 60 to 80 feet (18 to 24 meters) tall. Their fan-shaped leaves grow in bunches at the end of short stalks. Many people roast and eat ginkgo seeds, which are like nuts.

Chinese and Japanese Buddhists have planted ginkgo in their temple gardens for centuries. People in many countries plant ginkgo trees for decoration. Some people use ginkgo leaves as an herbal medicine. They believe that ginkgo may help to relieve various medical conditions.

Other articles to read include: **Seed; Tree**

Seeds   **Ginkgo**   Leaf

Ginkgo trees bear seeds but not fruits or cones. The seeds have an unpleasant odor.

Ginseng

Ginseng *(JIHN sehng)* is an herb grown for its root. The ginseng root is used as a medicine in a number of countries. However, its medical value has not been proven.

Manufacturers may add ginseng to such products as shampoos, skin creams, and soft drinks. The root is dried, sold whole, and then ground into a powder. It may be processed into tablets.

Ginseng is a low plant with three to five leaves on top. Each leaf has five leaflets.

Ginseng has a long, fleshy root that resembles a human body. The plant's name comes from Chinese words meaning *likeness of a man*.

Wild ginseng has almost disappeared. The plant is now grown mainly in China, Korea, and the United States. Most ginseng grown in the United States is exported to China.

Other articles to read include: **Herb; Root.**

Ginseng

Gladioluses

Gladiolus

The gladiolus *(GLAD ee OH luhs* or *gluh DY uh luhs)* is a plant with large, silky flowers. The flowers bloom along a long, straight stem. Gladioluses are grown commercially. They are most often used by flower shops in arrangements. There are many kinds.

Gladiolus flowers come in a variety of colors. Some are white, and others are shades of red or orange. Blue gladiolus comes mainly from South Africa. The individual flowers are cup shaped and grow one above the next. The bottom flower opens first. The others follow in turn.

A gladiolus grows from a *corm,* an underground stem that looks like a bulb. The corm should be dug out of the ground each fall and stored in a warm place. The corm can be replanted the next spring.

Other articles to read include: **Flower.**

Glucose

Glucose *(GLOO kohs)* is a kind of sugar. It is the main source of energy for most living things. Glucose is made by plants through *photosynthesis (foh tuh SIHN thuh sihs).*

Photosynthesis is the process by which plants make food. Plants take in water and the gas carbon dioxide. They use the energy in sunlight to combine these chemicals. This process creates glucose. It also releases the gas oxygen.

Plants use glucose to live and to grow. Animals get glucose by eating plants or by eating animals that have eaten plants. Honey and such fruits as grapes and figs contain large amounts of glucose. Pure glucose is a white crystal. It is about three-fourths as sweet as table sugar.

Other articles to read include: **Photosynthesis; Sugar.**

Goldenrod

The goldenrod is a common wildflower. There are many kinds. The two most common goldenrods are called the early goldenrod and sweet goldenrod. Goldenrods grow in many kinds of places, including forests, along roadsides, and in fields.

Goldenrod blossoms are bright yellow or deep golden. The plant blooms in late summer and fall. They grow in thick bunches at the top of a slender stem. Some kinds of goldenrods have smooth leaves. Others have leaves with jagged edges.

Goldenrod is a popular flower in the United States. It is the state flower of Kentucky and Nebraska. Some people brew a tea from the leaves of the sweet goldenrod.

Other articles to read include: **Flower.**

Goldenrod

Gourd

Gourds are vegetables that are closely related to pumpkins and squashes. Gourds bear fruits of many colors and shapes. They may have stripes of red, white, orange, and green. Some gourds are round. Some gourds are long and curved at one end and round at the other. Other gourds are shaped like pears or bottles. Many gourds are smooth, but some are covered with wartlike bumps.

Gourds grow on the ornamental trailing vines.

Gourds grow wild in North and South America, Africa, and the Pacific Islands.

The leaves are large with pointed lobes, and the flowers are usually yellow. The stems grow like vines along the ground or climb on walls or other supports.

Gourds are easy to grow. The seeds need to be planted in a sunny area after the threat of frost has passed.

Other articles to read include: **Pumpkin; Squash; Vegetable.**

Gourds bear fruits of many colors and shapes.
Luffa
Dipper gourd
Bottle gourd
Aladdin's turban
Striped pear gourd
Warted gourd
Spoon gourd
Bicolor gourd

Grain

Grains are cereal plants. They rank among the most important food crops. Around the world, farmers grow such grains as wheat, corn, rice, barley, sorghum, oats, rye, and millet. People eat the seeds of these crops. The word *grain* also refers to these seeds.

People use grain as food for themselves and as feed for animals. Some grains are cooked and eaten whole. But most grains are ground up into a fine powder. This powder is made into flour, meal, syrup, oil, or starch. These products are used to make such foods as bread, breakfast cereal, and cooking oil.

Wheat is the most important food grain in many areas of the world. Most wheat is milled into flour and used for making baked goods and pasta. For most Asians, rice is the main food grain. Rice is typically cooked and eaten as a grain. It also can be made into flour. Millet is an important source of food in dry regions of Africa and Asia.

Any grain can be made into livestock feed. In the United States, the grains most widely used as livestock feed are corn, sorghum, and oats. Grain also is used to make beer, whiskey, and other alcoholic beverages. Grain can be used to make fuels, makeup, drugs, plastics, and many other products.

Other articles to read include: **Barley; Cereal; Crop; Farm and farming; Oats; Rice; Rye; Seed; Wheat.**

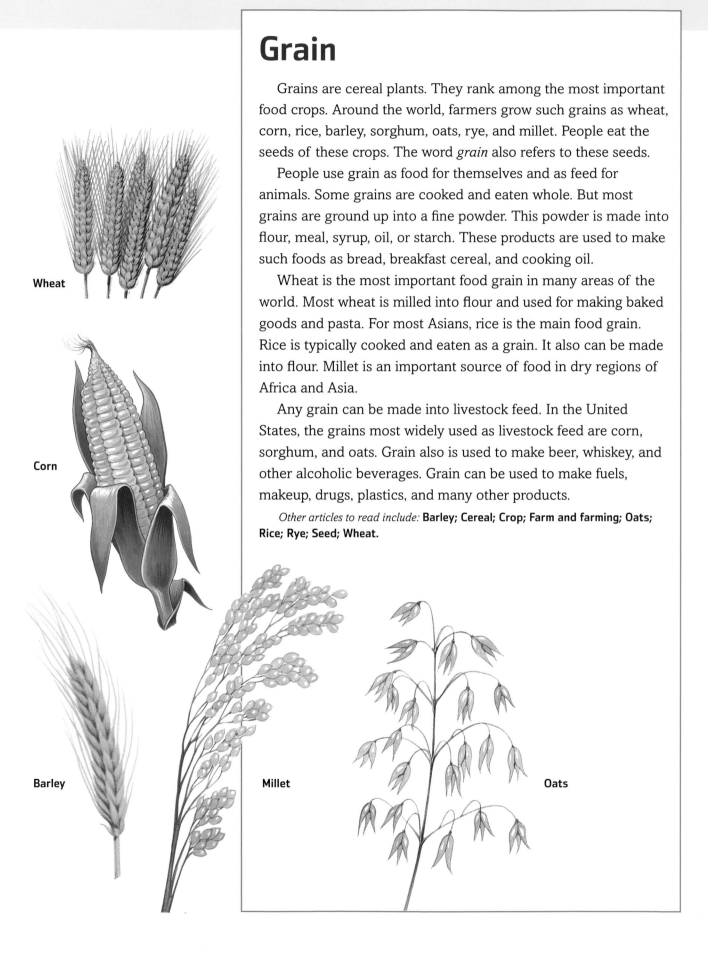

Wheat

Corn

Barley

Millet

Oats

Grape

Grapes are juicy berries that grow in bunches on woody vines. Grapes have a smooth skin and may be black, blue, golden, green, purple, red, or even white.

Most grapes are used for making wine. Some kinds are eaten fresh. These are called *table grapes*. Grapes can also be dried into raisins, made into juice or jelly, or canned with other fruits.

Some grapevines grow from seeds. But most grapevines are grown from cuttings from other vines. When the cuttings are placed in sandy soil, they put out roots and new plants begin to grow. Grapes need a lot of sunshine to grow. But they can grow almost anywhere the temperature is at least 50 °F (10 °C) and above.

After a grapevine has grown from a cutting, it sprouts leaves and tiny buds. The buds become the grapes. Bunches of grapes can have as few as 6 berries or as many as 300.

Ancient Egyptian tomb paintings show that people have grown grapes for at least 4,400 years. Today, most grapes are grown in Europe, especially in France, Italy, and Spain. California produces most of the grapes grown in the United States. Grapes also are grown in Australia, South Africa, and parts of South America.

Other articles to read include: **Berry; Fruit; Vine.**

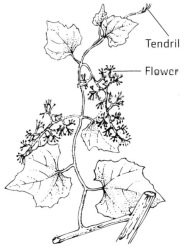

Tendril

Flower

Grapes grow on a woody vine. Grapes grow in clusters of as few as 6 to as many as 300 berries. The tendril is a twisting, threadlike part that attaches to an object to support the plant's weight.

White table grapes grown in Sicily, Italy. Grapes grow in many parts of the world. The berries may be black, blue, golden, green, purple, red, or white.

Grapefruit

Grapefruit

The grapefruit is a big, round fruit with sour flesh. People enjoy eating grapefruit and drinking grapefruit juice. Grapefruit is rich in vitamin C.

The grapefruit tree has dark green leaves and white flowers. It grows about 30 feet (9 meters) tall. The skin of a grapefruit is thick. It is yellow, or yellow with a little pink. The inside is made up of long, juicy pieces. Yellow grapefruits have light yellow flesh. Pinkish grapefruits have pink or red flesh. Most grapefruits have a few small seeds.

Grapefruits grow in warm areas around much of the world. Most of the grapefruit in the United States comes from Florida.

Other articles to read include: **Fruit.**

Grass

Grasses are masses of green plants that cover fields, lawns, and pastures. Some kind of grass can be found on almost all the land surfaces of Earth. They grow in swamps and deserts. They grow in polar regions and tropical lands. Grasses are even found on rocky land and cold, snowy mountains.

Cereal grasses, such as wheat, corn, barley, and rice, provide food for people. Farmers also raise grasses to feed livestock. Some grasses are used to make fuels, plastics, and many other products. Much of the sugar we eat comes from a grass called sugar cane. People use corn and barley to make alcoholic drinks. Some paper is made from the leaves and stems of certain grasses.

Continued on the next page

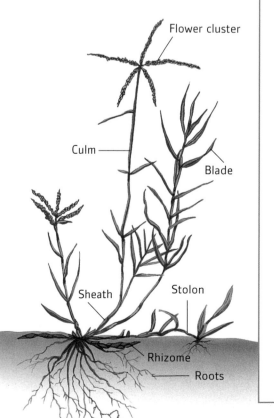

Flower cluster

Culm

Blade

Sheath

Stolon

Rhizome

Roots

The parts of a Bermuda grass plant include two types of creeping stems, called *stolons* and *rhizomes.* Stolons develop above the ground, and rhizomes grow below the ground. Leaves grow from stems called *culms.*

Grass, like other plants, is usually green because it contains a green-colored substance called *chlorophyll*. Through a process called *photosynthesis*, this substance helps change sunlight into energy that plants—and the animals that eat plants—can use.

Grass also makes the world more beautiful. It grows on lawns, parks, and playgrounds. The threadlike roots of grasses protect the land, too. They hold the bits of soil together so they are not easily blown away by wind or washed away by water.

Grass roots grow in a thick mat under the soil. Grasses have jointed stems and long, narrow leaves. Grass stems may be solid or hollow. The flowers of grasses produce the fruits and seeds that make new grass plants. Most grasses have clusters of flowers and many seeds. The seeds of grasses such as wheat, rice, and barley are called *grains*. The plants themselves may also be called grains.

Some grasses die at the end of the growing season. New seed must be planted at the beginning of the next season. Other grasses live through the winter and grow again each year.

Grass may be divided into six main types based on how they are used. The types are (1) grazing grasses, (2) turfgrasses, (3) ornamental grasses, (4) cereals, (5) sugar cane, and (6) woody grasses.

Grazing grasses feed such animals as cattle, goats, horses, and sheep. Turfgrasses are used to cover sports fields, golf courses, lawns, and playgrounds. Ornamental grasses are grown in gardens and parks for their beauty. They have featherlike flower clusters.

Cereals are among the world's most important food crops. The seeds of cereals provide grain that can be ground up into flour. Cereal grasses include wheat, rice, corn, oats, sorghum, barley, rye, and millet.

Sugar cane provides more than half of the world's sugar. Sugar cane also is used to make fuel. Sugar cane plants grow up to 15 feet (4.6 meters) tall.

Woody grasses include bamboos. The strong, woodlike stems of bamboos are used for building houses, rafts, bridges, and furniture. Bamboo may grow as high as 120 feet (40 meters).

Other articles to read include: **Bamboo; Barley; Bluegrass; Cereal; Corn; Farm and farming; Grain; Grassland; Oats; Pampas; Rhizome; Rice; Rye; Wheat.**

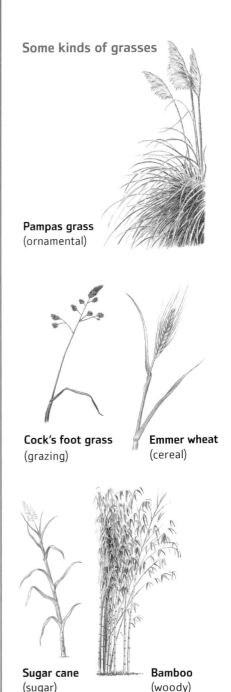

Some kinds of grasses

Pampas grass
(ornamental)

Cock's foot grass
(grazing)

Emmer wheat
(cereal)

Sugar cane
(sugar)

Bamboo
(woody)

Sheep graze on the grassland in Inner Mongolia, a part of China.

Grasslands

Grasslands are large, open areas where most of the plants are grasses. In many areas of the world, most grasslands are used to grow crops.

Some grasslands have short grasses and dry soil. These areas are called *steppes (stehps)*. Such grasslands include the Great Plains of the United States and Canada, the Veld of South Africa, and the plains of northern Kazakhstan and southern Russia.

Other grasslands have taller grasses and rich soil. These areas are called *prairies*. Prairies receive more rain than steppes. Some prairies also have hills and clumps of trees. Rivers and streams run through them. Prairies are common in the American Midwest, eastern Argentina, and parts of Europe and Asia.

Other articles to read include: **Grass; Prairie; Savanna; Steppe.**

The grasslands and savannas of Africa support a variety of animals, including topis, gazelles, and impalas.

Prairies are covered by tall grasses. Few natural prairie regions remain in the world because most have been turned into farms or grazing land.

Gray, Asa

Asa Gray (1810-1888) was the most respected plant-life expert of his time. His book *Manual of Botany* was published in 1848. This book helped people learn about plants of the northeastern United States. It also helped make *botany* more popular. Botany *(BOT uh nee)* is the study of plants.

Gray believed that each kind of plant started to grow in one place. He said the wind spread each kind to new areas.

Gray was born in Sauquoit, New York. He studied medicine but later became more interested in botany. He spent his spare time looking for different kinds of plants. He earned a medical degree in 1831 but never became a doctor.

Other articles to read include: **Botany.**

Asa Gray

Great Plains

The Great Plains is a dry grassland in North America. It runs south for about 2,500 miles (4,020 kilometers) from northern Canada into New Mexico and Texas in the United States. It also stretches east for about 400 miles (640 kilometers) from the Rocky Mountains to western Saskatchewan in Canada; and on to

Continued on the next page

The Great Plains is a large, dry grassland region in North America, running from northern Canada into New Mexico and Texas.

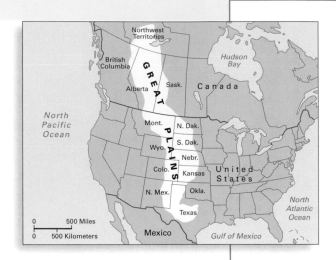

The Great Plains is an important agricultural and mining region of Canada and the United States.

Great Plains *Continued from the previous page*

eastern South Dakota, Nebraska, Kansas, and Oklahoma in the United States.

Few people live in the western part of the Great Plains. The Great Plains is an important farming region where vast crops of wheat are grown. Oil and coal also come from the Great Plains.

A large variety of plants and animals live in the Great Plains. Grasses called blue grama, buffalo grass, and crested wheatgrass grow there. Animals such as lizards, opossums, prairie dogs, weasels, raccoons, rattlesnakes, and skunks can be found in the Great Plains.

American Indians were the first people to live on the Great Plains. In the 1500's, Spaniards became the first Europeans to explore the region. In the late 1800's, railroads brought many settlers to the Great Plains.

Other articles to read include: **Grass; Grassland.**

Guavas develop from small, white flowers. Guavas have many hard seeds.

Guava

Guava *(GWAH vuh)* is a fruit that grows in warm regions. Guavas are round, oval, or pear-shaped. Their skin is yellow or light green. The insides are white, yellow, or pink with small seeds. Guavas contain vitamin C.

Some kinds of guavas are sweet, and some are sour. Sweet guavas can be eaten raw. Sour guavas are made into jam, jelly, or juice. They are used in pies, cakes, and ice cream.

Guavas grow on trees with shiny, smooth bark and drooping branches. They first grew in Colombia and Peru. Growers now raise them in Australia, Brazil, India, the Philippines, Thailand, and other warm areas. In the United States, they grow in California, Florida, and Hawaii.

Other articles to read include: **Fruit.**

Gum

Gum is a sticky substance. It is used to hold things together. Gum is also used in ice cream and pudding to make those desserts thick and smooth.

Most gum comes from plants. Gum is made from waxes and milky liquids called *latexes* from plants and from sticky liquids called *resins* from plants and trees. The best-known natural gum is called *gum arabic*. It comes from the sap of acacia trees in Africa. Other gums come from plant seeds, seaweeds, or chemicals. Chewing gum was once made from a latex called chicle. Today, most chewing gums are made from a variety of plant gums.

Other articles to read include: **Sap.**

Gum is a sticky substance produced by trees and other plants.

Gymnosperm

Gymnosperms *(JIHM nuh spurmz)* are a large group of plants with naked, or uncovered, seeds. They are among the largest and oldest living plants. There are hundreds of kinds of gymnosperms. Most are ever-green trees that bear cones. The plant's seeds are housed on the cones. Gymnosperms do not produce flowers.

Until about 130 million years ago, gymnosperms were the only seed plants on Earth. Today, angiosperms *(AN jee uh spurmz)* make up the vast majority of plants. Angiosperms produce seeds in a protective case. They produce flowers and fruits.

Conifers make up the largest group of gymnosperms. Conifers include such trees as *pine, fir, spruce,* and *balsam.* Unusual gym-nosperms include cycads and the ginkgo. A cycad resembles a palm tree with a large cone. The ginkgo produces seeds with an unpleasant odor. Gymnosperms are the source of many valuable products, including rosin, tar, timber, and turpentine.

Other articles to read include: **Angiosperm; Conifer; Cycad; Evergreen; Fir; Ginkgo; Pine; Seed; Spruce**

Pine cone

Scale

Winged seed

A gymnosperm is a plant that has exposed seeds. Most gymnosperms bear seeds in cones.

Hh

Habitat

Habitat *(HAB uh tat)* is the kind of place where something lives in the wild. All living things have certain needs, such as the right climate or foods. Living things can survive only in habitats that meet their needs.

Each plant requires a particular kind of habitat. For example, a water lily needs a pond. It could not survive in the desert. But a cactus needs the dry, hot conditions found in deserts. It could not survive in a pond.

Many different kinds of plants and animals can share a habitat. Trees, wildflowers, and mosses may live in a forest. A forest also provides a habitat for birds, deer, insects, and bears.

Many plants and other living things are at risk of dying out completely. Habitat destruction ranks as the greatest threat to most living things. For example, people have cut down or burned large areas of forest. This habitat destruction threatens many plants and animals.

Other articles to read include: **Biome; Deforestation; Endangered species; Environment; Forest.**

Aquatic plants such as water lilies (below) thrive in a mild, wet habitat. They could not survive in a desert habitat (below right). Such desert plants as cactus thrive in hot, dry areas. They could not survive in a wet habitat. Each kind of plant requires a particular kind of habitat.

Hemlock

The hemlock is a kind of pine tree. It grows in the forests of North America, Japan, China, and India. Hemlocks have soft needles. The needles are joined to the twig by small woody stalks.

There are different types of hemlock trees. The Eastern hemlock, or Canadian hemlock, may live up to 800 years. Its bark is used to tan leather. Its wood is used for lumber. The Eastern hemlock is the state tree of Pennsylvania.

The Western hemlock grows in the Pacific Northwest. It can grow to a height of 200 feet (60 meters). Its trunk can reach up to 8 feet (2.4 meters) across. The Western hemlock is the state tree of Washington.

Other articles to read include: **Pine; Tree.**

60 to 75 ft
(18 to 23 m)

Needles   Cone

The Easterm hemlock grows from southern Canada through the Appalachian regions of the United States.

Herb

An herb *(urb)* is a low-growing plant that has a juicy stem when it is young. The stems of some herbs get hard and woody when they grow old. Some herbs live for only one growing season. Others produce new plants year after year.

People use the leaves, stems, flowers, roots, and seeds of herbs. Herbs can be used fresh or dried for later use. Some herbs are used in cooking to make foods taste better. Such herbs include caraway seeds, mint, parsley, rosemary, saffron, sage, and vanilla. Other herbs are used in perfumes and as medicines.

Continued on the next page

Peppermint is an herb related to mint. It is used to add flavoring to foods and medicines.

Psyllium *(SIHL ee uhm)* is an herb grown in France, Spain, and India. Psyllium seeds are used to make laxatives. One species is used in some breakfast cereals.

Herb *Continued from the previous page*

People often grow herbs in their gardens. Many kinds of herbs can also be grown indoors.

Other articles to read include: **Balm; Basil; Ginseng; Horseradish; Lavender; Mint; Parsley; Rape; Rosemary; Saffron; Sage; Spearmint; Vanilla.**

Herbs can grow outdoors in gardens or in pots. Some herbs can be grown indoors on windowsills.

Basil   Sage   Borage   Mint

Parsley   Chives   Thyme   Savory

Herbal medicine

Herbal medicines are often sold as liquids in capsules or vials.

Herbal medicines are plants or plant products that are used to improve health. The plants are called *herbs.* People sell hundreds of herbal medicines in a variety of forms. Many are sold as dried plants or plant parts, without packaging. Others are sold as powders, capsules, tablets, and liquids. Sometimes the herbs are combined with other ingredients.

Popular herbal medicines include echinacea, ginkgo, and ginseng. Echinacea, made from cone flowers, is thought to relieve cold symptoms. Ginkgo and ginseng are said to improve memory and alertness. An herbal medicine called *St.-John's-wort* may help with mild depression. Some herbs used in cooking are also used in herbal medicine. For example, garlic may reduce the risk of heart disease.

Continued on the next page

Many people consider herbal medicines to be milder or safer than other drugs. However, many scientists question whether most herbal medicines actually work. In the United States, medicines are controlled by the Food and Drug Administration (FDA). But herbal medicines do not have to meet FDA rules for safety, effectiveness, and quality. Even though herbal medicines are natural, they may cause side effects. They may also affect other medications you may be taking. It is important to consult a doctor before taking herbal medicines.

Other articles to read include: **Herb.**

Some herbal medicines are prepared by grinding the herbs using a mortar and pestle.

Herbicide

An herbicide is a chemical used to kill plants. Herbicides are sometimes called *weed killers.* Farmers use herbicides to protect their crops from weeds. People also use herbicides to get rid of weeds in lawns, parks, and other areas.

Some herbicides kill only certain kinds of plants. For example, they may kill weeds but not harm grass or crops. Other herbicides destroy all plants. People use such herbicides to clear the ground around railroads and driveways.

Herbicides can be sprayed on plants or mixed into the soil. Herbicides can harm the environment. Some herbicides are poisonous to human beings and other animals.

Other articles to read include: **Pest control; Weed.**

People may apply herbicide to a lawn to prevent the growth of weeds.

Heredity

Heredity *(huh REHD uh tee)* is the passing of certain *traits* (characteristics) from one generation to the next. Heredity explains why offspring are like their parents. Heredity explains why a dandelion has offspring that are also dandelions. A dandelion will not produce an oak tree or a bluebird.

All living things are made up of cells. Traits are carried by a part of the cell called a *gene.* Genes are chemical instructions that direct how a living thing grows and functions. Among plants, a gene may carry instructions for building roots, stems, leaves, flowers, and fruit or other traits.

Living things pass on their genes to their offspring. Plants usually produce offspring through *sexual reproduction.* A plant made through sexual reproduction gets half of its genes from one parent and half from another parent. Plants sometimes produce offspring through *asexual reproduction.* A plant made through asexual reproduction gets all its genes from only one parent. Its genes are an exact copy of the parent's genes.

Other articles to read include: **Asexual reproduction; Cell; Gene; Mendel, Gregor Johann; Reproduction.**

In the mid-1800's, Gregor Mendel, an Austrian botanist and monk, studied hereditary traits in pea plants. The diagrams below show the main steps in Mendel's experiments on seed color.

Mendel first experimented with purebred strains of pea plants—one with yellow seeds and one with green seeds. He crossed these strains, and all the resulting hybrid seeds were yellow. He concluded that yellow seed color was the *dominant (controlling)* trait.

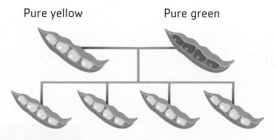

Pure yellow   Pure green

First generation (Hybrid yellow)

Plants grown from the hybrid yellow seeds produced yellow and green seeds in a ratio of about 3 to 1. The inheritance patterns Mendel discovered in this experiment and similar ones led him to formulate the first correct theory of heredity.

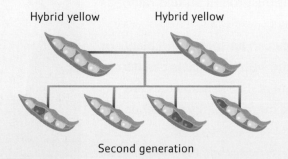

Hybrid yellow   Hybrid yellow

Second generation

Hollyhock

The hollyhock is a plant with spikes of colorful flowers. The flowers can be white, yellow, pink, red, or purple. They are round and open wide. Hollyhocks bloom from July to early September. There are many kinds.

Hollyhock flowers grow on the top of tall, heavy stems. Leaves also grow from the stems. The leaves are large, fuzzy, and heart-shaped.

Hollyhocks grow where there is a lot of sunlight. Many people grow hollyhocks as decoration along fences. When the flowers stop blooming, some people cut them down. People who want hollyhock seeds sometimes leave a few plants standing after the flowers are gone. A plant disease called *rust* can attack hollyhocks.

Other articles to read include: **Flower.**

Hollyhock

Honey

Honey is a sweet liquid that bees make from *nectar (NEHK tuhr).* Nectar is a liquid made by flowers.

People have raised bees for thousands of years for their honey. People eat honey raw and add it to many foods. The color and flavor of honey depend on the kinds of flowers that supply the nectar. Honey ranges in color from white through dark amber. It can have a mild or strong flavor. The most common honey plants are alfalfa, clover, aster, sunflower, citrus, goldenrod, and various wildflowers.

Worker bees make honey by drinking flower nectar. The bees store the nectar in a special pouch in their bodies called a *honey stomach.* Special chemicals in the pouch transform the nectar. The chemicals break down the nectar's sugars into simpler forms.

The bees store the nectar in a part of the hive called the *honey-comb.* There, the nectar loses much of its water. As the nectar loses water, it becomes honey. Bees eat honey for the energy it provides.

Other articles to read include: **Alfalfa; Clover; Flower; Goldenrod; Nectar; Sunflower.**

Bees store honey in their hives in tiny, six-sided containers called cells.

Tatarian honeysuckle

Honeysuckle

Honeysuckle is a shrub or vine with smooth, oval leaves of dark green. Honeysuckles often produce beautiful, trumpet-shaped flowers. The flowers can be white, yellow, pink, purple, or bright red. Berries form when the flower petals drop off. The berries can be red, yellow, white, black, or blue. People grow honeysuckles for decoration. Most of them are hardy and easy to grow. They grow in mild climates all over the world. Some honeysuckles are evergreens. There are many kinds.

Many birds like to eat honeysuckle berries. As they eat the berries, the birds carry away seeds to other places. There, new honeysuckle plants grow. Hummingbirds, bees, and moths like the sweet nectar of honeysuckle flowers. They carry pollen to and from the flowers as they feed on the nectar. Some honeysuckles are also called *woodbine*.

Other articles to read include: **Flower; Shrub; Vine.**

Horseradish

Horseradish is an herb. It has long leaves, a large root, and a number of side roots. The main root is used to make a sharp-tasting relish for food. It is most commonly served with prime cuts of beef.

To prepare horseradish for use, the root is first *grated* (worn down) into very small pieces. The pieces are then preserved in vinegar. Whole roots keep their sharp taste for long periods.

During the horseradish harvest, workers remove the plants' side roots. These roots are used to plant the next crop. Horseradish is native to Europe.

Other articles to read include: **Herb; Root.**

Horseradish

Horsetail

A horsetail is a plant with a hollow, jointed stem. The stem holds a rough material called *silica*. People once scrubbed metal with horsetail to make it shine. Horsetail is sometimes called *scouring rush* for this reason.

Most horsetails are small. The stalks of some horsetails look like tiny trees. Horsetails were common many millions of years ago. At that time, some grew to be large trees.

Horsetail grows from creeping roots. A horsetail does not produce flowers or seeds. Instead, it reproduces using tiny cells called *spores.* Horsetails are closely related to ferns.

Other articles to read include: **Fern; Stem.**

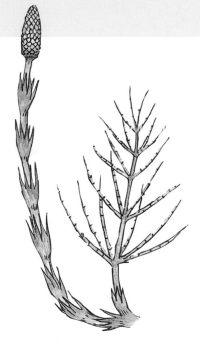

Horsetails have hollow, jointed stems.

Horticulture

Horticulture *(HAWR tuh kuhl chuhr)* is the science of growing fruits, vegetables, flowers, and decorative plants. It is a branch of agriculture *(AG ruh kuhl chuhr),* the growing of plants and animals for the benefit of people. Most horticultural plants are raised in greenhouses, nurseries, and orchards.

Continued on the next page

A horticultural scientist checks redwood seedlings in a research lab in Santa Cruz, California. Horticultural scientists try to find new and better ways to grow healthy plants.

Gardening is the most popular horticultural hobby.

Horticulture *Continued from the previous page*

Horticulture has played a crucial role in the development of civilization. Horticulture and agriculture supported the first permanent human settlements, which gave rise to the first cities.

Today, horticulture is both an industry and a hobby. The horticulture industry produces most of the world's fruits and vegetables. Horticultural hobbies such as gardening and flower arranging are practiced around the world.

Horticultural scientists try to find new and better ways to grow healthy plants. They try to figure out which food and lighting conditions are best for particular plants. They also improve plants using genetic engineering, techniques that change an organism's characteristics. Horticultural scientists often conduct experiments in special research centers called *horticultural experiment stations.*

Other articles to read include: **Agriculture; Botany; Farm and farming; Flower; Fruit; Vegetable.**

Humus

Humus *(HYOO muhs)* is a dark brown substance in soil. It is made from dead plant and animal matter. Humus greatly increases the ability of soil to support the growth of plants.

Humus holds many *nutrients.* A nutrient is a substance living things need to grow and live. Humus is spongy and can hold much water. It also helps to hold soil together. Humus thus helps to prevent soil from being carried away by wind or water.

Humus is made by living things called *decomposers.* Decomposers include different kinds of *microbes* (very small organisms). Earthworms and insects also are decomposers. Decomposers feed on dead plant and animal matter. Eventually, decomposers turn this material into humus.

Other articles to read include: **Decay; Soil.**

Hybrid

A hybrid plant is the offspring of two different *varieties* of plant. Varieties are members of a *species* (kind) of organism that differ in some ways but can still reproduce. People create hybrids to combine *traits* (characteristics) from different varieties.

For example, people may want a type of corn that resists a certain pest and can also grow in cool weather. They can take one corn plant with each trait and combine them to make a hybrid with both traits.

Much of the alfalfa, barley, corn, rice, and wheat grown by farmers are hybrids. Vegetables that have been hybridized include broccoli, carrots, cauliflower, onions, pumpkins, and tomatoes. Hybridized fruits include apples, grapes, pears, and plums. Some flowers are hybrids, including marigolds, orchids, and roses.

The word *hybrid* can also describe the offspring of different species. For example, a mule is the hybrid off-spring of a donkey and a horse. Like most such hybrids, mules can almost never reproduce.

Other articles to read include: **Agriculture; Crop; Gene; Heredity; Species.**

Most hybrid corn results from single-crossing. In this process, selected corn plants are bred with other plants of the same variety. This procedure produces *inbred seed.* Two inbred varieties are then bred, resulting in *single-cross seed.*

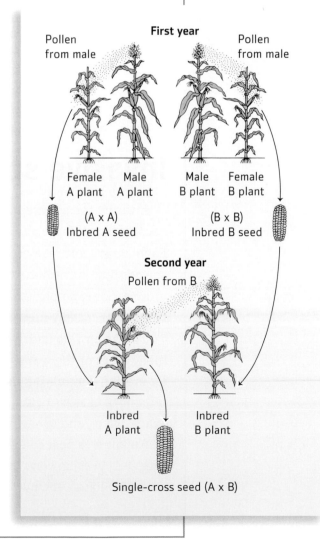

First year

Pollen from male

Pollen from male

Female A plant   Male A plant   Male B plant   Female B plant

(A x A) Inbred A seed

(B x B) Inbred B seed

Second year

Pollen from B

Inbred A plant   Inbred B plant

Single-cross seed (A x B)

Impatiens

Impatiens *(ihm PAY shuhnz)* is a flowering plant known for its exploding seed pods. As the seed pods ripen, water pressure builds up inside. The gentlest touch makes the pod walls burst, throwing seeds in all directions. For this reason, some kinds of impatiens are called *touch-me-not* and *snapweed.* There are many kinds of impatiens. The plant's flowers may be pink, reddish-orange, orange, yellow, purple, or white.

Wild impatiens grow around much of the world. Most kinds of wild impatiens grow along riverbanks and in woods, swamps, and damp thickets. But some kinds grow in gardens. Two types of impatiens commonly grown in pots are the *garden balsam* and the *busy Lizzy,* which is a shade plant.

Other articles to read include: **Flower; Seed.**

The busy Lizzy is a type of impatiens often grown in containers.

Invasive species

Invasive species are living things that spread to new places, causing harm. A species is one particular kind of living thing. People transport many species from place to place. Invasive species flourish because there are few natural limits on their growth. For example, the animals that normally feed on the species are usually missing from its new home.

The Asian vine kudzu has become an invasive species in many areas of the world. In the United States, kudzu was planted for erosion control. But the fast-growing kudzu soon spread out of control in areas of the American South. Stands of kudzu take space, water, and sunlight from other plants.

An invasive pest can alter an entire *habitat* (place in which an organism lives) in ways that threaten many native species. In areas of Florida, the number of forest and brush fires has

Continued on the next page

increased dramatically since paperbark trees were introduced. These trees have highly flammable bark and leaves. The intense fires kill many native plants. Paperbark trees flower several times a year and produce many seeds. For this reason, they can quickly take over the habitat, preventing the regrowth of native plants. The loss of native plants has harmed the animal species that rely on the plants for food and shelter. The most effective way to prevent the spread of invasive species is to keep them out. Many governments ban travelers from bringing foreign plants into their country. People also may uproot invasive plants or kill them with poisons. But killing off an invasive species can be extremely difficult after it has spread.

Other articles to read include: **Balance of nature; Endangered species; Habitat; Species.**

The Asian vine kudzu has become an invasive species in the southern United States. Thick stands of kudzu harm native plants, even killing adult trees.

Iris

The iris *(EYE rihs)* is a plant with large, unusually shaped flowers. It has three sets of petals. The lower petals flare out and down. The upper petals curve up into a dome. A third set of petals covers the flower's center.

Irises can be any color. The flowers may be from 1 inch (2.5 centimeters) to over 1 foot (30 centimeters) across. Iris plants grow from 6 inches (15 centimeters) to 6 feet (2 meters) tall. They bloom in mild climates in spring and early summer.

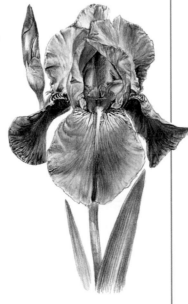

The leaves of iris plants rise from underground stems called *rhizomes (RY zohmz).* Iris rhizomes are poisonous. Eating them can cause upset stomach. Some dried iris rhizomes are used in perfumes and powders.

Other articles to read include: **Flower; Rhizome.**

Bearded iris

An irrigation canal carries water through the desert to farms near Yuma, Arizona. Irrigation has enabled large desert areas in the southwestern United States to be turned into productive farmland.

Irrigation

Irrigation is the watering of land by people. People transport water from lakes, rivers, streams, and wells to irrigate land that does not get enough rain.

Farming would be impossible in desert regions without irrigation. In other areas, rain falls only part of the year. Irrigation allows farming to continue during the dry season. Even places with regular rainfall sometimes have a *drought (drowt)*. A drought is a long period without rain. Irrigation can save crops during droughts.

To irrigate, people must find ways to transport water to where it is needed. Most farms use a network of canals to carry water from streams, rivers, and lakes to the fields. Water from wells is often pumped to the surface. The pump lifts the water into a ditch or pipe that carries it to the crops.

Irrigation water may be flooded over the surface of the field or sprayed over the field with sprinklers. It may be dripped onto the field through plastic tubes on the ground. It also may be soaked into the plant roots from underground pipes.

Other articles to read include: **Desert; Drought; Farm and farming.**

Ivy

Ivy is a vine that grows along the ground or on trees or walls. Some people grow ivy for decoration.

Many different kinds of plants are called *ivy*. One kind is English ivy or common ivy. It grows in North America and Europe. Its leaves feel waxy. They stay dark green most of the year.

Boston ivy, or Japanese ivy, looks like a green carpet. It grows on the shady side of many buildings in the eastern United States and in Asia and Europe. In the fall, its green leaves turn red and fall off.

The leaves of poison ivy are covered with an oil. The oil can make people itch or cause blisters on the skin. The leaves are red in the early spring. They are green from late spring through summer. They turn red or orange in autumn.

Other articles to read include: **Poison ivy; Vine.**

Ivy is a climbing vine that is often grown on walls.

Jack-in-the-pulpit

Jack-in-the-pulpit is an American wildflower. It grows mostly in the eastern half of the United States. Jack-in-the-pulpits grow in moist woodlands, flood plains, and swampy areas. They are sometimes called *Indian turnips* or *bog onions*.

A jack-in-the-pulpit has a cluster of small flowers atop a thin stem. This cluster is called a *spadix (SPAY dihks)*. A large leaf forms a hood over the spadix. This leaf is called a *spathe (spayth)*. It looks like a flower petal. The spadix is nicknamed the "preacher," and the spathe is nicknamed the "pulpit." A preacher is a minister. A pulpit is the raised platform from which a preacher speaks.

The color of the spathe ranges from green to purple or bronze. The spathe may be striped. The flowers bloom from April to June. In late summer, the spathe falls away. It leaves behind clusters of scarlet or red-orange berries. The jack-in-the-pulpit is considered poisonous when eaten raw. The plant's tissues contain bundles of needlelike crystals that can injure the mouth and throat.

Other articles to read include: **Flower; Poisonous plant.**

Jack-in-the-pulpit

Jasmine

Jasmine *(JAS muhn* or *JAZ muhn)* is a shrub or vine known for its fragrant white flowers. People grow jasmines for their beauty. People also use the flowers to flavor tea. Jasmine is an ingredient in some perfumes. The plant grows in tropical and nearly tropical regions. There are many kinds.

Jasmines may grow upright or as a vine. Some jasmines lose their leaves each autumn. Others remain green the year around.

The common white jasmine is a vine with dark green leaves and white flowers. This plant is also called a jes-samine. The Spanish jasmine has larger flowers with a small amount of red underneath.

Other articles to read include: **Flower; Shrub; Vine.**

Jasmine

Joshua tree

Joshua tree

Joshua tree is a desert plant with stiff, pointed leaves. It is a kind of *yucca (YUHK uh).* The Joshua tree grows in southwestern North America. It is especially common in the Mojave *(moh HAH vee)* Desert. According to legend, Mormon pioneers named the Joshua tree after a figure in the Bible.

The Joshua tree may grow as high as 40 feet (12 meters). Its leaves reach about 14 inches (36 centimeters) in length. The Joshua tree provides food and shelter for many desert animals.

The rare Joshua tree can be found in Joshua Tree National Park in southern California.

Other articles to read include: **Desert; Tree.**

Juniper

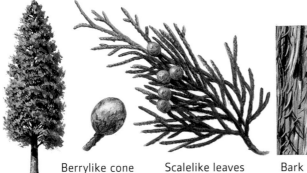

Berrylike cone   Scalelike leaves   Bark

40 to 50 ft
(12 to 15 m)

Junipers have fragrant berrylike fruits that range in color from blue to red.

Junipers *(JOO nuh puhrz)* are small evergreen trees with fragrant, berrylike cones. These cones are called juniper berries. Juniper trees are sometimes called *cedars* or *redcedars.* But junipers are not true cedars. There are many kinds of junipers. They grow in much of the world.

Juniper leaves may be needlelike and prickly. Other juniper leaves are like scales. They lie tightly against the twigs. Juniper berries range in color from blue to red.

Oils from some kinds of juniper berry are used in perfumes and as flavorings, especially for gin. The eastern redcedar has fragrant, reddish wood. It is used for cedar chests, furniture, and pencils. Its odor is thought to drive away moths.

Other articles to read include: **Berry; Cedar; Evergreen; Tree.**

Jute

Jute is a strong, natural fiber often used to make gunny sacks.

Jute *(joot)* is a long, soft, shiny fiber from the jute plant. It can be woven into rough, strong threads. Jute is one of the cheapest natural fibers. More jute is produced than any other natural fiber except cotton. Jute also ranks second to cotton in its number of uses.

Jute is often used to make cloth for wrapping bundles of cotton. It is used to make rough cloth bags called gunny sacks. Jute fibers are also woven into curtains, chair coverings, carpets, and coarse cloth called burlap. Jute is used in making twine and rope.

Jute grows best in warm, damp areas. China, India, and Bangladesh are the world's biggest growers. Jute fibers are off-white to brown and grow from 3 to 15 feet (0.9 to 4.5 meters) long.

Other articles to read include: **Cotton.**

Kelp

Kelp is a type of seaweed that grows in shallow ocean waters. Seaweeds are algae *(AL jee)* rather than true plants. Kelp is usually brownish-green. It grows in cold to mild waters around much of the world. It generally does not grow well in tropical waters. There are many kinds of kelp.

Kelps are different in size and shape. The largest is called giant kelp. It grows to 200 feet (60 meters) long. Many giant kelps live together in underwater forests.

Many animals depend on kelp for shelter. They hide from hunting animals among kelp forests. Animals also feed on kelp. These include certain snails and sea urchins. People also grow kelp for food on special farms in the ocean, especially off the coasts of East Asia.

Other articles to read include: **Algae; Seaweed.**

Giant kelp can grow up to 200 feet (60 meters) long.

Kingdom

A kingdom is a large group of related living things. It is one of the largest groups in *scientific classification*. Scientific classification is the method scientists use to group living things.

The living things in a kingdom share certain basic qualities because they share a common ancestor. For example, all plants belong to the kingdom Plantae (plant). Members of this kingdom have more than one cell, live in one place without moving around, and usually make their own food using sunlight.

Kingdoms are divided into smaller groups called *phyla* or *divisions*. Mosses make up the division Bryophyta. Kingdoms are sometimes grouped into larger *domains*. Plants, animals, fungi, and tiny creatures called protists all belong to the domain Eukaryota. All these organisms have cells with a *nucleus* (center).

Other articles to read include: **Classification, Scientific; Phylum.**

Continued on the next page

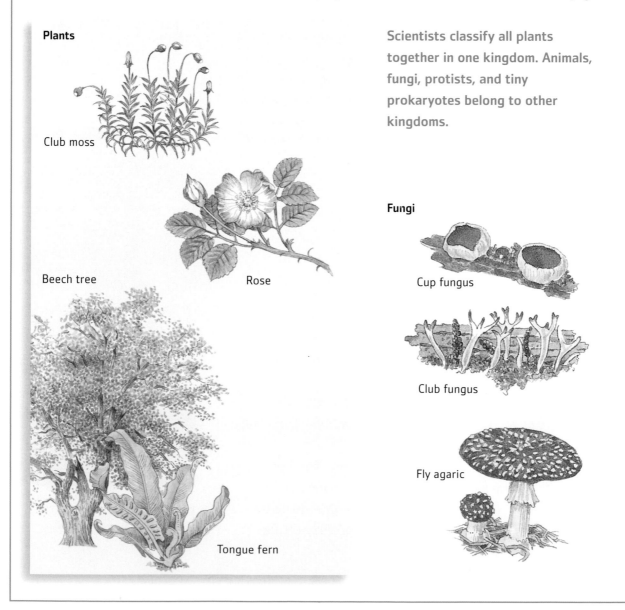

Plants

Club moss

Beech tree

Rose

Tongue fern

Scientists classify all plants together in one kingdom. Animals, fungi, protists, and tiny prokaryotes belong to other kingdoms.

Fungi

Cup fungus

Club fungus

Fly agaric

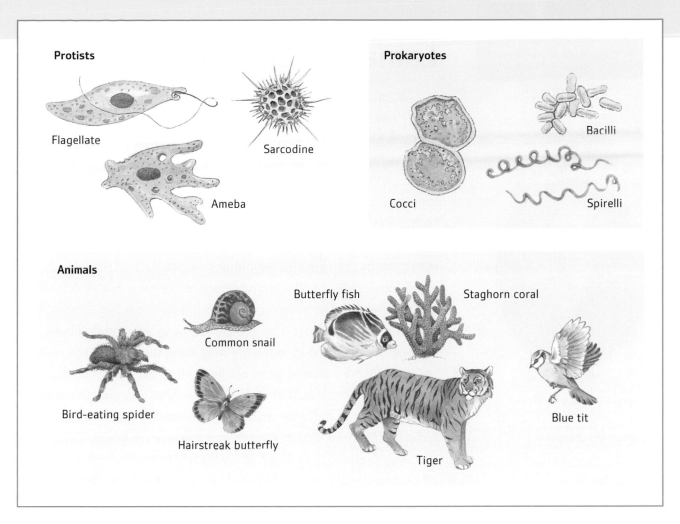

Protists

Flagellate

Sarcodine

Ameba

Prokaryotes

Bacilli

Cocci

Spirelli

Animals

Butterfly fish

Staghorn coral

Common snail

Bird-eating spider

Hairstreak butterfly

Tiger

Blue tit

Kiwi fruit

The kiwi *(KEE wee)* fruit is a brown, fuzzy fruit about the size and shape of an egg. It is a berry that grows on a vine. The name *kiwi* comes from the name of a small, brown bird of New Zealand. The largest growers of kiwi are New Zealand, France, and the United States.

Inside, the kiwi fruit is green and has tiny black seeds. The seeds can be eaten. Kiwi fruit has a sweet, mixed-fruit taste. People eat kiwi fruit fresh, frozen, or canned. They use kiwi fruit to make pies, ice cream, and wine. People also drink kiwi juice.

Kiwi fruit grows best in a place that does not have extreme cold or extreme heat.

Kiwi fruit is native to China. It was once called Chinese gooseberry.

Other articles to read include: **Berry; Fruit; Seed.**

The flowers and fruit of the kiwi plant.

Chevalier de Lamarck

Lamarck, Chevalier de

Chevalier de Lamarck *(SHEHV uh LIHR duh luh MAHRK)* (1744-1829) was a French scientist. He was one of the first scientists to propose ideas about *evolution*. Evolution is the slow change in living things over generations.

Lamarck found that plants and animals change in response to their surroundings. Adults then pass these changes to their offspring. For example, Lamarck believed that giraffes stretched out their necks reaching for leaves in trees. As a result, he thought, they gave birth to giraffes with longer necks.

Lamarck's ideas about evolution influenced the British scientist Charles Darwin. Darwin proposed a different theory of evolution that nearly all scientists now accept. Lamarck was wrong about changes that occur during the life of a living thing. Such changes are generally not passed on to offspring. Instead, living things evolve largely through a process called *natural selection*. In natural selection, organisms with characteristics useful in a particular habitat are more likely to survive and produce offspring. This tendency leads to the spread of useful traits.

Lamarck was born Jean Baptiste Pierre Antoine de Monet on Aug. 1, 1744, in Bazentin, France. He was made keeper of the royal herbarium plant collection in Paris in 1788. He was appointed professor of zoology at the Museum of Natural History there in 1793. He died on Dec. 18, 1829.

Other articles to read include: **Darwin, Charles Robert; Evolution; Natural selection.**

Lavender

Lavender

Lavender is a small bush with fragrant flowers and leaves. It grows wild in Mediterranean countries. Commercial and private gardeners also grow the plant in many parts of the world.

Lavender bushes grow from 3 to 4 feet (90 to 120 centimeters) high. They have long, narrow green leaves and pale purple flowers. This shade of purple is also called lavender, after the flowers. The flowers grow in clusters around the stem. When dried, they keep their pleasant odor for a long time.

Continued on the next page

The word *lavender* comes from a Latin word that means *to wash*. The plants may have gotten their name because ancient Romans used the leaves and flowers to give their bathwater a pleasing scent. Dried lavender flowers were once stored with linens and clothing. Today, the scent of lavender is added to a wide variety of products. The dried flowers are used in mixtures of dried flower petals and spices called *potpourris*. Oil from the flowers is used in some perfumes.

Other articles to read include: **Flower.**

Leaf

Leaves are the main food-making part of nearly all plants. The number of leaves on a plant ranges from only a few to thousands.

Most leaves are 1 to 12 inches (2.5 to 30 centimeters) long. But some plants have huge leaves. The largest leaves grow on the raffia *(RAF ee uh)* palm. The leaves of this tree grow up to 65 feet (20 meters) long. Some plants have tiny leaves. The leaves of asparagus plants are so tiny that they are hard to see without a magnifying glass. Leaves come in many shapes. Most leaves can be divided into three groups according to their basic shape. *Broad leaves* are the most common type of leaf. These leaves are fairly wide and flat. Plants that have such leaves include maple and oak trees, pea plants, and rosebushes. *Narrow leaves* are long and slender. Narrow leaves grow on grasses. Grasses include lawn grasses as well as barley, corn, oats, wheat, and other cereal grasses. Lilies, onions, and certain other plants also have narrow leaves. Needle leaves grow on firs, pines, spruces, and most other cone-bearing trees and shrubs. Needle leaves resemble short, thick sewing needles. A few other kinds of cone-bearing plants, including certain cedars and junipers, have scalelike leaves.

Leaves are important to people. Many people enjoy the beauty of leaves and the rustling sound they make when shaken by the wind. Leaves are eaten as food and used to flavor foods and make tea and other drinks. Some drugs come from leaves.

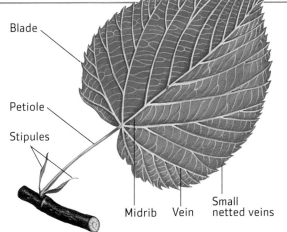

Blade

Petiole

Stipules

Midrib Vein Small netted veins

Lower side of a broad leaf

Most leaves have two main parts: (1) a *flat blade* and (2) a stemlike *petiole*. The leaves of many plants also have a third main part, two small flaps called the stipules. *Veins* are the *pipelines* that carry food and water in a leaf.

Continued on the next page

Leaf *Continued from the previous page*

People use certain leaves to make rope. Leaves also help to enrich the air that we breathe. When leaves make the plant's food, they give off a gas called oxygen. People and other animals must breathe oxygen to live.

A leaf makes its food using the energy in sunlight, water from the soil, and a gas in the air called carbon dioxide. This food-making process is called *photosynthesis (FOH tuh SIHN thuh sihs)*. Plants need this food to live, grow, and produce flowers and seeds. They store the food made by leaves in their fruits, roots, seeds, stems, and even in the leaves themselves.

Continued on the next page

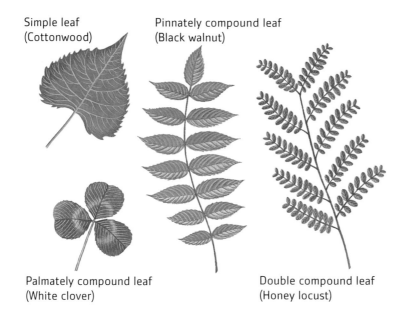

Simple leaf
(Cottonwood)

Pinnately compound leaf
(Black walnut)

Palmately compound leaf
(White clover)

Double compound leaf
(Honey locust)

A leaf may have one or more blades. If a leaf has only one blade, it is called a *simple leaf.* A leaf with more than one blade is known as a *compound leaf.* The blades of a compound leaf are called *leaflets.* They may be arranged in a *palmate* (palmlike or handlike) or *pinnate* (featherlike) pattern. A few plants have *double compound leaves,* in which each leaflet is further divided into still smaller leaflets.

Vein patterns differ among leaves. Most broad leaves have a pinnate or palmate vein pattern. Grasses have parallel veins. Needle leaves have one or two center veins.

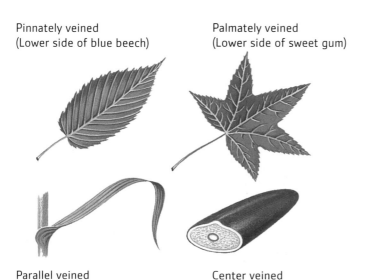

Pinnately veined
(Lower side of blue beech)

Palmately veined
(Lower side of sweet gum)

Parallel veined
(Upper and lower sides of rye)

Center veined
(Cross section of white pine)

Some leaves have special jobs other than making food. The spines of a cactus keep animals from eating the plant. The fat leaves on a tulip bulb store food underground in winter. Many plants that grow in dry places have thick leaves that store water. *Tendrils* are special leaves that hold climbing plants in place. Some leaves attract, trap, and digest insects.

A leaf begins its life in a bud. Buds are the growing parts of a stem. They form along the sides and at the tip of the stem. The bud contains a tightly packed group of tiny leaves. These leaves unfold and make food for the plant.

The leaf is green because it contains a green substance called *chlorophyll (KLAWR uh fihl)*. Chlorophyll enables the leaf to make food. The leaf also has other colors, but they are hidden by the green. Many trees lose their leaves as winter approaches. Before the trees lose their leaves, the green color disappears. The leaf may then show its other colors, such as yellow or orange-red. Some dying leaves turn red and purple. When the leaf dies, it dries up and drops to the ground.

On the ground, the dead leaf becomes part of the soil. It enriches the soil and supports new plant growth.

Other articles to read include: **Bud; Chlorophyll; Photosynthesis.**

Most plants have broad, flat leaves, such as those of a maple tree (above, far left). But wheat (above center) and other grasses have long, narrow leaves. Pines (above) and most other cone-bearing plants have needle leaves.

Leek

Leeks

The leek is a vegetable related to the onion. The leek has many flat leaves that join together at their base. The joined leaves form a thick neck. The neck measures 1 to 2 inches (2.5 to 5 centimeters) wide. It reaches 5 to 8 inches (13 to 20 centimeters) long. The neck is the edible part of the plant. It has a mild, onion-like flavor. It often is cooked or used as a flavoring for other foods. It also can be eaten raw.

Leeks live for two years. The plants are grown from seeds. They require a long growing season. Leek seeds are generally planted in a greenhouse in the early spring. In late spring, the seedlings are moved to a field or garden. Rich, fertile soil is packed around the neck. This practice improves the quality of the plant. Leeks are probably native to the eastern Mediterranean region.

Other articles to read include: **Onion; Vegetable.**

Legume

The many varieties of beans that people eat are the seeds and/or the seed pods of various legumes.

A legume *(LEHG yoom* or *lih GYOOM)* is any plant in the pea family. Legumes make up one of the largest groups of flowering plants. There are thousands of kinds of legumes. Legumes get their name from the seed pods they bear. These seed pods are also called legumes.

Many legumes are important crops. Beans, peas, and peanuts are nourishing foods. Alfalfa, clover, and vetch provide animal feed. Other legumes yield dyes, medicines, oils, and timber. Legumes also add *nutrients* (nourishing substances) to the soil. For this reason, farmers often use legumes to improve poor soil.

Legumes grow in most parts of the world. They may be trees, shrubs, or herbs. Many of them are climbing plants. The flowers of many legumes look like butterflies. The common sweet pea belongs to this group. The flowers of other legumes may be small and regular. Some legumes have irregular flowers with spreading petals.

Other articles to read include: **Bean; Crop; Flower; Nut; Pea.**

Lemon

Lemons are small yellow fruits. They belong to a group called citrus fruits, which also includes limes and oranges. Lemons are oval and have a yellow rind, or peel. Most lemons taste sour, so most people do not enjoy eating fresh lemons.

Lemons are used to flavor soft drinks, desserts, and many other foods. Cooks use lemon juice and oil from the lemon rind to flavor meat and fish. Lemon oil is also used as a scent.

Lemon trees grow up to 25 feet (7.6 meters) tall. They have thorns, pointed leaves, and sweet-smelling white blossoms. The trees often have flowers and fruit at the same time.

Lemon trees, which only grow in warm climates, can be damaged by freezing weather. Growers use heaters, big fans, or water sprays to help protect the trees from cold.

Other articles to read include: **Fruit; Tree.**

The lemon is a popular citrus fruit that is raised mainly for its tart juice and fragrant oil.

Lettuce

Lettuce is a leafy green vegetable. It usually grows close to the ground. It is used mainly in salads, and most people eat it raw.

There are three main kinds of lettuce. Head lettuce is the most common. Its leaves curl around the center and form a ball shape. Leaf lettuce grows in thick, leafy clumps instead of heads. Gardeners grow more leaf lettuce than any other kind. Romaine lettuce grows long and upright. The leaves curl inward. Romaine contains more vitamins and minerals than any other kind of lettuce.

Most lettuce is planted right in the ground, but some lettuce is started in buildings called greenhouses. Plants in greenhouses are protected from the cold. Lettuce must be packed, cooled, and shipped right after harvesting because it spoils easily.

Other articles to read include: **Vegetable.**

Iceberg lettuce

Leaf lettuce

Romaine lettuce

Varieties of lettuce include iceberg, leaf, and romaine, as well as bibb and Boston.

Lianas are vines that climb on or around tree trunks or other objects.

Liana

Liana *(lee AH nuh)* is a name for many kinds of vines. Lianas are usually found in tropical rain forests. They climb on or around the trunks and branches of trees, using the trees for support. They have flexible growing parts called *shoots.* Lianas grow quickly.

There are many kinds of lianas. Some of them cannot hold on to trees. They simply lean against trees as they climb. These lianas are called *scramblers* or *leaners.* Other lianas wrap around trunks and branches. Many lianas have twisting, threadlike parts called *tendrils.* The tendrils attach tightly to trees and other objects. One kind of liana with tendrils is the grapevine. Some lianas use special roots for attachment. These lianas include ivy and vanilla vines. Still other lianas have hooked thorns to help them climb.

Other articles to read include: **Rain forest; Vine.**

Lichen

A lichen *(LY kuhn)* is a living thing made up of a fungus and usually an alga. Lichens are an example of *symbiosis (sihm bee OH sihs).* In symbiosis, two or more living things have a close relationship. They often depend on one another for survival. In the case of lichens, the alga depends on the fungus for water. It needs this water to make food using the energy in sunlight. In exchange, the alga provides the fungus with food. The fungus cannot make its own food. In this way, each of these living things depends on the other for survival.

There are thousands of kinds of lichens. Lichens can be green, brown, yellow, orange, or gray. Some grow in soil. But most lichens grow on rocks or tree bark. Lichens can live where few plants can live. They can grow on bare rock because they do not have roots. Some lichens live in the Arctic. The Arctic is too cold for many plants. Other lichens live in deserts or on mountains.

In the Arctic, caribou (commonly known as reindeer) eat lichens during the winter. Snails and insects also eat lichens.

Other articles to read include: **Algae; Fungi; Symbiosis.**

Lichens cover much of the ground in the Arctic, providing winter food for caribou.

Life

Life is a special condition shared by all living things. People generally find it easy to tell living things from nonliving things. A butterfly, a horse, and a tree are obviously alive. A bicycle, a house, and a stone are obviously not alive. People consider a thing to be alive if it is capable of certain activities. Such activities include growing and reproducing. Living things are known as *organisms*.

The life of a typical plant begins when its seed sprouts and pushes the stem and leaves up above the soil.

Scientists have found it difficult to come up with a satisfactory definition of what life actually is. Part of the problem is that there are millions of different kinds of living things. Many of these organisms appear to have little in common. Some, including bacteria, are too small to see without a microscope. Others, such as redwood trees and blue whales, are huge.

Despite their differences, all living things are alike in some ways. The basic unit of life is the cell. A cell is like a tiny compartment. Many organisms are made up of a single cell. These single-celled organisms include bacteria. Other organisms have bodies made up of billions or even trillions of cells. These multi-celled organisms include plants and animals.

All living things can reproduce. That is, they can make more of their own kind. Some living things reproduce by dividing in two. Bacteria reproduce in this way. Most plants reproduce by combining cells from two parents. Special *sex cells* combine to form a cell called an *embryo*. An embryo can develop into a new individual. Among most plants, sex cells are made by flowers.

All living things grow. Most plants begin life as seeds. Even the tallest redwood grows from a tiny seed. This growth takes many years. A mature tree may live for hundreds or even thousands of years. But eventually, all living things die. Death makes it possible for new things to grow.

Continued on the next page

Life *Continued from the previous page*

Living things must use energy to live. Plants generally get their energy from the sun. They use the energy in sunlight to make sugar. This process is called *photosynthesis (foh tuh SIHN thuh sihs)*. Plants use this sugar to live and grow. Animals get their energy from plants.

Many living things move around. Others remain fixed in place. Plants generally depend on animals or the wind to spread to new places. For example, some seeds have a shape that catches the wind. Others have special hooks that catch on animal fur. Among adult plants, much of the movement takes place inside. Nearly all plants have special tubes that move water from their roots to their leaves. Other tubes move food from the leaves to the rest of the plant.

Living things also react to changes in their surroundings. For example, many plants can slowly turn their leaves to face the sun.

Most scientists believe life arose through natural chemical processes in the ocean. Scientific evidence suggests that the first life form appeared about 3 ½ billion years ago. This single life form was the ancestor of all living things today.

The *theory of evolution* describes how living things change over long periods of time. Evolution describes how a single life form could develop into the great variety of organisms alive today.

Other articles to read include: **Biology; Cell; Death; Evolution; Life cycle; Plant; Reproduction.**

Life cycle

The life cycle is a set of stages that a particular living thing must go through as it grows and reproduces. All living things have a life cycle. But the life cycle of one kind of living thing may be quite different from that of another.

Plants have a complicated life cycle. There are two major stages to the life cycle of a plant. This arrangement is called the *alternation of generations.* In one stage, the plant produces tiny cells called *spores.* During this stage, the plant is known as a sporophyte *(SPAWR uh fyt).* Nearly all plants that look familiar to us are in the sporophyte stage of their life cycle. For example, the flowers, grass, and trees in a lawn are all sporophytes.

Continued on the next page

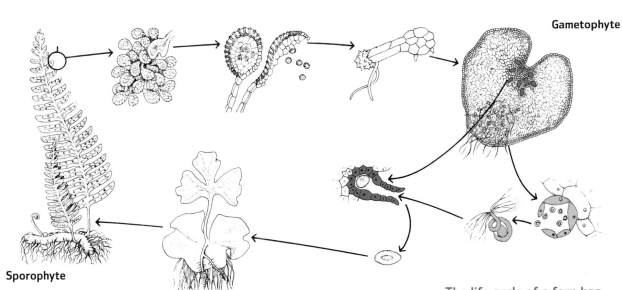

Gametophyte

Sporophyte

The life cycle of a fern has two major stages. In one, the plant grows into a heart-shaped *gametophyte.* The gametophyte produces *sex cells.* In the other stage, the plant grows into a *sporophyte,* which has the familiar form of a fern. The sporophyte makes *spores.*

Spores develop into a new form of plant. This form produces *sex cells,* also called *gametes (GAM eets).* This form of plant is called a *gametophyte (guh MEE tuh fyt).* The gametophyte of most plants is tiny. It usually cannot be seen because it is protected inside the body of the sporophyte. Among flowering plants, gametophytes are housed in flowers. Sex cells enable two parents to produce off-spring. The male sex cell is called a *sperm.* The female sex cell is called an *egg.* A sperm cell combines with an egg. That is, the sperm *fertilizes* the egg. A fertilized egg is housed within a seed. A seed that finds good soil can grow into a new sporophyte. It may take many years for the developing sporophyte to become an adult. The adult sporophyte can then produce spores, starting the cycle anew.

Among some groups of plants, the gametophyte is not hidden within the sporo-phyte. For example, among ferns, the gametopyte appears as a small, heart-shaped plant. The ferns we are more familiar with are in the sporophyte stage. Among mosses, the gametophyte is the familiar form. The sporophyte is housed within the gametophyte. This arrangement is the opposite of how flowering plants and other seed plants develop.

Some plants complete their entire life cycle in only one growing season. These plants are known as *annuals.* Others require two growing seasons. These plants are called *biennials.* Still others may live for many years. These plants are called *perennials.* Some trees may live for hundreds or even thousands of years.

Other articles to read include: **Annual; Biennial; Fertilization; Life; Perennial; Plant; Reproduction; Spore.**

Lilac

The lilac is a beautiful shrub known for its pleasant-smelling flowers. Many poets have written about the beauty of these plants. The common lilac, from southeastern Europe, grows to a height of 20 feet (6 meters). It has green leaves and white or purple flowers in clusters.

Lilac bushes can be grown in almost any garden but grow best in northern climates. The plant needs little attention. Nurseries have developed many different kinds of lilacs. Many of these have larger and more colorful blossoms than the common lilac. Their colors range from white to dark purple and deep red.

A light purple color is also called lilac. It is named after the light purple flowers of some lilac plants.

Other articles to read include: **Flower; Shrub.**

Lilac

Lily

Wood lilies have bright, orange-red petals with purple spots. There are thousands of kinds of lilies.

Lilies are flowering plants, usually with clusters of flowers on upright stems. The blossoms are trumpet-shaped and have six petals. There are many kinds of lilies. People grow lilies around much of the world. One lily, the Easter lily, is pure white and associated with the *resurrection* (rising from the dead) of Christ.

Lilies grow from scaly bulbs. The bulbs are planted 6 inches (15 centimeters) or deeper in late fall or early spring. Lilies grow best in rich, sandy soil that is not too wet. They need to be protected from strong winds and bright sun.

Some plants with *lily* in their name are not true lilies. For example, water lilies are not closely related to true lilies.

Other articles to read include: **Flower; Water lily.**

Lily of the valley

Lily of the valley is a fragrant garden flower. Each blossom is shaped like a tiny bell. It grows in North America, Europe, and northern Asia. Wild lily of the valley grows in the southern Allegheny regions of eastern North America.

The beautiful bell-shaped flowers are pure white. They hang in a long cluster along a slender stem. The flower stalk rises from a *rhizome* (underground stem). Each stalk usually has two or three wide, oblong leaves. The plant requires rich, well-drained soil with leaf mold and grows well in shade.

Lily of the valley is a perennial that flowers naturally in late spring. In greenhouses, it blooms during all seasons. It is often used in bridal bouquets. The plant will grow outdoors for many years without needing to be moved. In greenhouses, it should be kept at a temperature of about 65 °F (18 °C) to bloom.

Lily of the valley is famous for its fragrance. A French toilet water called *eau d'or* is made from the flowers.

Other articles to read include: **Flower; Rhizome.**

Lily of the valley

Lime

The lime is a small green fruit. It is round with slightly pointed ends. A lime is shaped much like a lemon, to which it is related. Limes are also sour like lemons.

People do not usually eat limes as fruit. Instead, limes are used to flavor foods and drinks.

Limes grow on trees in warm climates. Lime trees are only about 10 to 12 feet (3 to 4 meters) tall. White flowers bloom on the trees. Limes grow from the flowers in about three to four months.

Lime trees first grew in India. Now they are grown in countries around the Mediterranean Sea, in the Caribbean Islands, and in Mexico. They also grow in California and Florida, where most limes in the United States are produced. The type most commonly sold in the United States is the Persian lime, but the smaller Key lime is also sometimes available.

Other articles to read include: **Fruit; Lemon.**

Limes are green citrus fruits that grow in clusters on trees.

Linnaeus, Carolus

Carolus Linnaeus created a scientific system for naming plants and animals.

Carolus Linnaeus *(KAR uh luhs lih NEE uhs)* (1702–1778) was an important Swedish scientist. Linnaeus created a scientific system for naming plants and animals. In this system, every kind of living thing has a *scientific name*. The scientific name has two parts. The first part is its *genus,* or group. The second part is its *species,* or specific kind. For example, the scientific name of common wheat is *Triticum aestivum. Triticum* is the genus, and *aestivum* is the species.

Linnaeus was born in Rashult, near Kristianstad, Sweden. He studied medicine in school and became interested in plants. He wrote careful notes about all of the kinds of plants he knew. These notes became his books.

Linnaeus earned a medical degree in the Netherlands. He returned to Sweden to practice medicine. He later became a professor of botany at Uppsala University in 1742.

Other articles to read include: **Botany; Classification, Scientific; Genus; Species.**

Locust

The black locust blooms in spring.

The locust is a shrub or tree known for its fragrant white flowers. There are many kinds of locusts. The plants are native to North America. They also are grown in much of Europe.

One of the most common locusts is the black locust. It has prickly branches. Its fragrant white flowers hang in drooping clusters. The tree produces long, glossy brown pods. Each pod holds about a dozen wax-coated seeds. Black locusts have blue-green leaves. The bark and leaves of the black locust are poisonous.

Locusts grow rapidly in good soil. The trees sometimes reach about 80 feet (24 meters) in height. Locust wood is valued because it is hard and lasts for a long time. It is most often used for fence posts and mine timbers.

Other articles to read include: **Flower; Shrub; Tree; Poisonous plant; Wood.**

Lotus

Lotus is the common name for many different kinds of plants that grow in water. The best-known is the sacred lotus, or East Indian lotus. The Egyptian water lily and the American lotus are also widespread. They grow wild and are grown in water gardens.

The sacred lotus has long been considered a symbol of purity. It is sacred in many parts of Asia. It is the national flower of India and Vietnam.

The Egyptian water lily is a common sight along the Nile River and neighboring streams. It has white or rose-purple flowers. The plants rise only a little above the water. The leaves spread out on the water's surface.

The American lotus is also known as the *water chinquapin* and *yellow water lily.* Its yellow flowers and leaves grow on stout stalks. The flowers stand 2 to 3 feet (60 to 90 centimeters) above the water.

Lotus is also the scientific name of a group of plants commonly known as *trefoils.* These plants, which have compound leaves with three leaflets, do not grow in water.

The lotus flower blooms 2 to 3 feet (60 to 90 centimeters) above the water.

Other articles to read include: **Water lily.**

Lycophyte

A lycophyte *(LY kuh fyt)* is a type of plant that does not have seeds. Lycophytes reproduce using only *spores.* Spores are tiny cells that can grow into a new plant. Nearly all other plants make seeds. There are hundreds of different kinds of lycophytes. Lycophytes tend to grow in moist, shady areas. They have roots, stems, and leaves. The leaves have a single central vein. Many lycophytes grow grasslike or needlelike leaves. *Club mosses* and *quillworts (KWIHL WURTS)* are just two types of lycophytes.

Lycophytes today are small. But they were among the first plants to grow as large trees. Great forests of lycophyte trees grew more than 300 million years ago, long before the first dinosaurs appeared. Much of the coal that people burn for energy formed over millions of years from these lycophyte forests.

Other articles to read include: **Forest; Seed; Spore.**

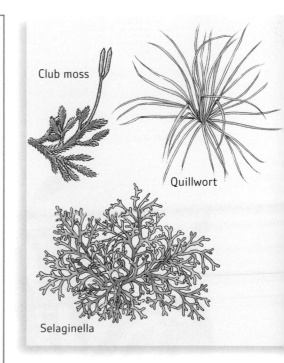

Club moss

Quillwort

Selaginella

Lycophytes have leaves with a single, central vein.

Magnolia

Magnolias are trees known for their large white or pink flowers. They also have cone-shaped fruits and large leaves. There are many kinds of magnolias. They are native to North and South America and Asia.

The *southern magnolia* is popular for its large, waxy flowers. It is the state tree and flower of Mississippi and Louisiana. The big-leaf magnolia has the largest flowers of any tree of the United States. The creamy-white flowers can be as large as 10 inches (25 centimeters) across. Many magnolias are grown for their flowers. People also use the wood to make furniture.

Other articles to read include: **Flower; Tree.**

The big-leaf magnolia tree has large flowers and leaves.

Summer and winter appearance

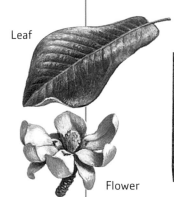

Leaf

Bark

Flower

Mango

Mangoes are fruits that grow in tropical regions throughout the world. Mangoes are an important food for many people in tropical countries. The mango is sometimes called the *king of the tropical fruits.* Mangoes are eaten fresh. They also are used in making desserts, preserves, and other foods. The fruit is an excellent source of vitamins A and C.

Most mangoes are kidney-shaped, oval, or round. They may be 2 to 10 inches (5 to 25 centimeters) long. They can weigh up to 5 pounds (2.3 kilograms). Mangoes have a smooth, leathery skin. It may be green, purple, or shades of orange, red, or yellow. The skin surrounds a juicy orange or yellow pulp and a hard inner pit. Some kinds of mango have a stringy pulp and an unpleasant smell. However, mangoes grown for eating have a soft, smooth pulp. They have a sweet, spicy taste and smell.

Other articles to read include: **Fruit.**

Mangoes, a tropical fruit, grow from clusters of tiny pinkish-white flowers on the evergreen mango tree.

Mangrove

The mangrove *(MAN grohv)* is a tree that grows in salt water. Mangroves can be found in quiet ocean waters along great lengths of tropical coast. A mangrove tree may look like a shrub on stilts. The "stilts" are actually roots growing down into the water. There are many kinds of mangroves. The best known is the *red mangrove.* As it grows, it sends down roots from its branches.

Mangrove seeds often begin to grow while the fruit is still on the tree. The seed grows a root that may hang down as far as 1 foot (30 centimeters). Eventually, the fruit falls. The fruit floats on the water, with the root hanging down. When the root's tip touches mud, a new tree begins to grow.

Large mangrove forests grow along bays, lagoons, and river mouths. These forests are important to many other living things. A variety of fish and other animals shelter in the roots. The roots also slow down flowing water and anchor soil. In this way, mangroves protect shorelines. Unfortunately, many mangrove forests have been destroyed. Many are cut down to make space for shrimp farms or rice farms. Some have been killed by pollution. Other mangrove forests have been cut down for their wood.

Other articles to read include: **Forest; Tree.**

Mangroves grow along great lengths of tropical coast. These mangroves are in Everglades National Park in the Florida Everglades.

Maple

The maple is a tree known for its sweet-tasting sap and for its beautiful color in the fall. The sap is made into maple syrup. There are many kinds of maple trees. Only some kinds produce maple syrup. Maples grow in areas with seasons around much of the world. Most maples are native to Asia.

Continued on the next page

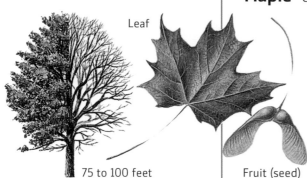

Leaf

75 to 100 feet
(23 to 30 meters)

Fruit (seed)   Bark

The sugar maple is found in eastern and northeastern North America. Its sweet sap is used to make maple syrup.

Maple *Continued from the previous page*

The leaves of maples grow in pairs on opposite sides of the branch. Each leaf has several *lobes,* or parts. Nearly all maples lose their leaves in the fall. In many kinds of maples, the leaves turn orange, red, or yellow before dropping off. The maple leaf is a national symbol of Canada.

Maples flower in the spring. Maple seeds grow in pairs. They are called *keys.* The keys have flat, thin wings. The wings make them spin and float in the wind as they fall. That helps carry the seeds to new locations.

The wood of maple trees is hard and strong. People use it for kitchen floors and to make furniture and musical instruments.

Other articles to read include: **Sap; Seed; Tree**

Marigolds

Marigold

The marigold is a popular garden flower. There are dozens of kinds of marigolds. They range from 6 inches to 3 feet (15 to 90 centimeters) tall. Most have yellow, orange, or reddish-brown blossoms. They have feathery, fernlike leaves. Most marigolds have a strong odor. Marigolds planted in gardens live for only one growing season.

Marigolds are easy to grow. They can survive dry weather better than most other garden flowers. Some marigolds produce an oil that repels certain garden pests. For this reason, home gardeners often edge vegetable gardens with marigolds to protect the other plants.

Marigolds are native to North and South America. They are now grown around the world.

Other articles to read include: **Flower.**

Marsh

Marshes are shallow wetlands where trees and bushes usually do not grow. Marshes are flooded with water for most or all of the year. Freshwater marshes often form around lakes, ponds, rivers, and streams. Plants such as bulrushes, cattails, horsetails, and reeds often grow in marshes. Many kinds of animals also live in marshes. These include dragonflies, frogs, muskrats, and turtles.

Salt marshes form where fresh water flows into the sea. Salt marshes are often found around the mouth of a river. Water levels in salt marshes change each day with the tides. Grasses such as cordgrass and salt-meadow grass often grow there.

Marshes provide shelter to many living things, especially young animals. Marshes also help to filter water and anchor the soil. Marshes can help to protect coastlines from hurricanes. Today, many marshes have been destroyed. People may drain marshes to build houses or plant crops. Water pollution also damages marshes.

Other articles to read include: **Bulrush; Cattail; Horsetail; Wetland.**

Salt marsh cordgrass grows in a salt marsh on Cape Cod, Massachusetts.

Horicon Marsh, in Wisconsin, is the largest freshwater cattail marsh in the United States.

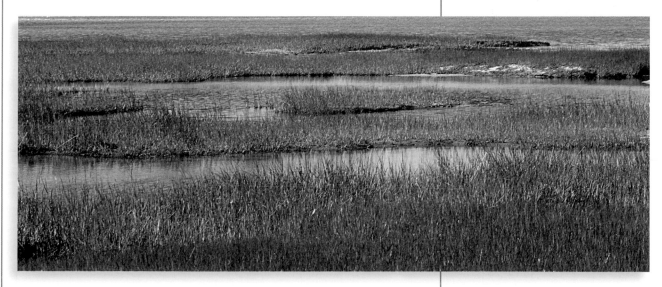

Barbara McClintock won the Nobel Prize for her research on genetics.

McClintock, Barbara

Barbara McClintock (1902-1992) was an American scientist. She won the Nobel Prize in physiology or medicine in 1983.

McClintock was a geneticist *(juh NEHT uh sihst),* a scientist who studies how traits pass from parents to their offspring. A plant's traits include such things as its height or the type of flowers it makes. These traits are carried by genes *(jeenz).* Genes are found inside cells, on threadlike parts called chromosomes *(KROHM uh sohmz).*

McClintock studied the genes of corn plants. In 1931, she showed that chromosomes can break and exchange parts. They do this during the formation of *sex cells.* Sex cells enable plants to reproduce. The process McClintock discovered enables each sex cell to contain a different combination of genes. That fact causes offspring to have different combinations of traits. In 1951, McClintock showed that certain genes can change their position on a chromosome. This change can cause the plant to have different traits.

McClintock was born June 16, 1902, in Hartford, Connecticut. She earned a Ph.D. degree from Cornell University. She died on Sept. 2, 1992.

Other articles to read include: **Cell; Gene; Heredity; Reproduction.**

The cantaloupe has a yellow-brown rind with rough ridges. Its flesh is yellow-orange.

Melon

Melons are the large fruits of several different kinds of gourd plants. The fruits come in different sizes and colors. They may be round or oval-shaped, like an egg. They can grow to 1 foot (30 centimeters) across or larger.

Some of the most popular melons are watermelons, cantaloupes, and honeydew melons. Watermelons have a smooth, thick green rind, or skin. The rind of a cantaloupe is yellow-brown, with rough ridges. Honeydew melons have a smooth green rind.

The flesh inside melons is also different colors. Watermelons can have pink, red, or yellow flesh. A cantaloupe's flesh is yellow-orange. Honeydews are green or white inside.

Gourds grow along the ground on long vine-like stems. The stems have *tendrils.* Tendrils are unusual leaves that look like curled-up wire.

Other articles to read include: **Fruit; Gourd; Watermelon.**

Mendel, Gregor Johann

Gregor Johann Mendel *(GREHG uhr YOH hahn MEHN duhl)* (1822–1884) was an Austrian scientist and monk. Mendel was a botanist *(BOT uh nihst),* a scientist who studies plants. Mendel discovered the basic rules of heredity *(huh REHD uh tee).* Heredity is the passing of *traits* (characteristics) from parents to their offspring.

Mendel was able to explain heredity by studying garden pea plants. He grew these plants in the garden of the monastery where he lived. Mendel bred and crossbred thousands of pea plants. He observed the traits of each new generation.

Gregor Johann Mendel was an Austrian scientist and monk. He discovered the basic rules of heredity by breeding pea plants.

Mendel found that plant traits are handed down through units of heredity. Today, these units of heredity are called *genes.* He reasoned that each plant receives a pair of genes for each trait. One gene comes from each of its parents.

Mendel discovered that each gene has different forms associated with different traits. For example, one form of a gene may cause a plant to bear round seeds. The other form may cause it to bear wrinkled seeds.

Mendel also found that one form of a gene could be *dominant* (strong) and the other form *recessive* (weak). If the plant has both forms of the gene, the trait of the dominant gene will appear in the plant. For example, the gene for round seeds is dominant. The gene for wrinkled seeds is recessive. So, a plant that inherits one "round seed" gene and one "wrinkled seed" gene will bear round seeds.

The importance of Mendel's ideas was not recognized during his lifetime. He is now considered the founder of *genetics,* or the study of heredity.

Mendel was born on July 22, 1822, in Heinzendorf, Austria. He became a priest in 1847. He later studied science and math. He taught high school biology and physics. He died on Jan. 6, 1884.

Other articles to read include: **Botany; Gene; Heredity; Pea; Seed.**

Mesquite

Mesquite

Mesquite (*mehs KEET*) is a thorny plant. Mesquites typically grow in deserts. There are many kinds of mesquite. The most common kind is the honey mesquite. It grows in southwestern North America and in the Caribbean region. It also grows in the Hawaiian Islands, where it was planted by missionaries.

A mesquite will grow in deserts too hot and dry for many plants. A mesquite that gets plenty of water may grow into a tree 50 to 60 feet (15 to 18 meters) high.

People use the wood of mesquite for fuel, to make fence posts, and to build houses. The seeds or beans serve as food for cattle and horses. Gum taken from mesquite is used to make candies and dyes.

As parts of the shrub die and decay, they enrich the soil. The soil around mesquite often is rich enough for other kinds of plants to grow.

Other articles to read include: **Desert; Shrub.**

Mint

Mint

Mint is a plant known for its pleasant aroma. There are thousands of kinds of mint. Familiar mints include lavender, rosemary, sage, and peppermint. Mints are especially common around the Mediterranean Sea.

The leaves of a mint plant contain oils. These oils provide the plant's aroma. The oils are released when the leaves are crushed. Most mint plants have white, bluish, or pinkish flowers. The flowers are small. Most mint plants produce small, roundish fruit.

Both the leaves and the oil of mint plants are used for flavoring. The leaves may be used fresh or dried. Some mints, such as rosemary and sage, are used in cooking. Other mints, such as peppermint, are used to add a sharp, cool flavor to candies or other sweets. Mints also are used in dental products, medicines, and perfumes.

Other articles to read include: **Lavender; Rosemary; Sage.**

Mistletoe

Mistletoe is a plant that grows on the trunks and branches of various trees. The *American mistletoe* and the *European mistletoe* grow most often on apple and oak trees. They also may grow on other trees.

Mistletoe is an evergreen with leathery leaves. It has tiny yellow flowers that bloom in February and March. Birds eat its white, shiny berries. However, the berries may be poisonous to people. Mistletoe is associated with many traditions and holidays, especially Christmas. In many countries, tradition says that a person caught standing beneath mistletoe must be kissed.

Other articles to read include: **Evergreen.**

Mistletoe is a plant that grows on the trunks and branches of other trees.

Mold

Molds are fungi *(FUHN jy)* that often grow on food. Like other fungi, molds are neither plants nor animals. They break down and absorb the food from their surroundings. There are many kinds of mold.

Mold often forms a cottony growth on bread, fruit, cheese, and other food. Molds grow from tiny cells called *spores*. When a spore lands on damp food, it swells and begins to grow, producing tiny threads. Rootlike structures connect these threads to the food. Soon, many stemlike growths called *fruiting bodies* begin to grow upward. Fruiting bodies make new spores. These spores float away to grow into new molds.

Continued on the next page

Some cheeses get their flavor from a mold that grows in them.

The parts of bread mold include rootlike growths and stemlike fruiting bodies that make spores.

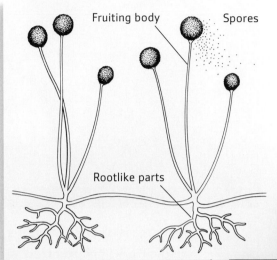

Fruiting body   Spores

Rootlike parts

Mold   *Continued from the previous page*

Molds can spoil food. They sometimes grow inside homes and can sicken people. But molds also enrich the soil by breaking down dead plant and animal matter. People use molds to add flavor to certain cheeses. Molds also provided penicillin, the first *antibiotic* known to medicine. Antibiotics are a type of drug that fight harmful *microorganisms* (microscopic living things).

Other articles to read include: **Fungi; Spore.**

Many common molds can grow on fruit and other foods.

Monkey flower

Monkey flower

Monkey flowers are plants with flowers that look something like a monkey's face. The flowers have two "lips." The upper lip is made up of two joined petals. The lower lip is made up of three joined petals. The petals often have spots.

There are many kinds of monkey flowers. They grow from 6 to 36 inches (15 to 90 centimeters) high. They grow in South and North America, mostly on the Pacific Coast. Monkey flowers can be grown in gardens or greenhouses. They grow well in shady places. They should be given plenty of water.

Other articles to read include: **Flower.**

Monocotyledon

A monocotyledon *(MON uh KOT uh LEE duhn)* is a type of flowering plant. Flowering plants have leafy structures called *cotyledons (KOT uh LEE duhnz)* within their seeds. Monocotyledons have only one cotyledon. Plants in the other major group of flowering plants have two cotyledons. These plants are called *eudicotyledons (yoo duh KOT uh LEE duhnz)*. A small number of flowering plants are neither monocotyledons or eudicotyledons. Among monocotyledons, the cotyledons typically absorb food stored in the seed. This absorption helps the young plant to grow.

Monocotyledons are sometimes called *monocots*. Grasses, irises, and palms are all monocots. Many monocots are important food crops, including bananas, coconuts, corn, pineapples, and rice. Bamboos and various grasses are monocots used to create buildings and furniture.

Other articles to read include: **Crop; Flower; Grass; Iris; Palm; Seed.**

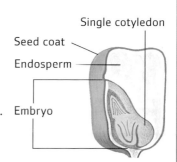

Single cotyledon
Seed coat
Endosperm
Embryo

A monocotyledon seed, such as this corn seed, has one cotyledon. Its food storage tissue is called the *endosperm*.

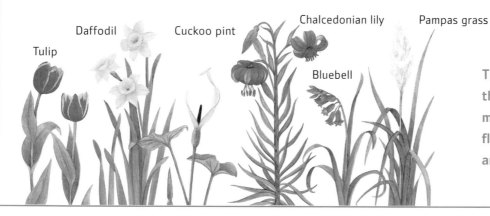

Tulip
Daffodil
Cuckoo pint
Chalcedonian lily
Pampas grass
Bluebell

There are many thousands of kinds of monocotyledons. The flower parts are usually arranged in threes.

Moor

A moor is a large area of land with few trees. These areas usually have poor soil and are not used for farming. Moors are found in Scotland and other parts of the United Kingdom. There are also moors in north-west Europe and North America.

Some moors are covered with a wet layer of spongy soil called *peat*. Peat is made of dead and rotting plants. Although the soil is poor, a kind of plant called peat moss grows on most moors. The moors of Scotland are covered with purple-rose shrubs called heather.

Other articles to read include: **Peat; Soil.**

Scotland is famous for its moors, which are covered with a purple-rose shrub called heather.

Hairy cap moss is common in North America.

Mosses tend to grow in bunches, and they often form dense mats that cover large areas (right). Peat moss, (above) is common in North America.

Moss

Mosses are small green plants with no flowers or seeds. Mosses tend to grow close together in large numbers. They form soft, thick mats on rocks, soil, or trees. Most mosses are found in moist, shady places. There are thousands of kinds of mosses. They grow throughout the world.

Unlike most plants, mosses reproduce using only *spores*. Spores are tiny cells that can grow into new plants. Mosses have no roots. Instead, they have threadlike parts that hold them to a surface. Moss stems are covered by tiny leaves in a spiral pattern. The leaves absorb water directly through their surfaces. Mosses generally measure less than 6 inches (15 centimeters) tall.

Mosses provide a home for many small animals, including mites and spiders. They also hold large amounts of water. As a result, mosses help to prevent flooding and keep soil from wearing away. When mosses die, they enrich the soil. This helps other plants grow.

Other articles to read include: **Spore.**

Muir, John

John Muir (1838–1914) was an American explorer, writer, and *naturalist*. A naturalist is a person who studies nature. Muir believed that people should protect and preserve nature. This idea is called *conservation*.

Muir convinced the United States Congress to pass an important conservation law in 1890. This law created the Yosemite and Sequoia national parks. Muir also helped the government set aside 148 million acres (60 million hectares) of land for forests. A redwood forest near San Francisco is named for him. It is called Muir Woods. In 1892, Muir founded the Sierra Club. It became a leading conservation group.

Muir was born on April 21, 1838, in Dunbar, Scotland. His family later moved to the United States. He wrote many books, including *The Mountains of California* (1894), *Our National Parks* (1901), and *The Yosemite* (1912). Muir died on Dec. 24, 1914.

Other articles to read include: **Conservation; Naturalist.**

American naturalist John Muir and U.S. President Theodore Roosevelt survey Yosemite National Park in 1906. Muir founded the Sierra Club in 1892 to protect the environment.

Mulberry

The mulberry is a tree or shrub with small, sweet fruits. The fruits are also called mulberries. They are white, purple, or red. Each "berry" consists of a cluster of tiny one-seeded fruits. Mulberry flowers are greenish white and grow in clusters. These clusters hang from stalks on the branches. The plants have oval or heart-shaped leaves.

There are several kinds of mulberries. Silkworm mulberries are important to the silk industry. Their leaves provide food for silkworms. They come from China. Russian mulberries are widely planted in the United States. They are sturdy shrubs that grow well as hedges. Growers often use them as windbreaks. Red mulberries grow wild throughout much of the United States. They also may be called American mulberries. Farmers feed their fruit to hogs and poultry. Black mulberries are grown throughout Europe. They produce juicy, crimson-black fruit. The fruit is eaten fresh. It is also used in making preserves and wines.

Other articles to read include: **Berry; Fruit; Shrub; Tree.**

Mulberries

Mushroom

Mushrooms are small, umbrella-shaped fungi *(FUHN jy)* that often grow in woods and grassy areas. Mushrooms come in many sizes and colors. They measure from less than ¼ inch (0.6 centimeter) to 18 inches (46 centimeters) across. Most mushrooms are white, yellow, orange, red, or brown. Some are blue, violet, green, or black.

A mushroom is actually only a part of the fungus. The rest grows just beneath the surface of the soil. This part consists of thousands of threadlike cells. These cells usually form a tangled web. They feed on dead plant and animal matter. This underground part may live and grow for many years.

The main parts of a mushroom are the *cap, stalk,* and *mycelium.* The underside of the cap consists of either *gills* or *tubes*. Tiny, club-shaped cells called *basidia* on the gills or tubes produce the *spores* from which new mushrooms grow. The mycelium is made up of white or yellow threadlike filaments. This part grows in soil or wood and absorbs food materials.

The mushroom above ground lives only a few days. It is called a *fruiting body*. The mushroom is the way the fungus reproduces. It grows up from the soil as a stalk and is topped by a rounded cap. Most kinds of mushrooms have thin growths on the underside of the cap. These growths are called *gills*. The gills release tiny cells called *spores*. The spores can grow into new fungi.

Many kinds of mushrooms are tasty and safe to eat. Many other kinds, however, are poisonous. Some mushrooms can kill people who eat them. People should never eat wild mushrooms unless they are certain the mushrooms are safe.

Other articles to read include: **Fungi; Spore.**

Continued on the next page

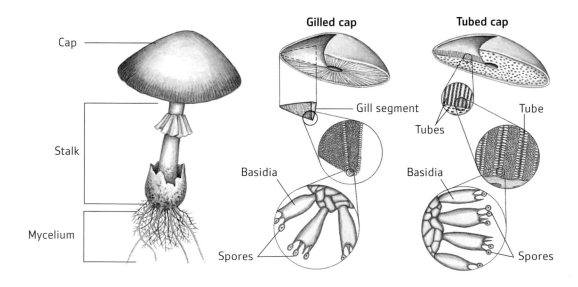

Cap

Stalk

Mycelium

Gilled cap

Gill segment

Basidia

Spores

Tubed cap

Tube

Tubes

Basidia

Spores

Mushrooms are divided into two groups. One kind has *gills* under its cap; the other kind has *tubes* under its cap. There are both poisonous and nonpoisonous mushrooms.

Gill-type mushrooms

Fly agaric
(poisonous)

Shaggy mane
(nonpoisonous)

Oyster mushroom
(nonpoisonous)

Jack-o'lantern
(poisonous)

Tube-type mushrooms

Edible bolete
(nonpoisonous)

Old man of the woods
(nonpoisonous)

Slippery jack
(nonpoisonous)

Larch suillus
(nonpoisonous)

Mustard

Mustards are leafy plants used to make tangy food seasonings. The seeds of certain mustards can be made into a yellowish powder or paste, also called mustard. It is used in salad dressing and pickles. It is sometimes used to flavor meat. The oil in mustard seeds gives mustard its strong flavor. Most mustard plants grow to about 4 feet (1.2 meters) tall.

There are several kinds of mustards. Many of the most popular mustard pastes in the United States are made from the seeds of white mustard, also called yellow mustard. Brown mustard is used to make spicy, French-style mustard. Mustard pastes made from this plant also are popular in Asia.

Mustards have large, deep-green leaves. The leaves are thick and jagged. They may be harvested while still tender and eaten as greens. Mustard leaves are an excellent source of vitamins A, B, and C.

Other articles to read include: **Spice.**

The dark green leaves of the mustard plant are rich in vitamins.

Nn

The poet's narcissus has a single, wide-open blossom on each stalk. The blossom has a yellowish cup and white petals.

Narcissus

The narcissus *(nahr SIHS uhs)* is a beautiful, fragrant flower. The flowers are yellow, white, or sometimes pink or orange. There are many kinds of narcissus. They are sometimes called daffodils *(DAF uh dihlz)*. Certain narcissuses are called jonquils *(JONG kwuhlz)*.

Narcissuses grow from brown bulbs. The bulbs are poisonous. Gardeners usually plant the bulbs in the fall. The plant blooms in early spring. It sends up shoots with sword-shaped leaves. The flowers have six petals around a trumpet-shaped or cup-shaped tube. The tube may be long or short.

Other articles to read include: **Daffodil; Flower.**

Nasturtium

The nasturtium *(nuh STUHR shuhm)* is a flower of the American tropics. It is also a popular garden flower. The nasturtium is a trailing or climbing plant. It can grow to about 10 feet (3 meters) long. The flowers are yellow, orange, or red.

Nasturtium flowers have five small *sepals (SEE puhls),* or outer petals. The three upper sepals form a long spur. The spur holds nectar. Inside the five sepals, there are five petals. The three lower petals have long, fringed claws. These petals are a little apart from the upper two petals. Nasturtium leaves are shaped like umbrellas. They have a spicy taste and are used in salads.

Nasturtiums grow well from seeds. Frost will kill the plants. But they can be grown indoors in the winter. Nasturtiums grow well in bright sunlight.

Other articles to read include: **Flower.**

The nasturtium is a North American garden plant. It has umbrella-shaped leaves and orange, red, or yellow blossoms.

Natural selection

Natural selection is a process by which certain *traits* (characteristics) become more common among living things over time. Each living thing is born with different traits. Certain traits make it more likely that an individual will survive and have offspring. Individuals without these traits are less likely to survive and have offspring. Over time, these traits become more common among members of a *species*. A species is a particular kind of living thing. Natural selection is sometimes described as *survival of the fittest.*

Natural selection is an important part of the *theory of evolution*. The theory of evolution describes how living things change over many generations.

Consider the example of trees competing for sunlight. Trees use the energy in sunlight to make food. Trees that grow taller may block the sunlight from reaching shorter trees. Thus, taller trees are able to make more food and produce more seeds. They are more likely to survive and have offspring. The offspring are more likely to grow tall, like their parents. Over time, taller trees will become more common than shorter trees. In this way, natural selection can cause the evolution of taller trees.

If a plant's surroundings change, different traits may become favorable to survival. The overall character of a plant species might then change. In this way, the species *adapts* (changes to fit) to its surroundings. If members of a species live in different environments, they will probably develop differently. Natural selection will favor different traits depending on where individuals live. Eventually, individuals may differ so much that they become two separate species.

Charles Darwin was a British scientist who first explained the theory of natural selection. Natural selection was the centerpiece of his theory of evolution. Today, nearly all scientists believe that natural selection and the theory of evolution are true. But some people reject these ideas because the ideas conflict with their religious beliefs.

Other articles to read include: **Darwin, Charles Robert; Environment; Evolution; Species.**

Natural selection is based on differences among closely related individuals. During his visit to the Galapagos Islands in 1835, Charles Darwin noticed that there was a huge variety of finches on the islands. The size and shape of the beaks of the finches varied according to the types of foods that the birds ate. Darwin argued that all the different finch species evolved from just a few species. Natural selection caused the birds to evolve as they moved into new habitats, with new types of food.

Naturalist

A naturalist is a person who studies nature. Naturalists may go on hikes in the countryside to see birds or wildflowers. In the city, they may visit zoos, museums, or gardens. Some organizations have nature study programs. Such organizations include the National Audubon Society, the Boy Scouts, and the Girl Scouts.

Many naturalists keep notebooks. In them, they write down what they have seen in nature. Naturalists may also make drawings or take photographs of animals or plants. Some naturalists collect living things, especially plants. But naturalists are careful not to collect plants that are rare or threatened. Collecting such plants can do harm and is illegal in many areas. Naturalists may also collect such things as rocks, seashells, or leaves.

Many naturalists have made important contributions to science. Carolus Linnaeus identified many kinds of plants and studied their growth. He created the modern system of scientific classification. Charles R. Darwin studied plants and animals all over the world. He proposed the *theory of evolution*. This theory describes how living things change over many generations.

Other articles to read include: **Darwin, Charles Robert; Linnaeus, Carolus.**

Naturalists often keep detailed notes and make drawings or take photographs of what they observe in nature.

Nectar

Nectar *(NEHK tuhr)* is a sweet liquid made by many flowers. Many kinds of animals feed on nectar. These animals include such insects as bees, beetles, butterflies, flies, and moths. Larger animals such as hummingbirds and bats also may feed on nectar. Honey bees turn nectar into honey.

Plants use nectar to attract animals. These animals help the plants to reproduce. Animals that feed on nectar pick up tiny grains of *pollen*. Pollen comes from the male parts of the flower. The animals then move on to other flowers. They carry the pollen with them. Some of the pollen rubs off on the female parts of other flowers. This exchange of pollen among flowers enables the plants to produce seeds. These seeds can grow into new plants. The exchange of pollen is called pollination *(POL uh NAY shuhn)*.

Other articles to read include: **Flower; Pollen; Reproduction.**

Hummingbirds feed on nectar produced by flowers.

Nettle

A nettle is a kind of plant. It is covered in tiny *bristles* (hairs). If an animal touches the plant, these bristles can break off and stick in the animal's skin. A watery juice inside the bristle causes pain or severe itching. The itching does not last long.

The leaves of a nettle grow opposite one another on the stem. Nettles also have tiny groups of flowers. Nettles grow in Asia, Europe, and North America.

People sometimes cook young nettles like spinach. Many people consider nettles a weed.

Other articles to read include: **Weed.**

Nettles

Nicotine

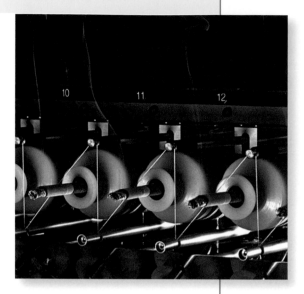

Nicotine is a substance found in the leaves, roots, and seeds of tobacco plants. Nicotine is a powerful poison. The tobacco plant makes nicotine to poison insects that try to feed on it.

Cigarettes and other tobacco products have nicotine. There is not enough nicotine in tobacco products to kill a person immediately. But nicotine is one reason why tobacco products cause disease and death. People also become *addicted* to the nicotine in tobacco. Being addicted means that a person struggles to stop using a substance, even when the person knows the substance is dangerous. Nicotine can make a person who is addicted to it feel refreshed and relaxed. But when tobacco users try to quit using nicotine, they usually feel cranky and anxious.

Other articles to read include: **Poisonous plant; Tobacco.**

Nicotine content in cigarettes is tested by machines at a government laboratory. Nicotine causes addiction to cigarettes.

Nightshade

Nightshade is a family of plants. They are grown for food, medicine, or decoration. There are thousands of kinds of night-shades throughout the world. Most nightshades grow in South America and Central America.

Nightshades eaten by people include the potato, the tomato, and peppers. The petunia and the tobacco plant are also night-shades. Some nightshades are poisonous, including henbane, jimson weed, and belladonna. They may be used as medicines in small amounts. Animals eat certain types of nightshades.

People in Europe once thought that witches used some types of nightshades. In the 1500's, people thought tomatoes and potatoes were poisonous.

Other articles to read include:
Pepper; Poisonous plant; Potato; Tobacco; Tomato.

Tomato plant

Petunia

Members of the nightshade family include the tomato and the petunia.

Nitrogen cycle

The nitrogen cycle describes how nitrogen moves through different parts of the environment. All living things need nitrogen to live and grow. Nitrogen moves from the air into soil and water. It also moves from soil and water to the air. In addition, nitrogen moves in and out of plants and animals.

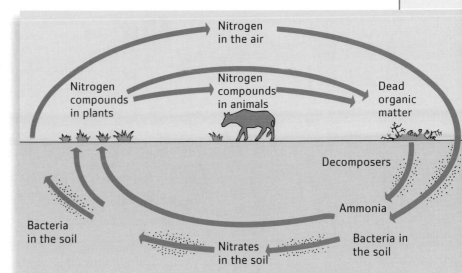

Nitrogen is the main chemical element found in air. It makes up about 78 percent of the *atmosphere,* the blanket of air that surrounds Earth. But this nitrogen is in a form that most living things cannot use. The form useful to most living things is called *fixed nitrogen.* Earth has a limited supply of fixed nitrogen. As a result, living things recycle nitrogen whenever possible.

In one part of the nitrogen cycle, nitrogen passes between living things and the soil. Dead plants and animals have large amounts of fixed nitrogen. Animal waste also has fixed nitrogen. Microbes in the soil break down this material. This process frees the nitrogen for other living things to use. Living plants take up the fixed nitrogen. Animals get their nitrogen by eating plants or by eating animals that eat plants.

In another part of the nitrogen cycle, microbes create more fixed nitrogen. These microbes are called *nitrogen-fixing bacteria.* These microbes can change nitrogen in the atmosphere into fixed nitrogen. Plants can then use the nitrogen. In fact, some plants provide a home for such microbes in their roots. The microbes help to supply the plants with the fixed nitrogen they need.

Different microbes return nitrogen in the soil to the air. Microbes also return nitrogen in the water to the air.

In living things, nitrogen is combined with other chemicals to make *proteins*. Proteins are an important part of cells. Cells are the tiny building blocks that make up all living things.

Some human activities affect the nitrogen cycle. Industry uses large amounts of nitrogen to make fertilizer. This fertilizer helps crops to grow. But much of the fertilizer washes off farmland. This nitrogen pollutes the water. In addition, factories and automobiles can release forms of nitrogen that pollute the air.

Other articles to read include: **Decay; Environment; Fertilizer; Life; Phosphorus; Soil.**

Nitrogen makes up about 78 percent of Earth's atmosphere, but most living things cannot use nitrogen in the air. Bacteria in the soil change nitrogen from the atmosphere and from decomposed *organic matter* (animal and plant material) into forms that plants can use. These forms are called *ammonia* and *nitrates*. Plants use these nitrogen compounds to grow. Animals get the compounds when they eat either plants or animals that ate the plants.

Nut

A nut is a dry seed or fruit. It grows inside a hard shell that looks like wood. People enjoy eating different kinds of nuts as snacks. They also use them in cooking to add flavor to food. Bread is sometimes baked with flour made from various nuts. Plants that make nuts grow in almost every part of the world.

A *true nut* is a dry, one-seed fruit surrounded by a hard shell that does not open on its own. Walnuts are true nuts. Nuts like almonds or peanuts are not true nuts.

Nuts can be used to make useful oil. Peanut oil and walnut oil are used in cooking. Walnut oil is also used to clean and polish wooden furniture.

Other articles to read include: **Almond; Bean; Cacao; Coconut; Fruit; Peanut; Pecan; Seed; Walnut.**

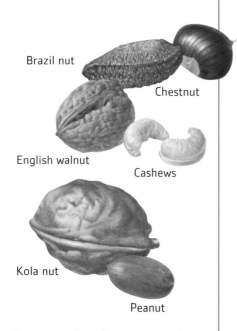

A *true nut* is a dry, one-seed fruit surrounded by a hard shell. Almonds and peanuts are not true nuts.

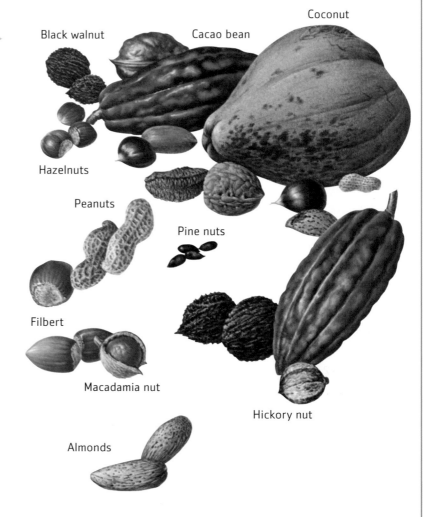

Oak

An oak is any tree or shrub that grows from an acorn. There are hundreds of different kinds of oaks. They grow in forests in Asia, Europe, and North America.

Some oaks only grow into small shrubs. Others reach heights of more than 100 feet (30 meters). Oaks produce small, yellowish-green flowers. Their acorns range in size from less than ½ inch (13 millimeters) to more than 2 inches (51 millimeters). The leaves of many oaks turn beautiful colors in the fall. Most oaks live for 200 to 400 years.

Other articles to read include: **Shrub; Tree.**

The English oak is found in forests of northern Europe. Its acorns grow on long stalks.

Oasis

An oasis *(oh AY sis)* is an area in the desert where underground water is close to the surface. This water enables trees and other plants to grow and thrive. The water at an oasis first fell as rain or snow in faraway mountains or hills. After seeping into the ground, the water slowly moved down through the underground rocks to the desert.

Soil in desert areas is usually able to support plant life. Because *oases* (the plural of oasis) have water, most of them that are lived in by people are farming areas. Some oases are so small that only a few people can live there. Others can support enough crops to provide for millions of people.

Fertile, vegetated areas along permanent streams in deserts are sometimes also called oases. Iraq's capital, Baghdad, which is on the Euphrates River, is such an area.

Other articles to read include: **Desert.**

An oasis is an area in a desert where underground water is close to the surface. Oases are scattered throughout the Sahara Desert in northern Africa.

Oats

Oats

Oats are an important grain crop. Farmers grow them mainly to feed livestock. Oats also provide healthy food for people. The seeds of oat plants are used in such foods as cookies, oatmeal, and breakfast cereals.

Oats are rich in protein and starch. Oats are a good source of vitamin B[1].

Oats grow well in areas that have a cool, moist climate and fertile soil. Oats can be planted by scattering the seeds over the field. Oats are also planted by sowing the seeds with a *grain drill,* a machine that drops the seeds and covers them with soil. Oats are harvested after the plants become dry and yellow and the seeds harden. Leading oat-growing countries include Australia, Canada, Poland, Russia, and the United States.

Other articles to read include: **Cereal; Crop; Grain.**

Oil

Oils are greasy substances that do not mix with water. Most oils are lighter than water and so float on the surface of water. There are many different kinds of oils. Oils come from plant, animal, or mineral sources. Most oils can be poured at room temperature. A few oils are solid at room temperature. These oils include lard and butterfat.

Many vegetable oils are pressed from corn, cottonseed, and soybeans. Olive oil and palm oil are taken from the fleshy fruit around the seed.

Margarine and salad oil are made of vegetable oils. Other products made from vegetable oils include candles, paint, and soap. Butterfat, lard, and tallow are the most important oils that come from animals. Butterfat, the main part of butter, comes from cream. Other animal oils are made by heating animal fat. Lard is made from the fat of hogs. Tallow comes from the fat of cattle, goats, and sheep.

Olive oil is a vegetable oil.

Oils give taste or smell to perfumes, chewing gum, toothpaste, and other products. The taste of such food flavorings as lemon, mint, and vanilla comes from their oil. These oils may be taken from the bark, flowers, leaves, roots, or twigs of plants.

Oil from mineral sources is called *petroleum* or *crude oil.* It differs chemically from plant and animal oils.

Other articles to read include: **Corn; Cotton; Fruit; Lemon; Mint; Olive; Palm; Seed; Soybean; Vanilla; Vegetable.**

Okra

Okra is a plant that people grow for its seed pods. People eat the pods as a vegetable. They often fry the pods or cook them in stews or soups. They are also pickled. The pods are cooked and canned when they are young and tender. Okra is also called *gumbo* or *okro*.

The okra plant grows up to 8 feet (2.4 meters) high. It has greenish-yellow flowers. Most pods grow up to 6 inches (15 centimeters) long. Gardeners plant okra seeds in the spring.

Okra is native to Africa, but it is eaten throughout the world. Okra is especially popular in the southern United States. It is the key ingredient in a traditional Southern stew also called *gumbo.*

Other articles to read include: **Seed; Vegetable.**

Okra

Oleander

The oleander *(OH lee AN duhr)* is a flowering shrub. It can grow to 15 feet (4.6 meters) tall. It has leathery leaves that are shaped like swords. Oleander flowers are shaped somewhat like roses. Most oleanders have either red or white flowers.

Oleander is native to Asia and the Mediterranean region. But gardeners around much of the world grow oleander.

Oleander is often raised from branch cuttings. Gardeners place the cuttings in jars of water. After a few weeks, the cuttings grow roots. They can then be planted in moist soil.

Gardeners plant the oleander outdoors in warm climates. However, they can be grown indoors in pots and tubs in temperate regions. It is a favorite porch plant in summer.

Other articles to read include: **Flower; Shrub.**

The oleander Is a flowering shrub. It produces leathery, sword-shaped leaves and colorful, roselike blossoms.

Olives are small fruits that grow on olive trees. They are grown chiefly for their oil, which can make up about half the flesh of the fruit.

Olive

Olives are the fruits of a tree native to the Mediterranean region. People grow olives for the oil of the fruit and for the fruit itself. The oil is used in a variety of ways, especially for cooking. The fruit is usually eaten whole.

Most olives are oval-shaped. As the fruit grows, it turns from green to yellow to red to purple-black. Olives have smooth skin. Their flesh surrounds a hard pit that contains a seed. Both the flesh and the seed contain oil. Fresh olives taste bitter and are unpleasant to eat. To improve their taste, olives are soaked in salt water and other substances. The olives people eat are either green or black.

Nations around the Mediterranean Sea grow most of the world's olives. Spain is the largest producer, followed by Italy, Greece, and Turkey. The olive crop in the United States comes almost entirely from California.

Other articles to read include: **Fruit; Oil; Tree.**

Onions come in many shapes, sizes, and colors. This drawing shows some common kinds of onions.

Onion

Onions are vegetables that have a strong smell and taste. They are one of the world's most popular foods. Onions are used mainly to add flavor to other foods. People eat them raw, cooked, dried, and pickled.

The leaves of an onion are long, hollow tubes that grow upright. They thicken at the base to form a bulb. The bulb is the part of the plant that people eat most often. Onion bulbs grow partly above the ground. Most bulbs are globe-shaped. Some are wide and flat, and others are narrow and upright. A thin, papery covering of dried outer leaves surrounds the bulb. Onion bulbs may be red, white, or yellow.

Other articles to read include: **Bulb; Leek; Vegetable.**

Southport Yellow Globe

Red Globe

White Globe

Ebenezer

Green onions

Bermuda

Orange

The orange is a citrus fruit. People typically eat oranges or drink their sweet juice. Oranges are a good source of many vitamins and minerals. Other citrus fruits include lemons, limes, and grapefruits.

Oranges grow on trees with dark green leaves and white flowers. The oranges grow from the flowers. The peel of an orange can be orange, pink, or dark red. Inside the peel is a spongy, white layer. Beneath this layer is the part of the orange that people eat. The inside of an orange is divided into 10 to 15 sections.

Oranges grow in warm places throughout the world. Brazil grows more oranges than any other country. In the United States, oranges are grown mostly in Florida and California. People have grown oranges for more than 4,000 years. Oranges probably originated in the part of Asia that now includes India, Myanmar, and southwestern China.

Other articles to read include: **Fruit; Tree.**

Oranges are popular citrus fruits that contain delicious juice and large amounts of vitamin C. In the United States, more oranges are harvested yearly than any other type of fruit.

Orchid

Orchids *(AWR kihdz)* are beautiful flowers. The flowers come in many shapes and colors. There are thousands of kinds of orchids.

Wild orchids grow around much of the world. Most kinds grow where there is plentiful rain. They grow on the trunks and branches of trees. Orchids in cooler areas grow on the ground. Orchid plants can be as short as ¼ inch (0.6 centimeter) tall. Some grow on vines up to 100 feet (30 meters) long.

An orchid's fragrance and the shape of its blossoms may attract certain types of animals. For example, many orchids look or smell like bees. These orchids attract bees. An orchid uses animals to spread its *pollen*. Pollen is tiny grains that flowering plants use to reproduce. Animals carry pollen on their bodies from one flower to another.

Continued on the next page

Phalaenopsis orchids got their name because they look like moths in flight. Botanist Carl Linnaeus gave the name *Phalaena* to a group of large moths.

Orchid *Continued from the previous page*

Orchids are prized for their beauty. People grow orchids in gardens and greenhouses. Vanilla orchids provide the seasoning vanilla. Many kinds of wild orchids have become rare. These plants are in danger of dying out completely.

Other articles to read include: **Flower; Pollen; Vanilla.**

Star orchid

Scorpion orchid

Order

An order is a large group of related plants, animals, or other living things. It is one of the categories that scientists use to *classify* (sort) living things. The living things in an order share certain basic qualities because they share a common ancestor.

Plants are divided into groups called kingdoms, divisions, classes, orders, families, genera, and species. Each order belongs to a larger group called a *class*. Members of an order are more closely related than are members of a class.

Orders can be divided into smaller groups called *families*. Members of a family are more closely related than are members of an order.

One example of an order is Ranunculales *(ruh nuhng kyuh LAY leez)*. This order of flowering plants includes the buttercup family. It also includes several other families. Ranunculales belongs to the class Eudicotyledones *(yoo duh KOT uh LEE duh nays)*. These plants are often called *eudicots*. They make up the majority of flowering plants.

Other articles to read include: **Class; Classification, Scientific; Family; Genus; Kingdom; Species.**

Osmosis

Osmosis *(oz MOH sihs)* is the process by which liquid moves from one *solution* to another. A solution is a mixture of two or more substances evenly spread throughout one another. In osmosis, the liquid moves through a membrane *(MEHM brayn)*. A membrane is a thin material that allows only some substances to pass through it.

Osmosis is an essential process for living things. Plants absorb most of their water by osmosis. Water is able to pass through the membrane surrounding roots by osmosis. The membrane does not allow such larger particles as soil to pass into the roots. The membrane also keeps substances the plant needs to survive from escaping into the soil.

Other articles to read include: **Root; Soil.**

Plants absorb most of their water by osmosis, through the membrane that surrounds the roots.

Oxygen

Oxygen is a kind of gas. Oxygen is found in the air, soil, and water. Nearly all living things need oxygen to stay alive. Oxygen combines with other chemicals in plant and animal cells to produce energy needed for cells to function.

Ordinary oxygen makes up part of the *atmosphere*. The atmosphere is the layer of air around Earth. Oxygen makes up about one-fifth of the volume of air. Oxygen in the air has no color, taste, or smell.

All of the oxygen in the atmosphere was produced by photosynthesis *(foh tuh SIHN thuh sihs)*. Photosynthesis is the process by which plants make their own food. During photosynthesis, a plant takes in water and the gas carbon dioxide. It uses the energy in sunlight to turn these ingredients into sugar. This process releases oxygen into the air.

Other articles to read include: **Photosynthesis.**

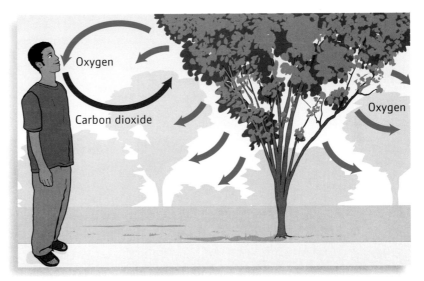

Plants give off oxygen that people and animals breathe. Plants use the carbon dioxide that people and animals breathe out.

Absorbing osmosis

Plants absorb most of their water through a process called *osmosis*. How does osmosis work? You can find out in this experiment, using any root vegetable, such as a potato or a yam.

1. Ask a teacher or other adult to cut the vegetable into two large slices or halves for you. Then, hollow out each vegetable slice so that each is about 1 inch (2.5 centimeters) thick.

2. Dissolve one spoonful of sugar in four spoonfuls of cold water in the cup. This makes a sugary liquid. Half fill one slice with this liquid. Half fill the other slice with cold water.

3. Place both slices in a dish. Pour cold water into the dish to a depth of ½ inch (1 centimeter). Cover the dish.

4. Look at the slices after a day. Do you see any difference in their water levels?

What you need:

- a knife
- one large root vegetable
- a spoon
- some sugar
- a cup
- cold water
- a large dish with a lid

What's going on:

The level of the sugary liquid will have risen. The water has entered the concentrated sugary liquid by osmosis.

http://bit.ly/WU1vik

Palm

Palms are plants that mostly grow in warm, wet places. Most palms have a straight, round trunk and leaves that are shaped like fans or feathers. The leaves grow at the top of the trunk.

Palms can be trees, vines, or shrubs. There are hundreds of kinds. Palms grow mostly in Southeast Asia, the Pacific Islands, and tropical North and South America.

People use palms in many ways. The fruits of some palms can be eaten. Such fruits include dates and coconuts. People use the fruits for food and oil and the sap for drinks. They also use the wood and leaves of palms to build houses. They make rope from palm fibers. People weave palm leaves into mats, hats, and baskets.

Other articles to read include: **Coconut; Fruit; Shrub; Tree; Vine.**

Palmettos are palm trees that have large, fan-shaped leaves. The leaves are sometimes used to make baskets, mats, and thatch for huts. They are native to Florida and to Caribbean islands.

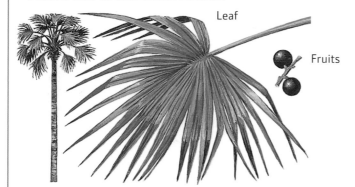

Leaf

Fruits

Fruits

The royal palm has a straight trunk that looks like a tall concrete pillar. It also has clusters of small dark fruits. Like most palms, the royal palm has huge leaves and no branches.

Pampas

Pampas *(PAM puh)* is a Guarani Indian word that means *plain*. Geographers use this word for many of the plains of South America. The word *Pampas* usually refers to the plain in Argentina that surrounds the capital city, Buenos Aires. The Pampas stretches from the Atlantic Ocean to the Andes Mountains.

Continued on the next page

An Argentine *gaucho* (cowhand) drives cattle across the plains of the Pampas. People use Argentina's Pampas for farming and ranching.

Pampas   *Continued from the previous page*

The Argentine Pampas has some of the richest soil in the world. It is excellent for growing such crops as wheat, corn, alfalfa, and flax. Herds of cattle feed on the dry grasslands of the western Pampas. Wealthy ranchers own huge farms on the Pampas. They rent land to farmers and hire workers to help plant and harvest crops.

Two-thirds of Argentina's people live on the Pampas. Most of the country's cities and industries are also on the Pampas.

Other articles to read include: **Crop; Grassland.**

Papaya

Papaya *(puh PY uh)* is a tropical fruit with flesh and seeds that can be eaten. People usually eat the fruit fresh. They also drink papaya juice. Papaya is rich in vitamins and minerals.

Papayas vary in shape. Many appear round or oval. Most grow between 5 and 6 inches (13 and 15 centimeters) long. They weigh about 1 pound (0.5 kilogram). The fruit's skin is usually greenish-yellow to orange when ripe. The flesh is from 1 to 2 inches (2.5 to 5 centimeters) thick. Its color ranges from light yellow to deep salmon-pink. The seeds are black and wrinkled.

Papayas grow on slender, hollow-stemmed plants. These plants may reach a height of 25 feet (8 meters) or more. The papaya is native to tropical regions of North and South America. But people grow the fruit in warm areas around the world.

Other articles to read include: **Fruit.**

Papayas

Papyrus

Papyrus *(puh PY ruhs)* is a reedlike water plant. People in ancient Egypt used it to make a paperlike material. They also used papyrus to make mats, sandals, and sails for small boats. Papyrus also grows in Ethiopia, southern Italy and Sicily, and Syria. The plant has long, thin stems. They grow 3 to 10 feet (0.9 to 3 meters) tall. As many as 100 flowers can grow from the top of each stem. The flowers may be more than 12 inches (30 centimeters) long.

The ancient Egyptians prepared sheets of papyrus for writing. They laid strips of papyrus on the ground and crushed them. The crushed strips could then be written on with ink.

The papyrus plant grows along the banks of the Nile River in Africa. The plant may reach up to 10 feet (3 meters) high.

Parasite

Parasite *(PAIR uh syt)* is a living thing that feeds off another living thing. The thing that is fed off is called a *host.* Predators hunting animals usually quickly kill and eat their food. But parasites feed on living hosts a little at a time.

Many kinds of parasites attack plants. Many of these parasites are varieties of fungi. For example, fungi called *smuts* live as parasites on cereal plants. Smuts harm plants by taking resources. The tiny spores the smuts use to reproduce also damage plants. *Blights* are another type of fungus that is a parasite on plants. *Rusts* are another type of fungus that attacks plants.

Other kinds of living things also live as parasites on plants. Tiny worms called roundworms or nematodes *(NEHM uh tohdz)* are parasites on plants. These worms typically feed on roots or other underground parts of plants. A variety of bacteria and viruses also attack plants. But these microbes are usually considered separately from other parasites.

Other articles to read include: **Food chain; Fungi.**

Many kinds of fungi are parasites of plants. Fungi typically produce hairy growths on leaves and stems.

Parsley

Parsley

Parsley *(PAHRS lee)* is a plant used mainly to decorate meats and salads. The leaves are also used as a flavoring in soups. The leaves can be dried. The most popular variety of parsley has crumpled leaves. Another variety has flat leaves. Parsley is a vegetable. It is sometimes considered an *herb*. An herb is a low-growing plant that has a fleshy or juicy stem when it is young.

Parsley is an excellent source of vitamins. It is especially rich in calcium, iron, and vitamins A and C. But parsley is usually eaten in small quantities. Thus, it has little effect on nutrition.

Parsley seed is often sown in greenhouses. It sends up leaves slowly and unevenly. The plants are later moved to the garden about a week before the last spring frost. A few leaves at a time can be picked off the plant. Parsley is sometimes grown indoors during winter.

Other articles to read include: **Herb; Vegetable.**

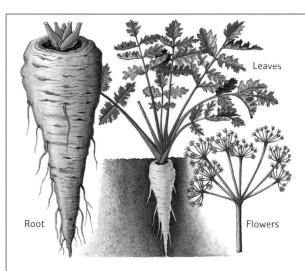

Leaves

Root

Flowers

The parsnip plant has a long root that looks like a carrot. People cook and eat the root.

Parsnip

The parsnip is a long, white root vegetable. It looks like a white carrot. It is grown mostly in home gardens, rather than on farms.

The part of the parsnip plant that people eat is the root. At the top of the root, many green leaves stick out of the ground.

Parsnips grow from seeds. The seeds are planted in early spring. At first, the parsnips grow slowly. In the fall, they start to grow quickly. Parsnips are often left in the ground through the winter. The winter cold does not hurt the roots.

People usually cook parsnips before eating them. Parsnips may be used as a side dish or added to stews and soups.

Other articles to read include: **Carrot; Vegetable.**

Pea

Peas are the seeds found inside the pods of pea plants. Peas may be green, yellow, white, gray, blue, brown, or spotted. They are cooked and eaten as vegetables. People add peas to soups, salads, and other dishes. Pea plants are also used to feed farm animals. Peas are a good source of protein, a substance the body needs to live and grow. Peas also contain vitamins.

Pea plants are vines with soft stems. Each leaf is made up of one to three pairs of tiny leaves. The leaves end in a curly thread called a tendril. Most pea plants have white flowers. Some have reddish-purple flowers. Pea pods have four to nine or more seeds.

Other articles to read include: **Legume; Seed; Vegetable.**

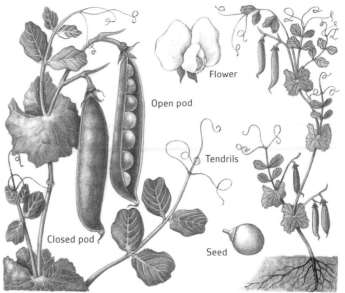

Peas grow inside seed pods. Thin growths called tendrils grab on to nearby objects, allowing the plant to spread as a vine.

Peach

The peach is a fruit that grows on trees. Peaches are round with fuzzy yellow or yellow-red skin. The skin protects the yellowish flesh, which is sweet and juicy. In its center, a peach has a hard stone that contains a seed.

People eat the flesh of peaches fresh, canned, or dried. Peaches are made into jams. They are also ingredients in a variety of foods, especially desserts.

Peach trees have thin leaves with jagged edges. Pink flowers appear in early spring. The fruit develops from the flowers. Peaches ripen from early summer to fall. Peaches are called *freestone peaches* or *clingstone peaches,* depending on how hard it is to remove the stone.

Other articles to read include: **Fruit; Tree.**

A peach contains a hard, rough *stone,* in which the fruit's seed develops. Surrounding the stone is the fruit's *flesh.*

Peanuts grow underground. People usually consider peanuts to be nuts, but they are actually legumes that grow seed pods. People eat peanuts and use the oil for cooking. Other products produced from the peanut plant include soaps, shaving cream, shampoos, and plastics.

Peanut

Peanuts are the nutlike fruits of a bushy plant. But peanuts are not actually nuts. Peanuts are legumes *(LEHG yoomz)*, plants that grow seed pods. Like peas, the peanuts grow within the pods. Usually there are two peanuts in each pod.

Peanuts are grown in warm climates in Asia, Africa, and the United States. Georgia grows more peanuts than any other U.S. state.

People enjoy peanuts roasted and salted. These peanuts are sold in the shell. The shell is easy to remove. Peanuts also are sold already shelled. Bakers often add peanuts to cakes, cookies, and pies. Cooks sometimes add them to main dishes. They also use peanut oil to fry food and flavor salads. Peanut butter is made from ground, roasted peanuts.

Peanuts have other uses. Peanut oil is used in soaps, powders, creams, paints, and shampoos. Peanut shells are used to make plastics and a material like cork. Every part of the peanut is useful.

Peanuts are native to South America. The U.S. scientist George Washington Carver made an extensive study of peanuts in the early 1900's. Carver is credited with having found more than 300 uses for the plant and its fruit. Since the 1930's, peanut farming has grown rapidly worldwide. In the United States, peanuts are grown widely in Virginia and North Carolilna.

Peanuts are a healthful food. But some people have allergies to peanuts. They must avoid peanuts and foods that include peanuts as an ingredient.

Other articles to read include: **Carver, George Washington; Fruit; Legume; Nut; Oil; Seed.**

Pear

The pear is a fruit that grows on trees. Pears have thin, smooth skin that may be yellow, red, or brown. Their whitish or yellowish flesh has a sweet taste. The center of the pear's flesh has a hollow core like that of an apple. A pear core may hold up to 10 seeds.

Some pears are large and round on one end. They get thinner toward the other end. Others are nearly perfectly round. Some are as small as a cherry.

The pear tree is closely related to the apple tree. It grows in warm areas throughout the world. There are hundreds of different varieties of pears.

Other articles to read include: **Apple; Fruit; Tree.**

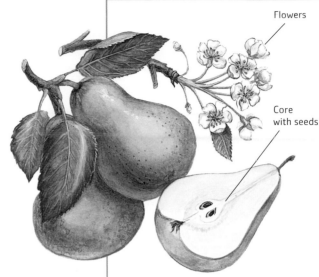

Flowers

Core with seeds

Many kinds of pears are wide at the bottom and thin at the top. The *core* (center of the fleshy part) of a pear looks like the core of an apple.

Peat

Peat is plant matter that is partly decayed, or rotted. It collects in swamps and marshes over long periods of time. Peat is usually the first stage in the formation of coal.

Peat forms in layers. The upper layers are made up of plants, herbs, and moss that have died. This plant matter has rotted in the water. Over time, the weight of the water and other plants pushes down on these layers. The plant matter turns into peat. The lower layers are almost all water and look like mud.

Machines are used today to dig, chop, and mix the peat. They shape it into blocks. The blocks are spread on the ground for drying. Dried peat is used as fuel in places where coal and oil are hard to find.

Other articles to read include: **Bog; Decay; Fertilizer; Marsh; Moss.**

A worker in a peat bog in Ireland collects blocks of peat. Dried peat may be used as fuel in places where coal and oil are scarce.

Pecan

Pecans

The pecan *(pih KAHN* or *PEE kan)* is a tree prized for its nuts. The nuts also are called pecans. Pecans are soft and easy to shell. They are often eaten by themselves. They also are an ingredient in a variety of dishes.

Pecan trees may reach 180 feet (55 meters) high. Their trunks are sometimes 4 to 6 feet (1.2 to 1.8 meters) wide. But most trees are smaller. The light brown or gray bark is deeply grooved. The leaves are 12 to 20 inches (30 to 51 centimeters) long. They are made up of from 9 to 17 lance-shaped leaflets. Pecan trees are native to North America. They also are grown in Australia, the Middle East, and South Africa.

Raising pecans is an important U.S. industry. It is especially important in the South. The pecan tree is grown chiefly for its nuts. But its wood is also valuable.

Other articles to read include: **Nut; Tree; Wood.**

Peonies

Peony

The peony *(PEE uh nee)* is a garden plant with large, showy blossoms. There are many *varieties* (types). Clusters of red and shiny green shoots grow into shrubby stems in early spring. The flowers appear in late spring or early summer. They are shades of pink, red, yellow, or white.

Many of the varieties of peonies grown in the United States are the offspring of the common peony of southern Europe cross-bred with the Chinese peony. The common peony has large white, red, or crimson blossoms. The blossoms do not have much fragrance. The Chinese peonies bear double blossoms with a sweet scent.

Peonies with woody stems are called *tree peonies*. These peonies have showy flowers in white and rose-colored hues. They grow on a stalk from 3 to 4 feet (91 to 120 centimeters) tall. Tree peonies grow slowly. They bloom season after season.

Other articles to read include: **Flower.**

Pepper

Pepper is a spice used to flavor foods. There are many kinds of pepper. They include black, white, red, and Jamaica pepper. Pepper comes from the fruit of the pepper plant.

The pepper plant makes a small green berry that turns red as it ripens. The berries are picked when they begin to change color. Then they are cleaned and dried. During drying, the berries turn black. The berries are ground up to make pepper. Most pepper comes from Brazil, India, Indonesia, Vietnam, and other countries with a hot climate.

Pepper contains a substance that gives it a sharp taste. Pepper also contains a mixture of oils that give it a special odor.

Other spices are sometimes called pepper. But these spices come from different plants. For example, a spice called red pepper, or cayenne pepper, is not a true pepper. It is made from an unrelated plant. Allspice, sometimes called Jamaica pepper, is not a true pepper either.

Other articles to read include: **Berry; Fruit; Spice.**

Berries

The pepper plant produces small green berries that turn red as they ripen. The dried berries, which turn black, are ground up to make pepper.

Perennial

A perennial *(puh REHN ee uhl)* is a plant that lives for more than two years or growing seasons. Some perennials, such as trees, can live for hundreds of years. Perennials are different from *annuals (AN yu uhlz)* and *biennials (by EHN ee uhlz)*. Annuals live for only a year. Biennials live for two years.

Some perennials are woody. They include trees and shrubs. The stems of woody perennials become wider each year. They do this by growing new material, mostly wood.

Other perennials are not woody. Their stems and other above-ground parts die each season. But the under-ground parts survive. They produce new shoots the next year. Nonwoody perennials include asparagus *(uh SPAR uh guhs),* rhubarb *(ROO bahrb),* and many spring flowers.

Other articles to read include: **Annual; Biennial.**

New York aster

Lilac

Lily of the valley

Perennials include many popular flowers, including lilacs, lilies of the valley, and New York asters.

Pink periwinkle

Periwinkle

The periwinkle *(PEHR uh WIHNG kuhl)* is a small ever-green shrub known for its intensely blue flowers. It grows wild in warm areas of the world. People also grow periwinkles in gardens and pots. There are several kinds.

Periwinkles grow 1 to 2 feet (0.3 to 0.6 meter) tall. They have shiny, dark green leaves. The leaves are 1 to 2 inches (2.5 to 5 centimeters) long.

Periwinkles bloom all summer long. The colors of the flowers range from white to pink to purple. The common periwinkle has pretty blue flowers. People sometimes use the word "periwinkle" to describe a particular light blue color.

Other articles to read include: **Evergreen; Flower; Shrub.**

Pest control

Pest control refers to ways of reducing or eliminating pests. In agriculture, pests may be weeds, living things that cause plant diseases, and insects that damage crops.

Most farmers control pests with chemicals called *pesticides.* Pesticides are classified according to the pests they control. The four main types of pesticides are (1) *herbicides,* which are used against pest plants; (2) *fungicides,* used against fungi; (3) *rodenticides,* used against such rodent pests as rats and mice; and (4) *insecticides,* used against insect pests. Pests may develop resistance to pesticides so that more pesticides are needed over time.

All pesticides must be used with extreme care. If they are used improperly, they may pollute the environment or the food supply. Improper use can also endanger the health of people and animals.

Farmers also use other methods of pest control that do not involve pesticides. For example, some farmers combat damaging insects by releasing other insects that prey upon the pests. Many pest control experts favor an approach called *integrated pest management.* This strategy combines the limited use of pesticides with natural control methods.

Other articles to read include: **Farm and farming; Herbicide; Weed.**

Petunia

The petunia *(puh TOO nee uh* or *puh TOO nyuh)* is a garden flower with beautiful, funnel-shaped blossoms. Petunias are one of the most popular garden flowers. There are many kinds of petunias.

A petunia's blossoms grow 4 inches (10 centimeters) or more across. They may be pink, rose, white, blue, or a mixture of colors. Some have a single set of petals. Others have a double set. Tiny hairs cover the stems and leaves of most garden petunias. People may grow petunias from cuttings or from seeds. The plants thrive in sunny locations. Their flowers bloom in summer and early fall. Petunias are native to South America.

Other articles to read include: **Flower.**

Petunias

Phosphorus

Phosphorus *(FOS fuhr uhs)* is a chemical that all living things need to live and to grow. It is most commonly found in nature in a form called *phosphate,* usually in rocks.

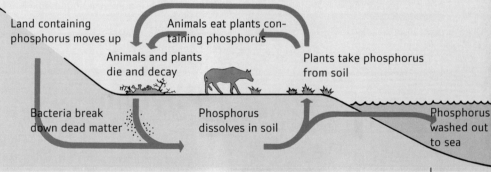

Land containing phosphorus moves up

Animals eat plants containing phosphorus

Animals and plants die and decay

Plants take phosphorus from soil

Bacteria break down dead matter

Phosphorus dissolves in soil

Phosphorus washed out to sea

Plants take in phosphorus from the soil. They need phosphorus for photosynthesis *(FOH tuh SIHN thuh sihs)*. Photosynthesis is the process by which plants make food using the energy in sunlight. Individual plant cells also need phosphorus. Phosphorus is part of a substance cells use for energy. Cells make this substance from food.

Farmers often add phosphorus fertilizers to soil to help crops grow. Rain may carry some of this phosphorus into such waterways as rivers and lakes. This phosphorus can cause tiny organisms called *algae* to multiply rapidly. A sudden increase of algae, also called a *bloom,* can quickly remove oxygen from the water. Low levels of oxygen can kill fish and other things. For this reason, phosphorus that enters waterways is considered a form of pollution.

Other articles to read include: **Fertilizer; Nitrogen cycle; Photosynthesis; Soil.**

Phosphorus moves through the environment in a process called the *phosphorus cycle.* These movements happen at different rates in different places.

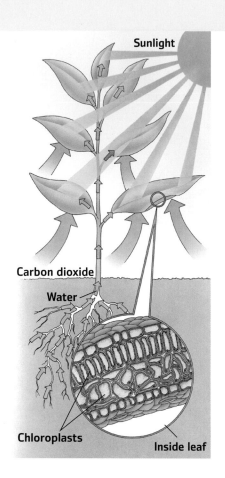

Sunlight

Carbon dioxide

Water

Chloroplasts

Inside leaf

Photosynthesis

Photosynthesis *(foh tuh SIHN thuh sihs)* is the way that green plants, algae, and certain microscopic living things make their food. During photosynthesis, these organisms use the energy from sunlight to turn water and a gas called carbon dioxide into food. This process releases another gas called oxygen into the air. Animals, including people, breathe in the oxygen and breathe out carbon dioxide. Photosynthesizers take in the carbon dioxide, use it, and then give off more oxygen.

Photosynthesis is the main job of a plant's leaves. A green substance called chlorophyll *(KLAWR uh fihl)* is stored in the leaves. The chlorophyll takes up the light the plant uses in photosynthesis.

Plants carry out photosynthesis by using the energy from sunlight to combine water and carbon dioxide. This combination, which takes place in structures in the leaves called *chloroplasts,* creates food.

Other articles to read include: **Chlorophyll; Chloroplast; Leaf; Oxygen; Respiration.**

Phylum

The phylum *(FY luhm)* is one of seven chief levels of groups that scientists use to *classify* (sort) all living things. The largest level of classification is called a *kingdom.* Each kingdom is divided into several *phyla* (the plural of phylum). In the plant kingdom, a phylum is often called a *division.* Members of a division are more closely related than are members of a kingdom. Phyla or divisions are further divided into *classes.* Members of a class are more closely related than are members of a division.

All of the living things in a phylum have certain basic features in common because they share a common ancestor. For example, in the plant kingdom, flowering plants make up the phylum Anthophyta *(an thuh FY tuh).* Members of this phylum grow flowers, though sometimes the flowers are small. All these plants produce seeds. The seeds are housed within fruits. Anthophyta is by far the largest phylum of plants.

Other articles to read include: **Class; Classification, Scientific; Kingdom.**

Pine

A pine is a type of evergreen tree. Pines have needlelike leaves and cones. There are many different kinds of pine trees. They grow mostly in sandy or rocky soils. Pines are common in the mountains of western and southeastern North America. They are also common in southern Europe and southeastern Asia. Some pines are as small as shrubs. Others grow as tall as 200 feet (60 meters).

Pines belong to a group of plants called conifers *(KOH nuh fuhrz)*. Conifers grow cones that house seeds.

Pine trees grow tall and straight, making them useful for lumber. Some pines make *resin*. Resin is a sticky yellow or brown substance. It is used to make turpentine, paint, and soap. The wood of many pines is made into paper.

Other articles to read include: **Conifer; Evergreen; Resin; Wood.**

Cone

Needles

The jack pine is one of the dozens of kinds of pine trees that grow in North America. It is found from the Great Lakes region to northwestern Canada. The cones of the jack pine are curved.

Pineapple

The pineapple is a plant known for its sweet fruit and juice. The pineapple probably got its name because the fruit looks like a large pine cone.

The skin of the ripe fruit is dark green, orange, or green and yellow. A group of spiky leaves sticks up at the top. The inside of the fruit is firm and light yellow or white. Most pineapples have no seeds.

The pineapple plant grows from 2 to 3 feet (60 to 90 centimeters) tall. It has blue-green, sword-shaped leaves that grow around a thick stem. Pineapple plants grow in warm places around the world. The Philippines and Thailand are the top producers of pineapples.

Other articles to read include: **Fruit.**

The fruit of the pineapple has a thick, hard skin called a *shell.* Inside the shell is juicy, edible flesh.

An ant crawls around the rim of the pitcher-shaped leaf of a pitcher plant. Attracted by a sweet smell inside the plant, the ant will soon crawl inside and become trapped.

Pitcher plant

The pitcher plant is a kind of *carnivorous* (*kahr NIHV uhr uhs*) plant. Carnivorous plants feed on insects and other tiny animals. Pitcher plants have long, tube-shaped leaves shaped like pitchers that trap insects. The leaves range from bright yellow-green to purple in color.

The top edges of a leaf form the lid of the pitcher. Sweet juice inside the leaf attracts insects. Thick hairs grow at the mouth of each pitcher. These hairs grow downward. When an insect crawls inside the leaf, the hairs keep it from escaping. The insect then slides down the tube. It drowns in rainwater that has collected at the bottom.

Pitcher plants do not capture insects for food. Like most other plants, pitcher plants make their own food using sunlight. Instead, feeding on insects provides pitcher plants with a substance called nitrogen. Nitrogen is a chemical that plants and other living things need to grow. Pitcher plants grow in soil that has little nitrogen.

Other articles to read include: **Carnivorous plant.**

The three main kinds of plains are *coastal plains* (near the sea), *inland plains* (in high interior areas), and *flood plains* (in low areas along rivers).

Plain

A plain is a large stretch of land that is nearly flat. Most plains are lower than the land around them. Plains may be found along a seacoast or farther inland. Coastal plains generally rise from sea level until they meet higher landforms, such as mountains or plateaus. Inland plains may be found at high altitudes.

Continued on the next page

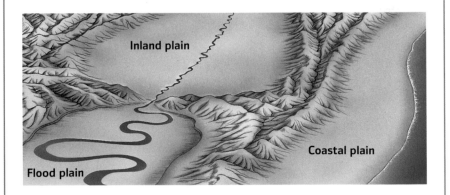

In warm, wet places, thick forests usually cover plains. Grasslands cover plains in areas that are drier, such as the Great Plains. The Great Plains extend from northern Canada through the midwestern United States into New Mexico and Texas. The soil on plains is usually good for farming.

Other articles to read include: **Forest; Grassland; Great Plains.**

Many inland and flood plains, such as Canada's Interior Plains, make productive farmland.

Plankton

Plankton is the mass of tiny living things that drift with currents in the ocean. Plankton also lives in inland seas and lakes. Plankton lives near the surface. Some kinds of plankton can swim. But they cannot swim strongly enough to stop the water from carrying them about.

There are two main kinds of plankton. They are called *phytoplankton (FY toh PLANGK tuhn)* and *zooplankton (ZOH uh PLANGK tuhn)*. Phytoplankton includes *organisms* (living things) that make their own food using the energy in sunlight. These plantlike organisms are also known as *algae*. Various kinds of tiny animals make up Zooplankton. These include water fleas and many other *crustaceans (kruhs TAY shuhnz)*. Crustaceans are animals with shells and jointed legs. Zooplankton also includes many kinds of *larvae*. These larvae are the young forms of crabs, fish, and other animals. As larvae mature, many become large enough to swim against the currents. They are no longer part of the plankton family.

Plankton provides food for a huge variety of living things. Phytoplankton also gives off large amounts of the gas oxygen. Human beings and other animals must breathe in oxygen to live.

Other articles to read include: **Algae; Life; Oxygen.**

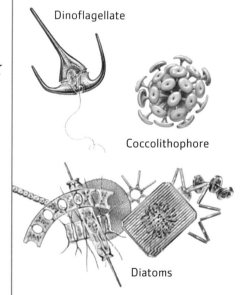

Dinoflagellate

Coccolithophore

Diatoms

Phytoplankton includes many kinds of plantlike organisms. These creatures use the energy of sunlight to make their own food. They are often eaten by zooplankton.

Plant

Plants are living things that grow in almost every part of the world. Plants grow on mountaintops, in oceans, in deserts, and in snow-covered areas.

Scientists believe there are more than 260,000 kinds of plants. Some are so tiny that they can hardly be seen. Others are much taller than people. Among the largest living things on Earth are sequoia *(sih KWOY uh)* trees. Some sequoias stand over 290 feet (88 meters) high with trunks wider than a house. Plants also are the oldest living things. One bristlecone pine tree in California is 4,000 to 5,000 years old.

Without plants, people and many other kinds of life could not survive. Plants help make the air we breathe and supply us with

Continued on the next page

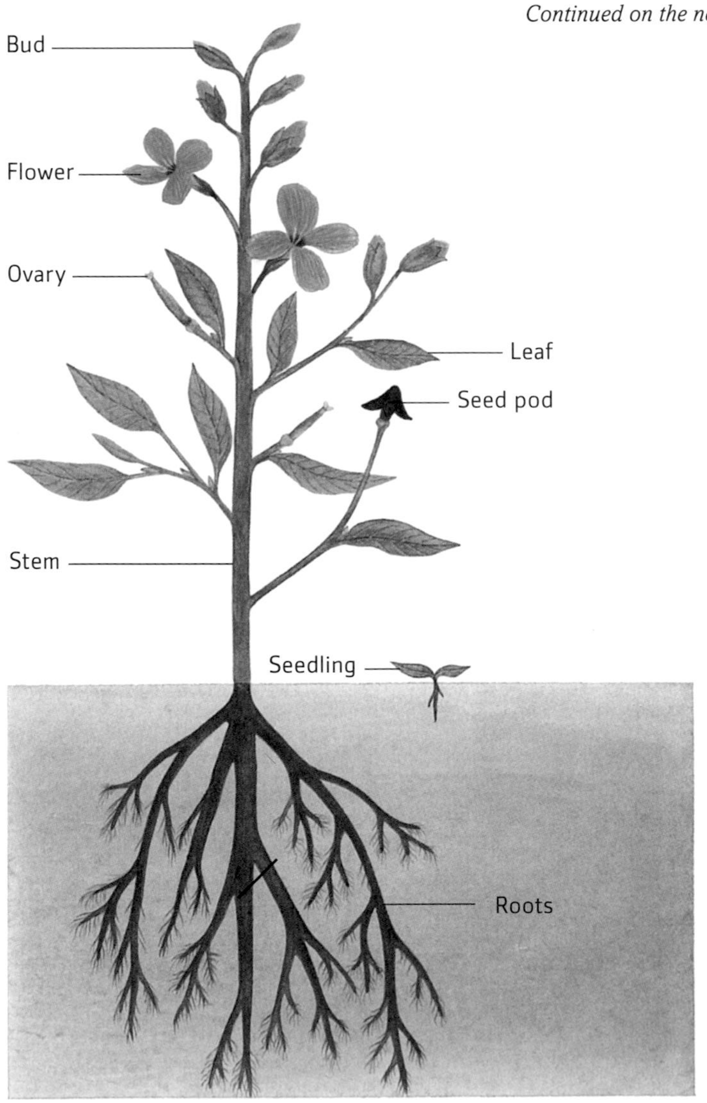

Bud

Flower

Ovary

Leaf

Seed pod

Stem

Seedling

Roots

The main parts of a typical flowering plant include *roots, stems, leaves,* and *flowers. Buds* may bloom into new flowers. After blooming, a flower's petals drop off, leaving the *ovary. Seeds* develop inside the ovary. In some plants, a *seed pod* develops, out of which the ripe seeds shoot and fall to the ground. If soil conditions are right, the seeds may grow into new plants, called *seedlings.*

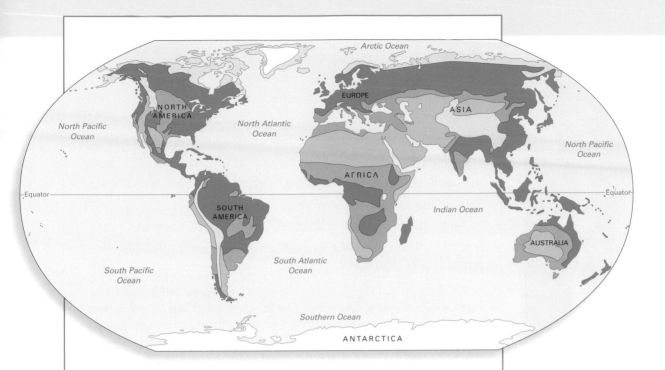

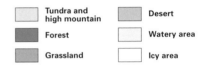

	Tundra and high mountain		Desert
	Forest		Watery area
	Grassland		Icy area

many useful things and materials. But certain plants are not helpful to people. Weeds choke off useful plants. Pollen from plants can cause such health problems as asthma and hay fever. Some plants, such as poison ivy and poison oak, cause rashes on the skin.

Most plants have four main parts. They are roots, stems, leaves, and flowers.

Most roots grow underground. They take in the water and minerals that the plant needs to grow. The roots hold the plant in place. Some plants also store food in their roots.

Stems help support the leaves and flowers. Stems hold the leaves up in the air where they can get more sunlight. Leaves make most of the food that plants need to live and grow. Flowers are the parts of plants that seeds grow in.

Most plants begin growing when a seed sprouts. The seed takes in water, which makes it swell. It swells until it splits open, and a tiny seedling appears. The lower part of the seedling turns into a root. This root holds the seedling in the ground.

All the other roots grow from this main root. Next, the upper part of the seedling begins to grow upward. At the tip of the seedling is the bud that produces the first leaves. Most plants grow at the tips of their roots and branches.

Continued on the next page

Plants grow in five major kinds of regions around the world. Cold-loving plants grow in tundra and on mountains. Forests include many tall trees and smaller plants. Grasslands are made up mainly of grasses and other flowering plants. Plants capable of surviving dry conditions are found in deserts, and plants that like wet conditions are in watery areas. No plants grow where there is ice all year.

Plant *Continued from the previous page*

When their leaves have unfolded, many plants produce food by a method called *photosynthesis (foh tuh SIHN thuh sihs)*. In photosynthesis, the plant makes food by using light from the sun, water and minerals from the soil, and a gas called carbon dioxide from the air. While the plant does this, it gives off oxygen into the air. People and animals need oxygen to breathe.

Some plants cannot produce their own food. They attach to living plants and take the food they need from these plants. Other plants grow on dead plants or animals.

Other articles to read include: **Angiosperm; Annual; Biennial; Biome; Botany; Bud; Carnivorous plant; Chlorophyll; Conifer; Evergreen; Flora; Flower; Forest; Fruit; Germination; Gymnosperm; Leaf; Perennial; Photosynthesis; Poisonous plant; Root; Seed; Shrub; Spice; Stem; Tree; Vegetable; Vine; Weed;** *and those on individual plants.*

The sequoia tree is one of the largest living things on Earth.

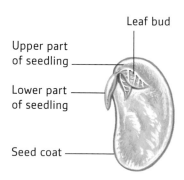

Leaf bud

Upper part of seedling

Lower part of seedling

Seed coat

A cross section of a bean shows the young seedling inside a seed coat.

A seed contains all the parts needed to form a new plant. The sprouting of a seed is called *germination*. The major steps in germination are shown here.

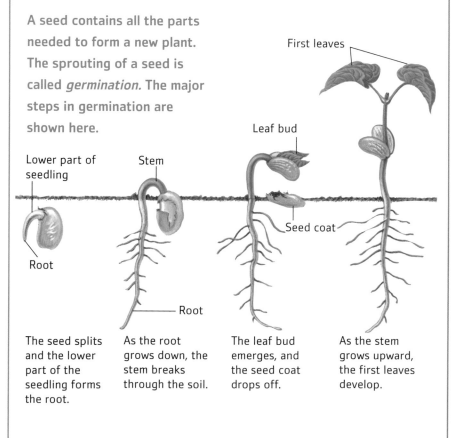

First leaves

Leaf bud

Lower part of seedling

Stem

Root

Seed coat

Root

The seed splits and the lower part of the seedling forms the root.

As the root grows down, the stem breaks through the soil.

The leaf bud emerges, and the seed coat drops off.

As the stem grows upward, the first leaves develop.

ACTIVITY

The power of plants: Rooting roots

All plants need water and light to thrive. But just how important are these things to a plant? Here are two experiments to show how hard plants will work to get water and light.

1. Soak the four dried beans in water overnight.

2. Stuff a glass jar full of paper towels or cotton balls and add enough water to wet them.

3. Place the beans between the towel and the glass jar, so you can see them. Place two of the beans facing the top of the jar, one facing the bottom of the jar, and one facing the jar's side.

   After a few days, the beans will sprout and begin to send out roots in search of water. The plant has used up most of the food that was stored in the bean, and now it needs to find a way to make more.

What you need:

- four dried navy beans
- water
- a glass jar
- paper towels or cotton balls
- a pen or pencil
- paper

4. After several days, in which direction do the roots grow? Why does the bean search in that direction to find water? Is it because that is where the water is found in the jar, or is there some other reason? Record your thoughts and observations.

5. Make sure the paper towel is moist and put the lid back on the jar. Turn the jar upside down and wait a few more days. In which direction are the roots growing now? How can you explain this?

What's going on:

Geotropism (jee OT ruh pihz uhm) is the tendency of certain parts of plants to grow in a certain direction in response to the pull of gravity. Roots grow toward the source of gravity (Earth), and stems grow away from the source of gravity.

http://bit.ly/YZTXgL

The power of plants: Plant workout

How hard will plants work to get light? This experiment will suggest an answer.

1. Soak a runner bean seed in a bowl of water overnight. Then plant it in a small pot filled with moist potting soil.

2. Cut away one short end of a shoebox. Stand the shoebox so the open end is on top. Set the pot inside the box toward one side.

3. Cut the two cardboard cards so that they are the same size as the end of the shoebox.

4. About ½ in (1.25 cm) from one end of each card, cut a square "window" about 2 in by 2 in (5 cm by 5 cm). Tape one of the cards inside the shoebox to make a shelf above the pot. Position the window on the side of the box away from the pot. Now put the cover back on the box and wait a few days. Write or draw what you think will happen.

5. After the bean sprouts, check in what direction its stem grows. How do you explain the growth?

6. Now tape the other card about 2 in (5 cm) above the first card, this time with the window on the opposite side. Predict what will happen. In what direction does the stem grow after a few days? Write down your thoughts and conclusions.

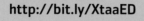
http://bit.ly/XtaaED

What you need:

- a runner bean seed
- a bowl
- water
- a small clay pot or other small container
- potting soil
- a shoebox
- two pieces of cardboard or tagboard
- scissors
- tape
- a pen or pencil
- paper

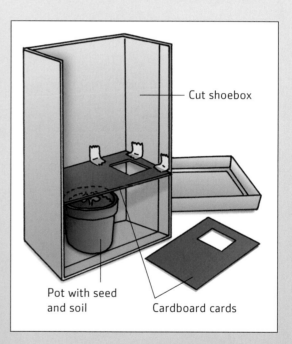

Cut shoebox

Pot with seed and soil

Cardboard cards

What's going on:

Phototropism (foh TOT ruh pihz uhm) is the tendency of certain parts of plants to grow in a certain direction in response to light. Your plant grows in a zig-zag pattern as it bends to where the light comes through the cards.

Plum

Plums are a popular fruit. People eat plums fresh. They also make plums into jams, jellies, and preserves. Some kinds are dried to make prunes.

Plums have smooth, thin skin. The flesh is juicy and sweet. A hard pit lies in the center of the fruit. Plums may be heart-shaped, oval, or round. They may be black, blue, green, purple, red, or yellow.

Plum trees have beautiful white blossoms in early spring. These blossoms develop into the fruits. The fruits ripen in late summer.

Other articles to read include: **Flower; Fruit.**

Plums grow on trees that have whitish blossoms. The tasty fruit grow from these blossoms.

Poinsettia

Poinsettia *(poyn SEHT ee uh)* is a popular house plant. It is often used as a Christmas decoration. It has tiny yellow flowers surrounded by large, colored leaves. These leaves resemble flower petals and are commonly bright red. On some poinsettias, these leaves are pink, white, or other colors.

Poinsettias are native to Mexico. A wild poinsettia may grow from 2 to 15 feet (0.6 to 4.6 meters) tall. A potted poinsettia grows from 1 to 4 feet (30 to 120 centimeters) tall.

The poinsettia was named for Joel R. Poinsett. Poinsett was the first United States ambassador to Mexico. He arrived in Mexico City, the capital, in 1825. He introduced the plant to the United States when he returned home. Other common names for the poinsettia include the Christmas flower, lobster flower, and Mexican flame leaf. The plant's hollow stems contain a milky sap that can irritate the skin and eyes.

Other articles to read include: **Flower; Leaf.**

Poinsettia

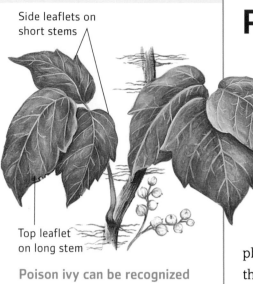

Side leaflets on
short stems

Top leaflet
on long stem

Poison ivy can be recognized
by its three pointed leaflets.
The leaflets contain a
poisonous oil that irritates
the skin, causing a rash.

Poison ivy

Poison ivy is a vine or bush that contains a poisonous oil that irritates the skin. It grows in parts of the United States and Canada.

Poison ivy leaves are made up of three small leaves. The leaves are red in spring and then turn shiny green. The plant has small, greenish flowers and white, waxy berries. Poison oak and poison sumac are related to poison ivy.

The oil in poison ivy sticks to the skin when people touch the plant. People can even be poisoned by touching clothing or shoes that have picked up the oil. This oil makes the skin itch, turn red, and blister. Washing the skin right after touching the plant reduces damage caused by the oil. A liquid called calamine lotion or pads soaked in Epsom salts or baking soda help stop the itching.

Other articles to read include: **Ivy; Poison oak; Poisonous plant; Sumac; Vine.**

Poison oak

Poison oak is a plant with sap that irritates the skin. It is related to poison ivy and poison sumac. It grows as a bush or vine. The leaves of poison oak are usually made up of three separate leaflets. The plant has small greenish or yellowish flowers and hairy, berrylike, light-colored fruits.

All parts of poison oak contain the irritating sap. A person who touches poison oak should wash the affected areas well with soap and water. If blisters or swelling are severe, the person should see a doctor.

Other articles to read include: **Oak; Poison ivy; Poisonous plant; Sumac; Vine.**

Poison oak has three leaflets
arranged in a similar way to
poison ivy. However, the
leaflets of poison oak have
rounded edges. The leaflets
contain a poisonous oil that
irritates the skin, causing a
rash.

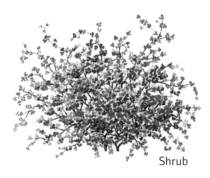

Shrub

Leaflets

Poisonous plant

A poisonous *(POY zuh nuhs)* plant is a plant that produces a poison that can hurt or even kill a human being or another animal. There are hundreds of kinds of poisonous plants.

Many plants are poisonous if eaten. Many of these look, smell, or taste bad. This helps warn animals not to eat them.

Some common food plants have poisonous parts. For example, the leaves of the potato plant are poisonous. But people can safely eat the potato vegetable. Fruits with poisonous parts include apricots, cherries, and peaches. Their flesh is safe to eat, but the hard *pit* at the center of each contains poison.

People should never eat or even chew a plant unless they are sure it is safe. If they think they may have eaten a poisonous plant, they should call a doctor or a poison control center right away.

Not all plants must be eaten to hurt a person or animal. For example, poison ivy irritates the skin. Some people are more likely to be irritated by these plants than are other people.

Other articles to read include: **Foxglove; Hemlock; Nightshade; Poison ivy; Poison oak; Potato; Sumac.**

The bean of the castor oil plant contains ricin. Even a tiny dose can kill an adult human.

The leaves and berries of deadly nightshade are highly poisonous. However, the medicinal drug atropine is made from the poison produced by the plant.

Pollen

Some plants rely on the wind to spread their pollen from one flower to another. The flowers of these plants, such as this pussy willow, release the pollen grains to the open air. Breezes then blow the grains to other flowers.

Pollen is tiny grains made by flowers. Most plants use pollen to *reproduce* (make offspring). Pollen is made in the stamen *(STAY muhn),* the male part of a flower. The movement of pollen from the male part of a flower to the female part of a flower is called *pollination.* Pollination enables most plants to make their seeds. Pollen grains vary in shape, size, and surface features. These differences make the grains of each *species* (kind) of plant different.

Some plants are pollinated by the wind. The wind carries pollen from one flower to another. The pollen of these plants may have a shape that catches the wind. Plants that rely on the wind usually make large amounts of pollen. Their flowers usually do not have bright colors or a fragrant odor.

Most plants with colorful flowers are pollinated by insects or other animals. These animals are drawn to flowers to feed on a sugary liquid called *nectar.* When animals drink the nectar, pollen sticks to their bodies. They then carry the pollen to another flower. Plants that rely on animals for pollination usually make sticky pollen.

Bees and other insects often carry pollen from one flower to another. The pollen is brushed onto the insects, such as this honey bee, when they visit flowers to drink sugary *nectar.* When the insects land on other flowers, the pollen may fall off.

Some plants are *self-pollinating.* In these plants, the pollen may stay inside the flower and fall down to the flower's female part.

Many people are allergic to pollen. Large amounts of pollen in the air cause them to develop hay fever. This allergy results in headaches, red and itching eyes, a runny nose, and sneezing. Pollen from the ragweed plant is the most common cause of hay fever in the United States.

Other articles to read include:
Fertilization; Flower; Nectar; Reproduction.

Pomegranate

The pomegranate *(POM GRAN iht)* is a gold-red fruit about the size and shape of a large orange. It has a hard rind. The fruit contains many seeds. Each seed is inside a layer of crimson pulp. The pulp has a pleasant, refreshing taste. It is used mainly to make cooling drinks.

The pomegranate plant grows wild in western Asia and northwestern India. In the wild, it is bushlike. Pomegranate is also grown commercially in the United States. On farms, the pomegranate is trained to grow as a small tree. The tree reaches a height of 15 to 20 feet (4.6 to 6 meters). Scarlet flowers grow at the ends of its slender branches.

Other articles to read include: **Fruit; Seed; Tree.**

Pomegranate

Popcorn

Popcorn is a type of corn that is eaten as a popular snack food, especially in the United States. A popcorn kernel has a hard outer shell that surrounds a soft, moist, starchy center. When a kernel is heated, its moisture turns rapidly to steam. The steam builds up pressure inside the shell until the shell bursts. The release of the steam causes a small explosion that turns the kernel inside-out. The soft center expands and becomes filled with air. Kernels expand to 30 to 40 times their original size when popped.

Popcorn is probably native to Central America and is one of the oldest forms of corn. American Indians grew popcorn for more than 1,000 years before the arrival of European explorers in the 1400's and 1500's. Indians used popcorn for food as well as for decoration and in religious ceremonies.

Most of the world's popcorn is grown in the United States. It is generally served with butter and salt added.

Other articles to read include: **Corn.**

Popcorn is a type of corn that is heated until it pops.
Popcorn is a popular snack, especially in the United States.

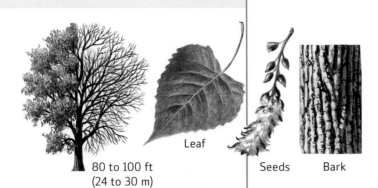

80 to 100 ft
(24 to 30 m)

Leaf

Seeds   Bark

The eastern cottonwood is a type of poplar that grows in most of eastern North America.

Poplar

The poplar is a tree that bears tiny seeds hidden in fluffy, cottony hairs. The wind carries the seeds through the air. Poplars grow in the northern parts of the world. They grow best in moist places. There are many different kinds of poplar. Three common kinds are *aspens, cotton-woods,* and *Lombardy poplars.*

Poplars have pointed leaves with toothed edges. They have small greenish flowers. The flowers appear early in spring, before the leaves. The flowers grow in drooping clusters called *catkins.* They bear the seeds. Many poplars grow fast but do not live long.

Poplar wood is whitish or light brown. It is used to make boxes, crates, and packing material. It is also used to make paper.

Other articles to read include: **Aspen; Tree.**

Poppy

The poppy is the name for several groups of beautiful flowers. There are many kinds of poppies. The common corn poppy grows wild in Europe. Many *varieties* (types) of poppies are grown in flower gardens. The Shirley poppy is one of the most common varieties. The Iceland poppy grows throughout much of North America. Its flowers are shades of white, orange, yellow, and red. The showiest poppy is the Oriental. It produces red, orange, white, or salmon crepe-paperlike blossoms. The Oriental has a blackish-purple center.

The Oriental is the showiest of poppies.

The most important kind of poppy is the opium. It is native to Asia and has been grown since ancient times. It has white, pink, red, or purple blossoms.

The opium poppy produces the *narcotic* (nerve-dulling) drug opium. The drug comes from the capsules where the seeds develop. Workers scratch the capsules late in the day. The milky juice that seeps out solidifies overnight. Workers collect it the next day. The opium is dried into powder. Drug manufacturers use products derived from raw opium to make medicines to treat people with severe pain. Heroin, an illegal drug, is also made from opium.

Other articles to read include: **Flower.**

Potato

The potato is an important crop that grows underground. Potatoes are round or oval and firm. Their skin is thin and may be brown, reddish-brown, pink, or white. The inside of a potato is white. There are many varieties of potatoes.

Potatoes can be cooked in many ways. People like to eat them baked, boiled, French-fried, and mashed. They can also be made into potato chips, instant mashed-potato powder, and other products. Potatoes have many vitamins and minerals.

Potatoes are native to the Andes Mountains of South America. Today, China grows more potatoes than any other country. Other leading potato-growing countries include India, Russia, Ukraine, and the United States.

The part of a potato plant that people eat is the *tuber (TOO buhr)*. Tubers form underground on the plant's stems. Most potato plants have three to six of these growths.

The part of the plant that grows aboveground has spreading stems and rough, dark green leaves. It has pink, purple, or white flowers. The leaves of the potato plant are poisonous.

Other articles to read include: **Poisonous plant; Tuber; Vegetable.**

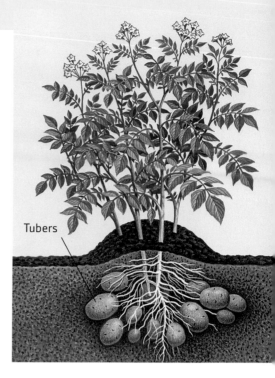

Tubers

A potato plant has leafy stems and whitish or purplish flowers. Growths called *tubers* form underground on the stems. Tubers are the part of the plant that people eat.

Prairie

Prairies are regions of flat or hilly land covered mainly by tall grasses. The North American prairie stretches from Texas in the United States to Saskatchewan in Canada. Other prairies include the Pampas of Argentina, the veld of South Africa, and the Canterbury Plains of New Zealand. Prairies also cover parts of Hungary, Romania, Russia, and Ukraine.

Prairies have hot summers and cold winters. Most of the rain falls in late spring and early summer.

Prairie soils are deep and rich in *nutrients,* which help plants grow. The richness results from the decay of plant matter over many years. The rich soil of prairies is good for growing crops. As a result, many prairies are farmed.

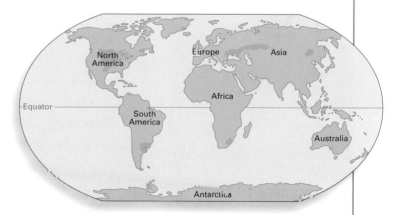

Prairies grow in several parts of the world (shown by the green areas). The world's largest prairie lies in North America.

Continued on the next page

Prairie   *Continued from the previous page*

Many kinds of grasses grow on prairies. Many varieties of wildflowers add splashes of color to a prairie's sea of grass. Cattails grow in wet areas, and some bushes grow among the grasses. A few scattered trees are found in river valleys on the prairie.

Other articles to read include: **Grass; Grassland; Soil.**

The natural vegetation of a prairie—a variety of grasses and wildflowers—can be seen at Grasslands National Park, in Saskatchewan, Canada.

The protist has a funnellike shape when viewed under a microscope. At the top of each funnel are hairlike *cilia,* which beat to draw food particles into the protist's body.

Protist

Protists *(PROH tihsts)* are a large group of mostly tiny living things. Protists make up one of the kingdoms of life. Other kingdoms include the plant kingdom and the animal kingdom. Some protists are like animals in many ways. Others are plantlike. Most protists are too small to be seen without a microscope. However, seaweeds and some other protists can be seen with the unaided eye.

Protozoans *(proh tuh ZOH uhnz)* are one type of protist. Protozoans have only one cell. Many must feed on other living things for energy. Like animals, protozoans can move around. Amebas *(uh MEE buhz)* are protozoans. An ameba moves by stretching out its body and flowing into new areas. Other protozoans swim using tiny hairs called cilia *(SIHL ee uh) .*

True algae *(AL jee)* are another type of protist. Like plants, algae make their own food using the energy in sunlight. Algae may have one cell or many cells. Seaweeds are among the algae with many cells.

Protists can be found almost every place on Earth. Many protists float in surface waters. These protists make up a large part of the *plankton.* Plankton is the mass of tiny living things that drift with the currents. Many other protists live in the soil. Still other protists live as *parasites* inside the bodies of animals. A parasite feeds off another living thing, called its *host.*

Other articles to read include: **Algae; Cell; Kingdom; Life; Parasite; Plankton; Plant.**

Pumpkin

The pumpkin is a large vegetable that is usually orange. However, some pumpkins are white, yellow, or other colors. Pumpkins are a type of squash. They are round or oval. They have a hard outer shell and stringy pulp inside. The center is filled with seeds. Most weigh between 5 and 30 pounds (2.3 to 14 kilograms), though they may weigh more than 1,000 pounds (450 kilograms).

People cook pumpkin in different ways. Pumpkin pie is a popular holiday treat. Roasted pumpkin seeds are eaten as snacks. Farmers may use pumpkins as feed for their animals. In the United States, people carve pumpkins into jack-o'-lanterns to celebrate Halloween.

Pumpkin plants have large, prickly leaves. The plants may grow as either vines or bushes. Pumpkin plants need careful cultivation to produce healthy fruit.

Pumpkins are native to North America. Scientists have found seeds from related plants that people grew thousands of years ago in Mexico.

Other articles to read include: **Fruit; Seed; Squash; Vegetable.**

Seeds

Pumpkins are large fruits that are usually orange in color. The fruits are filled with protein-rich seeds.

Pussy willow

Pussy willows are bushes or small trees known for their fluffy flowers. These flowers grow in clusters on several long, straight branches. The flower clusters are called *catkins*. In the spring, the catkins are covered with silky, grayish-white hair. Some people think catkins look like tiny kittens clinging to the twig.

Pussy willows grow wild in eastern North America. They grow best in moist places. Most of the time, they do not grow taller than 20 feet (6 meters).

A cut flowering branch will sprout roots if the ends are in water. If planted, it will grow into another full bush.

Other articles to read include: **Shrub; Tree; Willow.**

Pussy willow branches have many hard flower buds (above left) from which grayish-white clusters of flowers break out in early spring (above right).

Rr

Radishes come in a number of different shapes, sizes, and colors. Many also have fancy names.

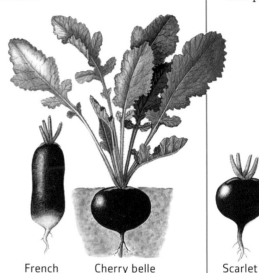

French breakfast   Cherry belle   Scarlet globe   White icicle

Radish

Radishes are plants with crisp, sharp-tasting roots. People eat the roots raw. They are most often sliced thin and served in salads or served whole on a relish tray.

Some radishes are round and some are oval. Others are long and pointed. Radishes may be red, white, yellow, pink, purple, black, or a mixture of red and white. Radishes may weigh less than 1 ounce (28 grams) or more than 2 pounds (1 kilogram).

Radishes grow best in cool weather. The plants are ready for harvesting 20 to 60 days after planting. Many people plant radishes in their home gardens.

Other articles to read include: **Root; Vegetable.**

The giant rafflesia produces huge flowers that smell like rotting flesh.

Rafflesia

Rafflesia *(ra FLEE zhuh)* is a plant with huge flowers. It has no leaves or stems. The flowers grow as parasites *(PAR uh syts)* on the stems and roots of bushes. A parasite is a living thing that feeds off another living thing.

One kind of rafflesia is the largest flower in the world. The giant rafflesia can grow more than 3 feet (90 centimeters) wide.

Rafflesia flowers have five wide, fleshy flaps around the outside. The flowers smell like rotting flesh. The odor attracts flies and beetles. These insects become covered in tiny grains called *pollen.* The insects carry the pollen from one rafflesia flower to another. This *pollination* enables the plant to reproduce.

Other articles to read include: **Flower; Parasite; Pollen.**

Ragweed

Ragweed is a North American weed. Many people are allergic to ragweed pollen. It is produced in great amounts from midsummer to early fall and spread by the wind. People who are allergic to the pollen typically suffer most when the plants are in bloom. Ragweed often grows along roadsides. It also grows in pastures, fields, and vacant lots.

There are many kinds of ragweed. Common ragweed is a coarse plant with finely divided leaves. It is also called bitterweed and hogweed. It usually grows from 1 to 3 feet (30 to 90 centimeters) high. Its small, hard fruit has short, sharp spines near the end. Giant ragweed commonly grows from 3 to 6 feet (1 to 2 meters) tall. It sometimes reaches 10 feet (3 meters) tall. Its leaves usually are divided into three broad parts. It is sometimes called kinghead. Perennial ragweed grows from long, spreading roots. It looks something like the common ragweed. But its fruit lacks the spines found on the fruit of common ragweed.

Other articles to read include: **Pollen; Weed.**

Ragweed

Rain forest

Rain forests are forests of tall trees that grow in areas with hot, wet weather. Most rain forests grow in the tropics. Africa, Asia, and Central and South America have large rain forests. Smaller rain forests are found in Australia and on islands in the Pacific.

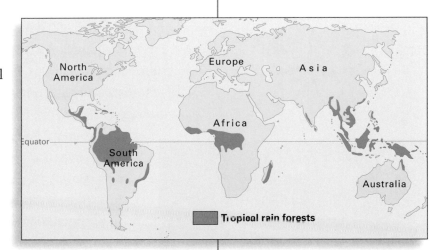

Tropical rain forests have more *species* (kinds) of plants than any other place on land. More than half of all plants and animal species on land live in tropical rain forests.

The tallest rain forest trees reach heights of 165 feet (50 meters). The treetops form a leafy covering called the canopy *(KAN uh pee)* high above the ground. Smaller trees form two

Continued on the next page

Tropical rain forests have a rich variety of plant life, which thrives in the warm, wet conditions of these environments. The trees in tropical rain forests stay green all year.

The largest tropical rain forests occur in parts of Central and South America, Africa, and Asia. Smaller tropical rain forests exist on the northeastern coast of Australia and on some islands.

Rain forest   *Continued from the previous page*

more layers, the *subcanopy* and the *understory* below it. These layers shade the ground. The ground gets very little sunlight, so few bushes grow there. People can walk through most parts of a rain forest. More light reaches the ground around riverbanks or clearings. There the plants form jungles of thick, tangled growth.

Most rain forests are very warm. Some have thundershowers more than 200 days a year, so the air below the canopies is almost always damp. The trees also give off water through their leaves. Water from the leaves makes up almost half of the rain in some rain forests.

Different areas of the same rain forest may have different species of plants and animals. For example, the Amazon rain forest has both mountains and lowlands. The kinds of trees that grow in the mountains do not grow in the lowlands.

Tropical rain forests are always green. Most of the trees lose their old leaves and grow new ones all year round. But some kinds lose all of their leaves for a short time. Different kinds of trees have flowers and fruit at different times of the year.

In a tropical rain forest, plants called epiphytes *(EHP uh fyts)* grow on tree branches. They get nourishment from the air and rain. Other plants, called lianas *(lee AH nuhz),* twine around the tree trunks and branches as they grow toward the sun.

Rain forests also have trees called strangler trees. These trees start growing as epiphytes. But they grow roots that reach down to the ground. The roots surround the tree on which the strangler lives. In time, the strangler may kill the other tree by cutting off its light, air, and water.

In a tropical rain forest, the plants themselves hold most of the nutrients *(NOO tree uhnts)*. Nutrients are substances that plants need to grow. Only a few nutrients are found in a thin layer of topsoil, where dead

A rain forest on the coast of the northwestern United States thrives in a cooler climate than most rain forests but receives a great deal of rainfall.   *Continued on the next page*

plants have decayed. So the roots of most rain forest plants are shallow and close to the topsoil. Some trees form large growths at the bottom of the trunk. These growths help hold the trees steady in the thin soil.

All the plants and animals of the rain forest depend on one another. Insects, birds, and other animals carry pollen from the flowers of rain forest trees to other flowers. Then new seeds form. As they visit the flowers, the animals receive food from the nectar of the flowers.

Rain forests are home to many people. Some groups have lived in the rain forest for thousands of years. They tradition-ally hunt, fish, and collect forest products. Some forest peoples have lost their home when the forests were destroyed.

People have cut down rain forests to clear land for farms and buildings. Digging mines and cutting trees for lumber have also destroyed rain forests. Scientists are afraid that thousands of kinds of plants and animals are dying out because they are losing their forest homes. Many people are working to save the rain forests.

Other articles to read include: **Amazon rain forest; Biome; Conservation; Deforestation; Endangered species; Epiphyte; Forest; Liana; Topsoil; Tree.**

The clearing of land in tropical rain forests, such as the rain forest in Malaysia, threatens thousands of kinds of plants and animals. People clear trees from the rain forests to make room for farms, homes, and businesses.

Rape

Rape is a flowering herb and a valuable crop. Varieties called *rapeseed* are grown for their seeds, which bear oil. Canola oil comes from one variety of rapeseed. This oil is used in cooking and to make such products as margarine. Canola oil is popular because it is thought to be more healthful than many other oils.

Rape is grown around much of the world. Some varieties are grown for stock to graze on. One variety of rape, the *rutabaga*, has an edible, turniplike root.

The rape plant reaches about 2 to 6 feet (61 to 183 centime-ters) tall. It has slender, branched stems. These stems produce bluish-green leaves. The plant bears pale yellow flowers. The flowers are about ½ inch (1.3 centimeters) long. Some varieties of the plant live only one year. Others live for two years.

Other articles to read include: **Canola oil; Crop; Herb; Oil; Rutabaga.**

Rape

Red raspberries

Raspberry

The raspberry is a fruit that looks like a cluster of tiny beads. Raspberries grow on small, thorny bushes. Raspberries are eaten fresh or used to make jams and jellies. Frozen raspberries are also popular. Most raspberries found in stores are red. Raspberries can also be black, purple, white, or yellow.

Raspberry plants grow best in cool areas of North America and Europe. They can be found in the wild. However, most raspberries sold in stores are grown on farms. The countries of Eastern Europe produce more than three-fourths of the world's raspberries.

Raspberries are not true berries. A true berry is made up of a single fruit with many seeds. For example, a grape is a true berry. Each of the tiny beadlike parts of a raspberry is a separate fruit. Each contains only one tiny seed. Raspberries are actually *compound fruits*.

Other articles to read include: **Berry; Fruit; Seed.**

Ray, John

John Ray (1627-1705) was one of the first scientists to classify plants and animals in an organized way. From 1662 to 1666, he traveled throughout western Europe with a pupil named Francis Willughby. Together, they collected plant and animal samples and attempted to classify them. At first, Ray classified plant life and Willughby classified animal life. After Willughby died, Ray continued Willughby's work on animal life.

John Ray

Ray was born on Nov. 29, 1627, in Black Notley, in the county of Essex, England. He died on Jan. 17, 1705.

Other articles to read include: **Classification, Scientific.**

Redwood

A redwood is a type of forest tree. Redwoods grow along the West Coast of the United States. They grow in foggy areas along the mountains facing the Pacific Ocean.

The world's largest living tree is the *coast redwood*. Many grow 200 to 300 feet (61 to 90 meters) high. But some are even higher. Their trunks may be more than 12 feet (3.7 meters) wide. Coast redwoods have green needles about 1 inch (2.5 centimeters) long.

Redwoods do not lose their needles in the fall. Their bark is reddish in color and deeply grooved.

Another kind of redwood is called the *sequoia (sih KWOY uh)*. Sequoias grow the thickest trunks of any tree. Sequoia trunks may be 100 feet (30 meters) around at the base.

Other articles to read include: **Conifer; Sequoia; Tree.**

A hiker is dwarfed by a giant redwood tree in Sequoia National Park in California. The tallest known redwood, in northern California, stands more than 365 feet (112 meters) tall.

Regeneration

Regeneration is the way that many plants replace lost or damaged parts. Regeneration is common in plants.

If a tree or a shrub is cut off near the ground, new parts called *shoots* may spring up from the stump. A potato may be cut into many pieces, each of which has an eye bud. Each piece can grow into a new potato plant if it is buried in soil.

Gardeners often use pieces cut from the stems of flowers and other plants to develop new plants. If these pieces are placed in water or moist soil, they usually develop new roots and grow into new plants.

Many plants that grow as weeds may be difficult to kill because they can regrow lost parts by regeneration. For example, a dandelion will regrow new stems and leaves even if only its roots are left in the soil.

Other articles to read include: **Asexual reproduction; Bud; Weed.**

Reproduction

Reproduction *(REE pruh DUHK shuhn)* is the way living things make more of their own kind. All living things reproduce—from the biggest plants and animals to the smallest creatures. Without reproduction, all forms of life would die out.

Living things make young that are like themselves. They can do this because all living things have *genes.* Genes are chemical instructions inside cells. They direct the growth and function of a living thing. During reproduction, genes are passed from parents to offspring.

There are two kinds of reproduction. Plants usually reproduce using *sexual reproduction.* In sexual reproduction, two parents produce offspring. This offspring has genes from each parent. The parents' genes are in *sex cells.* The male sex cell is called sperm. The female sex cell is called an *egg.* A sperm combines with an egg. That is, the sperm *fertilizes* the egg. A fertilized egg is housed within a seed. A seed that finds good soil can grow into a new plant.

The other kind of reproduction is called *asexual reproduction.* In this kind of reproduction, an offspring develops from only one parent. This offspring has a copy of all the parent's genes. Many plants use asexual reproduction at certain times. For example, a small piece cut from a plant can grow into a new individual. The piece might be a stem from a flower placed in water or moist soil. This piece of stem may develop new roots. It can then grow into a new flower.

Other articles to read include: **Asexual reproduction; Cell; Fertilization; Flower; Gene; Pollen; Seed.**

Flowering plants begin reproduction by a process called *pollination.* A *pollen grain* delivers *sperm cells* to the female *egg cell* inside the ovary. When a sperm fertilizes an egg, a seed begins to develop. The seed can grow into a new plant.

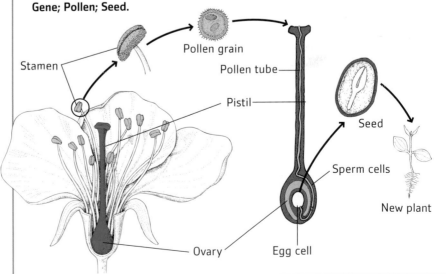

Stamen

Pollen grain

Pollen tube

Pistil

Seed

Sperm cells

New plant

Ovary

Egg cell

Resin

Resin *(REHZ uhn)* is a material that is typically gummy, oily, sticky, or waxy. It is used in varnishes, medicines, soaps, paints, and other products.

Natural resins are made by plants. Scientists divide natural resins into three groups. The first group comes from plants that are cut. Resin seeps from the cut. The second kind is taken from wood using special chemicals. The third kind of resin, called *amber,* is fossilized, ancient tree sap.

Synthetic *(sihn THEHT ihk)* resins are made in a laboratory or factory. They are made of complex chains of chemicals. Many plastics and other molded products are made from synthetic resins.

Other articles to read include: **Pine; Sap.**

Natural resin is collected from a pine tree. Turpentine is made from this resin. Turpentine is used as a thinner for oil paints.

Respiration

Respiration *(REHS puh RAY shuhn)* is the way living things get and use the oxygen they need to live. Oxygen is a gas in the air around us. Respiration also involves getting rid of carbon dioxide. Carbon dioxide is a gas that is given off when living things use oxygen.

Respiration can be divided into two processes. One process involves the movement of gases in and out of the living thing. The other process involves chemical reactions in cells.

In most plants, gases pass in and out through small openings in the leaves. Gases also pass through the outer layers of cells in the roots and stem. This movement of gases enables oxygen to reach plant cells. In cells, respiration involves a series of chemical reactions that require oxygen. These reactions release energy from food. This energy enables cells to function.

Plants make their own food through a "reverse respiration" process called photosynthesis *(foh tuh SIHN thuh sihs).* In photosynthesis, a plant uses the energy in sunlight to make sugar. During this process, the plant takes in carbon dioxide and gives off oxygen. The sugar made by photosynthesis can later be used for respiration inside the cell.

Other articles to read include: **Cell; Leaf; Oxygen; Photosynthesis.**

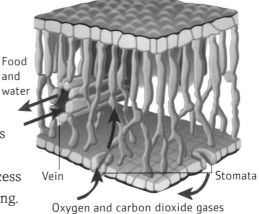

Food and water

Vein

Stomata

Oxygen and carbon dioxide gases

In the leaves of plants, respiration occurs through tiny openings called *stomata.* Plants also undergo a "reverse respiration" called *photosynthesis,* in which water and carbon dioxide are used to produce food and oxygen.

Roots grow down and shoots grow up

What you need:

- jar
- pea or kidney bean seeds
- some blotting paper or paper towels
- water

1. Soak the seeds in water for a few hours. Pour some water into the jar—the water should be about ½ inch (1.25 centimeters) deep. Dampen the blotting paper or paper towels.

2. Arrange the seeds between the blotting paper or towels and the side of the jar, as shown.

3. Put the jar in a warm place. Always keep about ½ inch (1.25 centimeters) of water in it.

4. The root from each seed will burst through the seed coat in a few days. In what direction is it growing? The shoot will appear a little later. In what direction is it growing?

5. Now turn the jar on its side so that the root and shoot of each seed are pointing sideways. Leave the jar on its side overnight. In the morning what do you see?

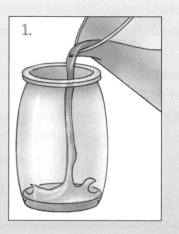

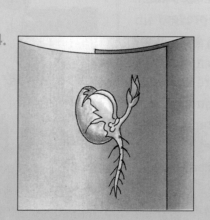

http://bit.ly/YfNnNb

Root *Continued from page 239*

Many plants have fibrous roots. These threadlike roots grow out in all directions. The first root does not remain larger than the other roots that grow from it. Grasses have fibrous roots. which may stretch for long distances. The roots of a rye plant, for example, may have a total length of about 380 miles (612 kilometers).

Other articles to read include: **Beet; Carrot; Soil; Sweet potato; Yam.**

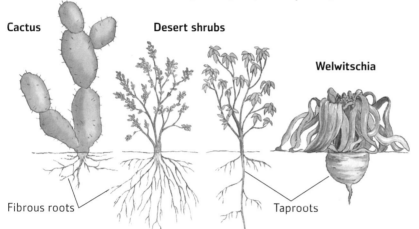

Cactus   **Desert shrubs**

Welwitschia

Fibrous roots   Taproots

The two main kinds of root systems are fibrous roots and taproots. In fibrous root systems, the secondary roots grow in all directions and may be longer than the primary root. In taproot systems, the primary root grows straight down and stays longer than the secondary roots. Plants such as the welwitschia have fleshy, swollen taproots.

Rose

Roses are among the most beautiful of all flowers. They come in many colors, including pink, red, yellow, white, and light purple. Some roses smell like tea or fruit. Others have a sweet smell, and some have almost no smell at all.

There are thousands of varieties of roses. These can be divided into three basic groups. They are: (1) wild roses, (2) old garden roses, and (3) modern roses. Wild roses grow as shrubs that bear thorns. Their flowers have one layer of five petals. Old garden roses include roses bred before 1867. They have double blossoms with petals in several layers. Modern roses include roses developed after 1867. Many roses grown by gardeners lack thorns.

Roses grow in many parts of the world. But they prefer mild climates or temperate climates, which have warm summers and cold winters. Many states and nations have adopted the rose as a national symbol. These include Iran, United Kingdom, and the United States.

Other articles to read include: **Flower.**

Hybrid tea roses are usually large flowers. In most cases, only a few of these flowers grow on each plant. Hybrid tea roses smell like tea or fruit.

Rosemary

Rosemary is an herb used for seasoning. It comes from the leaves of an evergreen shrub. The leaves have a pleasant aroma. They may be used fresh or dried. The dried leaves also may be used as a moth repellent. They are also brewed in tea to relieve stomachaches and headaches. The plant yields an oil used in perfumes. Europeans traditionally carry rosemary at weddings and funerals because they believe it will help them remember the event.

The rosemary plant grows from 2 to 6 feet (60 to 180 centimeters) tall. It bears shiny, dark green leaves and small, pale blue flowers. Rosemary grows wild in areas around the Mediterranean Sea.

Other articles to read include: **Evergreen; Herb.**

Rosemary

Rubber

Rubber is an important raw material. Rubber is used in thousands of products. For example, a car has about 600 rubber parts. Many sports are played with rubber balls. Rubber is useful because it is *elastic.* That means it can be stretched or pounded and still return to its original shape. Rubber can also hold air and keep out water. For these reasons, it is good for such items as cushions and waterproof diving suits. Electricity does not move through rubber easily. That makes rubber good for covering electric wires.

Natural rubber comes from the juice of the rubber tree. The tree's milky white juice is called latex *(LAY tehks)*. Workers cut holes in trees to collect latex. Machines form liquid latex into sheets of rubber. Most natural rubber is produced in India, Indonesia, and Thailand.

Rubber that is made from chemicals is called synthetic *(sihn THEHT ihk)* rubber. Most of this rubber is made in China, Japan, and the United States.

Other articles to read include: **Gum; Sap; Tree.**

Milky white latex is collected from a rubber tree by cutting a downward-pointing groove into the bark of the tree. At the bottom of this cut, a metal spout is stuck into the tree. The latex flows from this spout to a cup. About a teacupful of latex is collected at each tree. Then, the latex is taken to a factory, where machines make it into rubber.

Rutabaga

A rutabaga *(ROO tuh BAY guh)* is a plant with a root that can be eaten. Rutabagas look and taste a lot like turnips. Rutabagas are usually larger than turnips, and they have smooth, waxy leaves.

Rutabagas are yellow at the bottom. The top is purple. Inside, rutabagas are white. The roots are rich in vitamins and minerals. The blue-green leaves also may be eaten. The leaves are usually harvested in early summer. They become soft and bitter in hot weather. The plants usually grow best in cool weather.

Rutabagas first appeared in eastern Europe in the 1600's. Today they are a popular food in northern Europe. Rutabagas are also called Swedish turnips and Russian turnips.

Other articles to read include: **Root; Turnip; Vegetable.**

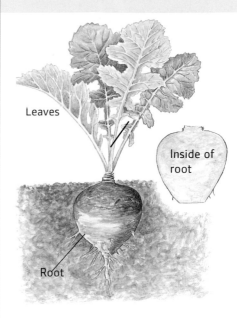

Leaves

Inside of root

Root

Rutabaga plants have smooth, waxy leaves aboveground and a fat, turniplike root belowground.

Rye

Rye is a kind of grain that is similar to wheat and barley. The rye plant has slender spikes of seeds with long, bristly hairs. The roots of a rye plant are deep, long, and widespread. They may have a total length of about 380 miles (612 kilometers).

Rye can be used to make bread and alcoholic beverages. The straw from rye plants can be used as packing material and as thatching for roofs. Rye straw can also be used to make hats, stuffing for mattresses, and paper. Farmers may plant rye to prevent soil from being carried away by wind or water.

Rye is grown in Asia, Europe, and North America. Major rye-producing countries include Germany, Poland, and Russia.

Other articles to read include: **Barley; Cereal; Crop; Grain; Seed; Wheat.**

Rye seeds grow on thin spikes at the top of long stems. The seed spikes also have many stiff, bristly hairs called *awns.*

Ss

Safflower

Safflower *(SAF LOW uhr)* is a plant grown to make oil. The oil comes from its seeds. Most safflower plants have yellow or orange flowers and spiny leaves. Some safflower plants have red or white flowers.

Safflower plants are grown in warm, dry regions. These regions include Australia, India, Mexico, Spain, and the southwestern United States.

Safflower seed oil is popular with health-conscious consumers because it contains low levels of saturated fats, which have been linked to heart disease. Safflower oil also contains high levels of essential fatty acids, which are necessary for good nutrition. The oil is used in cooking and in salad oils, margarine, mayonnaise, and shortening. Safflower oil is also used in paints and varnishes.

Other articles to read include: **Flower; Oil; Seed.**

The safflower has large blossoms and thistlelike leaves and stems. Safflower seeds are used in making nutritious oil and *meal* (ground-up grain).

Saffron

Saffron *(SAF ruhn)* is a valuable spice that is also used as a yellow dye. Saffron comes from the female parts of a flower called the saffron crocus. People must collect these saffron threads by hand. About 60,000 flowers yield only 1 pound (0.45 kilogram) of saffron. Saffron is prized as a food seasoning. It has a sweet odor but tastes bitter. It also is used to color foods and fabrics.

Other articles to read include: **Crocus; Spice.**

Saffron is a valuable spice that comes from the female parts of a flower called the saffron crocus.

Sage

Sage is the name of a large number of herbs and shrubs. One member of this group, called the common sage, is an important herb used for seasoning. The common sage has a strong odor. Its leaves and stems have a bitter taste. Cooks use the leaves to season cheeses, dressings for meat, sauces, and sausages. The leaves are also brewed to make tea. The common sage also may be called garden sage.

The common sage has white, woolly stems. The stems reach 2 feet (61 centimeters) tall. The grayish-green leaves have a rough, pebbled texture. The flowers grow in circular clusters at the tips of the stems. The flowers may be violet-blue, pink, or white. The common sage grows wild in areas around the Mediterranean Sea. It is now raised in many other areas.

Other articles to read include: **Herb; Shrub; Spice; Tea.**

Sage

Sagebrush

Sagebrush is a shrub of the western United States. It grows well in dry soil. Much sagebrush grows in northeastern California, eastern Oregon, Nevada, Utah, Wyoming, and Colorado.

Sagebrush can grow from 2 to 12 feet (0.6 to 3.7 meters) in height. It has a tall, straight stem and small leaves. The leaves grow close together. The plant has tiny yellow or white flowers.

Summer heat and dryness can dry up sagebrush. The plant may look dead. The wind can pull up the plant and blow it around. This is how the seeds are scattered.

Other articles to read include: **Desert; Shrub.**

Sagebrush

Saguaro

Fruit

Spine cluster

Saguaro

The saguaro *(suh GWAH roh)* is the largest cactus in the United States. It can grow up to 60 feet (18 meters) tall. The saguaro is shaped like a tall tree with a big trunk and thick branches. It can weigh as much as 10 tons (9 metric tons).

The saguaro grows only in the deserts of the southwestern United States and northwestern Mexico. Its flower is the state flower of Arizona.

During May and June, the saguaro grows greenish-white flowers. The flowers are shaped like a funnel. They grow 3 to 4 inches (7.6 to 10 centimeters) long. Bats, birds, and insects drink a sweet liquid called *nectar* from the flowers.

Other articles to read include: **Cactus; Desert.**

Saint-John's-wort

Saint-John's-wort

Saint-John's-wort is a shrub with large yellow flowers. There are many kinds of Saint-John's-wort. The larger kinds form rounded bushes when grown alone. The smaller ones are herbs. They make good low borders in gardens. Some St.-John's-worts are evergreen. The flowers of these plants bloom in clusters in the summer. Rarely, these flowers are pink or purplish. Many people use St.-John's-wort as a remedy for mild depression. But scientists are not certain whether the herb can treat mental illness.

Other articles to read include: **Flower; Herb; Shrub.**

Sandbur

Sandbur is a troublesome weed that grows in sand. It is sometimes called *bur grass.* Sandbur is native to prairies of the western United States. Today, sandbur grows in many warm and sandy parts of the world. *Cockspur* is a plant related to sandbur. It grows in the southern United States.

Sandbur has several stems. The stems are 1 to 2 feet (30 to 61 centimeters) high. Small spikes grow at the ends of the stems. Each spike has 10 to 20 shiny, sharp burs. The burs can prick the flesh, causing painful wounds.

Other articles to read include: **Grass; Weed.**

Sandbur

Sap

Sap is a liquid in the leaves, roots, and stems of plants. Sap has some of the same uses in plants that blood has in animals.

Some sap is found in plant cells. This sap is called *cell* sap.

Other sap travels through tubes called phloem *(FLOH ehm)* and xylem *(ZY lehm).* It is called *vascular sap.* Vascular sap carries useful materials through a plant's body. Phloem carries a sugary sap from the leaves to other parts of the plant. Xylem carries a sap of water and minerals from the roots to the leaves.

Some saps are collected for human use. For example, the sweet sap of some maple trees is made into maple syrup.

Other articles to read include: **Cell; Gum; Maple; Resin; Rubber.**

Sap containing nutrients flows through stems in tubes called *phloem,* from leaves to other parts of the plant. Sap containing water and minerals flows through stems in tubes called *xylem,* from the roots to the leaves.

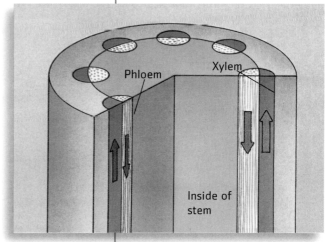

Savanna

A savanna *(suh VAN uh)* is a grassland with widely scattered trees and bushes. Savannas have dry and rainy seasons. Most savannas are found in warm areas. They usually lie between deserts and rain forests. Savannas cover much of Africa. They also cover areas of Australia, India, and South America.

Grasses are among the most common plants on savannas. There are usually few trees. Wetter savannas have taller grasses and more trees. Acacias *(uh KAY shuhz)*, baobabs *(BAY oh babz)*, and palms are some of the trees that grow on savannas.

Other articles to read include: **Baobab; Biome; Grass; Grassland; Palm; Tree.**

Savannas are grasslands with widely scattered trees. This savanna is found in southern Australia.

Savannas are found in many parts of the world.

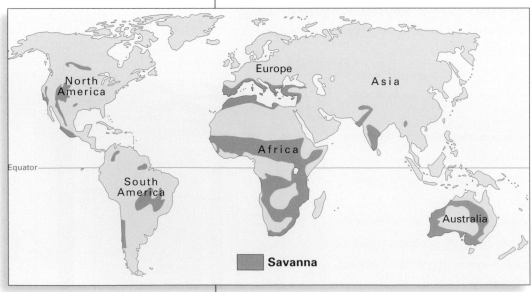

Seaweed

Seaweed is the name given to almost anything that looks like a plant and lives in the sea. Seaweeds can be found growing from the sea floor, floating on top of the water, attached to rocks and docks, or washed up on shore.

There are thousands of kinds of seaweeds. All of them are kinds of algae *(AL jee)*. Algae are not plants. They do not have true roots, stems, leaves, or flowers. A rootlike part called a *holdfast* helps the seaweed hold onto objects. A frond, which looks like a stem and leaf, grows from the holdfast. The soft fronds of a seaweed can bend and sway with the water without being torn apart. True plants that grow in the ocean are called *sea grasses.* Unlike seaweeds, they grow roots, stems, leaves, and flowers.

Like green plants, seaweeds use sunlight to turn water and carbon dioxide into food. This process is called photosynthesis *(FOH tuh SIHN thuh sihs)*.

Many seaweeds are rich in vitamins and minerals. Some kinds are eaten by people and sea animals. For example, thin sheets of seaweed are used to make sushi rolls. Seaweeds are also used in products that range from lipsticks to buttons.

Other articles to read include: **Algae; Kelp; Photosynthesis.**

Seaweeds come in a wide variety of shapes and colors.

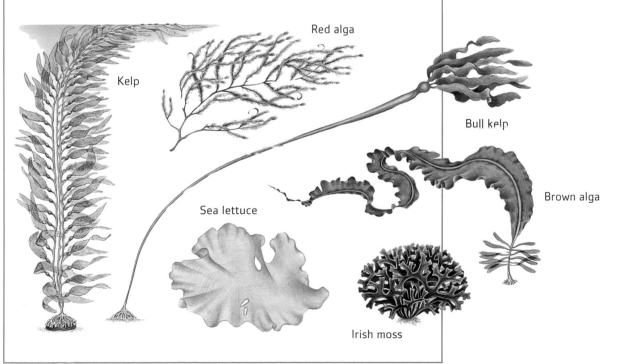

Kelp

Red alga

Bull kelp

Sea lettuce

Brown alga

Irish moss

Seed

Seeds are the part of a plant that can develop into a new plant. Most plants that make seeds are flowering plants. These plants include most trees, shrubs, and herbs. Conifers (cone-bearing plants) also make seeds.

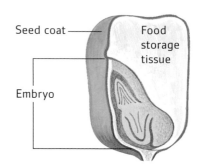

Seeds have three parts: the *embryo, food storage tissue,* and the *seed coat.*

Seeds vary greatly in size. Some seeds weigh less than 1 ounce (28 grams). Others weigh as much as 50 pounds (23 kilograms).

Seeds have three main parts: (1) the embryo *(EHM bree oh),* (2) the *food storage tissue,* and (3) the *seed coat.* The embryo develops into a new plant. Food storage tissue provides food for the new plant until its leaves can begin to make food. The seed coat protects the seed from injury, pests, and loss of water.

A seed is formed when a male sex cell (called a sperm) combines with a female sex cell (called an egg). Among flowering plants, seeds form inside flowers. The flowers grow into fruits that cover the seeds. The number of seeds produced by an individual plant varies according to the size of the seeds. A coconut tree has only a few large seeds. But an orchid or pigweed plant produces millions of tiny ones.

Seeds are spread in many ways. Some seeds are carried by the wind or water. Seeds inside fruit may rely on animals to reach new locations. Birds or other animals eat the fruit. They carry the seeds in their guts. Then they pass the seeds with their droppings. The plant grows where the seed is dropped.

Many seeds are important sources of food for people. Such seeds include those of corn, oats, rice, and wheat. Other seeds that we eat include beans, peas, and peanuts.

Other articles to read include: **Angiosperm; Flower; Fruit; Germination.**

In this germinating wild oat seedling, the lower part of the embryo has broken through the seed coat and is growing down into the soil. This part develops into the main root. The developing roots anchor the seedling and absorb minerals and water that the embryo needs to grow.

Seeds have a variety of features, such as little wings or sticky spines, that help them spread to new areas. Seeds may be spread by the wind or water, by animals, or by being *discharged* (shot out) by the plant.

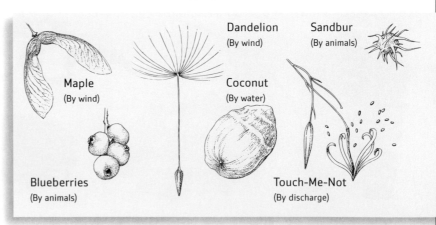

Maple
(By wind)

Blueberries
(By animals)

Dandelion
(By wind)

Coconut
(By water)

Sandbur
(By animals)

Touch-Me-Not
(By discharge)

ACTIVITY

What do seeds need to germinate?

Seeds will not germinate until they receive three things—water, warmth, and oxygen—all at the same time and in the correct amounts. You can prove this for yourself by carrying out a simple experiment.

What you need:

- self-adhesive labels
- a felt-tipped pen
- four small jars with tight fitting lids
- eight paper tissues
- a small spoon
- a packet of seeds, such as grass, mustard, or lettuce
- water
- some moist steel wool
- a kitchen cabinet
- refrigerator
- paper or notebook

1.

1. Number your jars 1, 2, 3, and 4. Lay the jars on their sides. Put two paper tissues into each jar. Use the spoon to sprinkle some seeds into jar 1. Screw on the lid.

2. Put a little water into the other three jars to make the tissues damp, but not soaking wet.

2.

3. Sprinkle some seeds on the damp tissues. Screw on the lids of jars 2 and 3. Put the steel wool into jar 4, and screw on the lid.

3.

Continued on the next page

A puffball fungus ejects spores. Spores are tiny cells that plants and some kinds of bacteria and fungi use to reproduce.

Spore

Fern leaf with spores

A spore is a special structure that can grow into a living thing. All plants make spores. So do some kinds of bacteria and fungi. But mosses and other plants that do not make seeds depend on spores to make offspring and spread from place to place.

Most spores are very small. They can only be seen with a microscope. They are made of just one cell. However, some fungi produce complex, multicelled spores. All spores contain *cytoplasm* (the living substance of a cell outside of the nucleus) and food.

Some spores have a thick wall around them. This helps the spore to deal with harsh weather, chemicals, and other conditions that might otherwise kill the organism.

Spores called zoospores have tails and can swim. Others move from place to place on air currents.

Other articles to read include: **Cell; Fungi; Moss; Reproduction.**

Spruce

The spruce is a type of evergreen *conifer* (cone-bearing tree). Spruce trees grow tall. Most are shaped like pyramids. In old trees, the drooping lower branches may brush the ground.

Spruce trees grow leaves that look like blue-green needles. These leaves are four-sided, stiff, and less than 1 inch (2.5 centimeters) long. Woody, peglike parts join the needles to the twig. Spruce trees grow cones that hang straight down.

Some spruces grow north of the Arctic Circle. Others grow as far south as the Pyrenees Mountains in Europe. In North America, they grow as far south as North Carolina and Arizona.

175 to 250 ft (53 to 61 M)

Spruce

Needles

Cone

Bark

Continued on the next page

Important spruces in North America include the white, black, and red spruces of the North and East. The Sitka, Engelmann, and blue spruces of the West are also important. The most important spruce in Europe is the Norway spruce.

Spruce wood is widely used for wood pulp in the papermaking industry. The timber is strong, light, and flexible. Spruce is also used to make boxes. It forms sounding boards for musical instruments. Spruce wood is also used for interior finishing in houses.

Other articles to read include: **Conifer; Evergreen; Tree; Wood.**

Squash

Squash is a gourd-shaped vegetable. Both the plant and its fruit are known as squash. The fruit is the part that most people eat. Squashes can be prepared in many ways. Acorn and butternut squash are often baked and buttered. Zucchini is often served raw in salads. People also fry and eat squash flowers. There are many different kinds of squashes.

Squashes provide large amounts of vitamins A and C. They are low in calories.

Squashes have large, five-pointed leaves. They grow yellow-orange flowers. Their fruits have many different colors, shapes, and sizes. The two major groups are *summer squashes* and *winter squashes.*

Summer squashes grow on bushes. The fruit is picked when it still has a soft rind. A squash that grows too large and ripe loses some flavor. Summer squashes should be eaten soon after harvesting. Common types include cocozelle, pattypan, white scallop, yellow crookneck, and zucchini.

Winter squashes grow on vines or bushes. They are frequently not picked until several days before the first freeze. At this time, the fruit is fully ripe and has a hard rind. Winter squashes can be stored for several months in a cool, dry place. Popular winter varieties include acorn, banana, butternut, Hubbard, and vegetable spaghetti.

Other articles to read include: **Fruit; Vegetable; Vine; Zucchini.**

Hubbard

Acorn

Butternut

White scallop

Zucchini and yellow crookneck

Squash is a nutritious vegetable that grows on bushes and vines. There are many different kinds of squashes, which differ in color, shape, and taste.

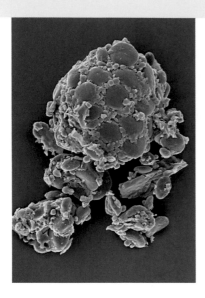

A grain of starch from baking flour as seen through a microscope.

Starch

Starch is a white, powdery substance made by plants. It can be found in the seeds of beans, corn, rice, and wheat. Starch is also found in the roots, stems, and *tubers (TOO buhrz)* (underground stems) of potatoes, arrowroot, and cassava plants.

Plants use starch to store food energy. Plants use the energy in sunlight to make sugar. This process is called photosynthesis *(foh tuh SIHN thuh sihs)*. Plant cells then change this sugar into starch. When the plant needs energy, it turns the starch back into sugar.

Starchy foods are an important source of direct energy for people and other animals. Starch is a *carbohydrate,* one of the three main classes of *nutrients* (nourishing substances).

Manufacturers also use starch. Starch is used in a product called *sizing,* which makes cloth stiff. It is also used to make certain kinds of paper stronger and smoother.

Other articles to read include: **Photosynthesis; Root; Seed; Stem; Tuber.**

Stem

A stem is a part of a plant. It grows and holds the buds, leaves, flowers, and fruit. Most stems hold the plant's leaves in the sunlight. The leaves need sunlight to make food. Stems also carry water and minerals from the roots to the leaves. In addition, they carry food made in the leaves to other parts of the plant.

Most plants have stems. But the stems of different plants vary in size and appearance. For example, lettuce plants have very short stems. Their stems can barely be seen under the large leaves. The trunks of California redwood trees are huge stems.

Most stems support the plant's flowers and leaves. Stems are woody or *herbaceous (hur BAY shuhs)* **(not woody). A woody stem has a rough, brown surface. A herbaceous stem has a smooth, green surface.**

They may grow 12 feet (3.7 meters) wide and more than 350 feet (107 meters) high.

Most stems grow up from the ground. A few kinds grow underground or along the ground.

Other articles to read include: **Bud; Flower; Fruit; Leaf; Lettuce; Redwood.**

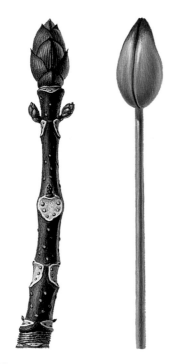

Woody stem   Herbaceous stem

Steppe

A steppe *(stehp)* is an area covered mainly by short grasses. Steppes are found in dry areas that have hot summers and cold winters. Most steppes receive a range of 10 to 20 inches (25 to 50 centimeters) of rain a year. This amount of rain is less than a prairie gets. But it is more than a desert receives. In North America, steppes cover most of the Great Plains from northern New Mexico to southern Alberta, in Canada. In Europe and Asia, steppes extend from southwestern Russia into central Asia.

Most steppe plants grow less than 1 foot (30 centimeters) tall. They do not grow as thickly as the tall grasses of prairies. Plants of the North American steppes include blue grama *(GRAH muh),* buffalo grass, cactuses, sagebrush, and spear grass. Before people farmed the steppes, many bison, deer, jack rabbits, prairie dogs, pronghorns, hawks, and owls lived there.

Today, people use steppes as grazing areas for livestock and as places to grow wheat and other crops. Summer fires are common on steppes. Such fires can be dangerous because flames spread quickly through the dry grass.

Overgrazing, plowing, and excess salts left behind by water have harmed some steppes. Strong winds may blow away loose soil after plowing, especially during a drought. A combination of plowing, winds, and drought has caused major dust storms in the Great Plains region of the United States.

Other articles to read include: **Farm and farming; Grass; Grassland; Great Plains; Prairie.**

Camels graze across the steppe, a dry area of short grasses, in northern China. Steppes surround much of the Gobi Desert, which stretches across southern Mongolia and northern China.

People use steppes to graze livestock and to grow wheat and other crops.

Strawberry plants produce tiny white flowers and heart-shaped red fruit. The delicious fruit can be eaten fresh or made into jam, jelly, and other food products.

Strawberry

The strawberry is a sweet, juicy fruit. When ripe, strawberries are red with many tiny yellow seeds on their skin. The fruit is rich in vitamin C and is often eaten fresh. Strawberries can also be canned or frozen. Strawberries are made into jam, jelly, and other food products.

The strawberry is not a true berry, because its seeds are on the outside. True berries, such as blueberries, have seeds inside the fruit.

The strawberry plant belongs to the rose family. Strawberry plants have long thin stems, called *runners*. These stems spread across the surface of the ground. Small white flowers grow from the stems.

Strawberries grow best in cool, moist areas. The main strawberry-growing states in the United States include California, Florida, Michigan, Oregon, and Washington.

Other articles to read include: **Berry; Fruit.**

A succulent

Succulent

A succulent *(SUHK yuh luhnt)* is a type of plant that has large leaves, stems, or roots in which water is stored. Cactuses are among the most familiar succulent plants. Succulents grow in deserts and other places where there is little water. By using the water stored in their leaves and stems, succulents can survive long periods without rain.

There are three main kinds of succulents. In *leaf succulents,* nearly the whole leaf is made up of water storage tissue. Leaf succulents have very short stems. *Stem succulents* have few or no leaves. The leaves that do appear tend to live only a short time before they shrivel up and fall off. *Root succulents* can survive long periods of dry conditions by storing nutrients and water below the surface of the ground.

Other articles to read include: **Cactus; Desert; Leaf; Stem.**

Sugar

Sugar is a sweet food product. People sprinkle sugar on such foods as grapefruit and cereal to make them taste sweeter. Some people add sugar to coffee, tea, and other drinks. In addition, food companies add sugar to many foods. Many candies, jams, jellies, and soft drinks contain large amounts of sugar. Sugar is also added to many baked goods, including cookies and cakes.

All green plants make sugar. But most of the sugar that people use comes from sugar cane or sugar beets. The sugar made by these plants is called sucrose *(SOO krohs)*. This sugar is the kind people keep in a sugar bowl. Sugar beets store sucrose in their roots. Sugar cane is a tall grass that stores sucrose in its stalks.

Sugar belongs to the group of foods called carbohydrates *(KAHR boh HY drayts).* Carbohydrates give energy to plants and animals. But eating large amounts of sugar may increase the risk of tooth decay and help cause a person to become overweight.

Other articles to read include: **Beet; Crop; Glucose; Grass.**

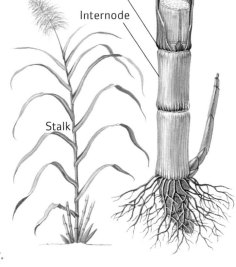

To obtain raw sugar from sugar cane, washed and shredded sugar cane is placed in a crushing machine, which forces a sugary juice called *cane juice* from the stalks. After the juice is heated and filtered, an evaporator and vacuum pan remove much of the water from it, forming a syrup.

A centrifuge separates sugar crystals from the syrup, producing raw sugar. A *centrifuge* is a machine that spins at high speeds to separate two substances from one another. The raw sugar is sent to a refinery to be prepared for use in sugar products. ▼

Sugar cane is one of the main sources of sugar. It grows in the form of stalks. The stalks are divided into *nodes* and *internodes.*

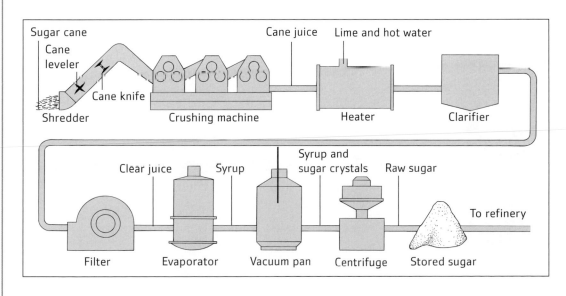

Sumac

Sumac *(SOO mak)* is a group of small trees and shrubs. Some kinds of sumacs are poisonous. Certain eastern Asian sumacs are important sources of natural waxes. One kind of sumac is the source of an important spice in Middle Eastern cooking. This spice is also called *sumac.*

There are dozens of kinds of nonpoisonous sumacs. They grow in regions with mild or warm weather. North American sumacs have long leaves. The leaves are made up of many smaller *leaflets.* The plants' fruits are small and mostly red in color. Most North American sumacs are fast-growing shrubs.

Several kinds of poisonous sumacs grow in Asia and North America. Oils in their sap cause rashes and irritation of the skin. *Poison sumac,* also known as *poison elder* or *swamp sumac,* thrives in bogs and swamps, especially in the Atlantic Coast and Great Lakes regions of the United States. It grows up to 25 feet (8 meters) tall. Its berries are white or yellowish and grow in drooping clusters.

Other articles to read include: **Poisonous plant; Shrub; Spice; Tree.**

Many sumacs have leaves that turn a brilliant red in fall. They also have small reddish fruits (inset).

Sunflowers

Sunflower

A sunflower is a type of tall plant that has large yellow flower heads with dark centers. There are more than 60 *species* (kinds) of sunflowers. Many sunflowers turn to face the sun throughout the day.

The most common species of sunflower grows up to 10 feet (3 meters) tall. It has one or more heads of flowers. Each head has a dark center made of many small tube-shaped flowers. These flowers are surrounded by large yellow petals.

Sunflower seeds are good to eat. They are rich in protein, which provides energy for the body. The seeds are also used to make a vegetable oil that is an ingredient in margarine and cooking oil.

Sunflowers are native to North America. They were brought to Europe in the 1500's.

Other articles to read include: **Flower; Oil; Seed.**

Sweet potato

The sweet potato is a vegetable that grows underground as a large root. The flesh and skin of sweet potatoes vary in color from purple to white. The most common flesh colors are orange, yellow, and white. Sweet potatoes are an important food in many countries. In the United States, sweet potatoes are sometimes called *yams*. However, true yams belong to a different family of plants.

Sweet potatoes have high amounts of carbohydrates *(kahr boh HY drayts)* and vitamins A and C. Carbohydrates give energy to plants and animals. People buy sweet potatoes fresh, canned, frozen, or dried. They are also used for animal feed, alcohol, and starch. The scientist George Washington Carver made 118 products and many recipes from the sweet potato.

Sweet potatoes probably first grew in South America. Today, they are grown all over the world. China is the world's largest producer of sweet potatoes.

Other articles to read include: **Carver, George Washington; Root; Vegetable; Yam.**

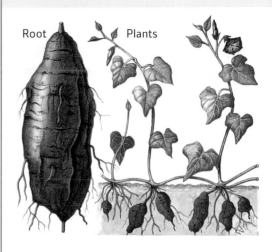

Sweet potatoes grow underground as large roots.

Switchgrass

Switchgrass is a tall North American grass. It grows 6 to 10 feet (2 to 3 meters) high. It has thick stems that grow in clumps. The stems produce a feathery head. Switchgrass's leaves are yellowish- to bluish-green. They grow to about 1 foot (30 centimeters) long.

Switchgrass once covered parts of vast prairies in the Great Plains of the United States. It provided food for huge numbers of buffalo, deer, and antelope. Most switchgrass was destroyed in the late 1800's. People plowed the switchgrass under to grow crops.

Scientists are studying switchgrass as a source of *biofuel*. Biofuels are made from plant matter or other remains of living things. Biofuels can be used in place of such traditional fuels as gasoline. Biofuels are a *renewable* source of energy. *Renewable* means that there may be an unlimited supply of the fuel. Traditional fuels such as gasoline are *nonrenewable*. Supplies of these fuels will eventually run out. However, biofuel made from switchgrass is expensive. Switchgrass will not become a major source of fuel unless scientists develop cheaper ways to *distill* (to make by refining) it.

Switchgrass

Other articles to read include: **Biomass; Grass; Great Plains; Prairie.**

80 to 120 ft   Leaf
(24 to 37 M)

Cone   Bark

Sycamore

Sycamore

The sycamore *(SIHK uh mawr)* is a shade tree. It may reach a height of 175 feet (53 meters). Its trunk can be 14 feet (4 meters) wide. The bark on the lower trunk is reddish-brown. The bark on the trunk breaks off in tiny scales. When these scales break off, they show an inner bark that is light cream in color. The leaves are broad and have large teeth. The fruits of a sycamore grow in small balls. Each ball is made up of many tiny dry fruits tightly packed together.

There are several kinds of sycamores. Some sycamores are known as buttonwoods. Others are called plane trees. The American sycamore is found in great numbers in the United States.

Other articles to read include: **Tree.**

Lichens growing on tree bark are an example of a symbiotic relationship. Lichens consist of fungus and algae cells living together in a way that benefits both.

Symbiosis

Symbiosis *(sihm by OH sihs* or *sihm bee OH sihs)* is when two *organisms* (living things), live together in a close relationship. Such organisms are said to have a symbiotic *(sihm bee OT ihk)* relationship. In a symbiotic relationship, at least one member always benefits from the relationship.

In one type of symbiotic relationship, one organism lives on or in another. The first organism, called a *parasite,* may cause great harm to the second organism, called the *host.* For example, a weed called dodder steals water and nutrients from such crop hosts as alfalfa, clover, and flax.

In another type of symbiotic relationship, one organism benefits from the host, which is not affected by the other organism. In a third type of symbiosis, both organisms benefit. The organisms may provide food or protection for each other.

Symbiosis is important for many types of plants. For example, many flowering plants have a symbiotic relationship with insects. The flowers provide the insects with sugary nectar. In turn, the insects carry tiny grains called *pollen* from one flower to another. This process enables the plants to make seeds and reproduce.

Other articles to read include: **Flower; Nectar; Parasite; Reproduction.**

Taiga

The taiga *(TY guh)* is a large area of forest in Earth's northern regions. It covers vast northern areas of Asia, Europe, and North America. The taiga is often called the boreal *(BAWR ee uhl)* forest. The word *boreal* means *northern*. The taiga includes some of the last great undisturbed forests on the planet.

The taiga is a biome *(BY ohm)*. A biome is a community of living things in a certain area of climate. The taiga has relatively short, cool summers and long, cold winters. Evergreen trees are the most common plants in the taiga. Large animals of the taiga include bears, moose, reindeer, and wolves.

Other articles to read include: **Biome; Evergreen; Forest.**

The taiga consists of vast evergreen forests that grow in northern areas.

Tea

Tea is one of the most popular drinks in the world. People make tea by pouring boiling water over dried leaves of the tea plant.

The tea plant is an evergreen that grows in warm regions. The finest tea comes from elevations of 4,000 to 7,000 feet (1,200 to 2,100 meters). The plant grows more slowly in the cool air at such elevations. The slow growth helps its flavor. Tea plants have small, white, sweet-smelling flowers. Each flower produces one to three seeds that look like hazelnuts.

There are three main kinds of tea—black, green, and oolong *(OO lawng)*. The leaves of the tea plant are treated differently to make the different kinds of tea.

Workers on a tea farm in Vietnam pick tea leaves, which they collect in baskets.

Continued on the next page

Tree

Trees are the largest kind of plant. The tallest trees are California's redwoods. They may tower more than 360 feet (110 meters), taller than a 30-story building. Some trees are also the oldest known things alive, surviving for thousands of years. Trees continue to grow as long as they live.

The main parts of a tree are the *roots,* the *trunk,* and the *leaves.* The roots hold the tree in the ground. They collect water and minerals from the ground. The trunk is a thick, woody stem. It usually has many branches growing out of it. The leaves grow from the branches. The leaves use energy from sunlight to make food for the tree. They do this by combining water with a gas called *carbon dioxide.* This process is called photosynthesis *(foh tuh SIHN thuh sihs).*

There are thousands of kinds of trees in the world. However, trees may be divided into six main groups: *broadleaf trees,* needleleaf trees, palms, cycad trees, tree ferns, and *ginkgo trees.*

The six main groups of trees—based on the types of leaves, seeds, or other structures that they have—are *broadleaf trees, needleleaf trees, palms, cycad trees, tree ferns,* and *ginkgoes.*

Silver maple

Fruit

Leaf

Red pine

Needles and cone

Royal palm

Fruit

Broadleaf trees bear flowers and green leaves in spring, and most lose their leaves in fall. Their seeds occur in fruits, which develop from the flowers.

Needleleaf trees have needle-like or scale-like leaves and bear their seeds in cones. Most of these trees stay green all year.

Palms form a large group of mainly tropical trees. Most palms have huge leaves and no branches.

Broadleaf trees are the largest group. This group includes ashes, elms, maples, oaks, walnuts, willows, and many other familiar trees. It also includes most of the trees found in tropical regions, such as mahogany and mangrove trees. Broadleaf trees have broad, flat leaves. Many broadleaf trees lose their leaves in the fall. The green leaves often turn yellow, orange, red, or brown before dropping. Broadleaf trees also have flowers. The flowers develop into fleshy fruits that surround the seeds.

Needleleaf trees include firs, pines, redwoods, and spruces. Most needleleaf trees have narrow, pointed leaves that look like needles. The leaves stay green all year long. They do not drop off in the fall. Needleleaf trees have their seeds in woody cones.

Palm trees are a large group of flowering trees. These trees grow in warm climates. Most palm trees have no branches. Their feathery or fan-shaped leaves stick out in a bunch at the top of the trunk. Some palm trees grow huge nuts called coconuts.

Cycad *(SY kad)* trees look something like palm trees. They have a thick trunk without branches and a crown of long, palm-like leaves. Cycads have their seeds in cones that look like large pine cones.

Continued on the next page

South African cycad

Leaves and cones

Cycad trees live in warm, wet parts of the world. They bear large, heavy cones that may grow to a length of 3 feet (91 centimeters).

West Indies tree fern

Leaflet with spore cases

Tree ferns are the only trees that have no flowers, fruits, or seeds. They reproduce by using tiny structures called *spores.*

Ginkgo

Seeds

Leaf

Ginkgoes bear seeds—but not fruit or cones. Only one kind of ginkgo survives.

The alpine tundra of Yukon, in Canada, blooms with yellow, white, and purple flowers during the warmer months.

The arctic tundra in Alaska is home to many small plants that grow near the ground, such as red bearberry and mosses.

Tundra

The tundra is a cold, dry region covered by snow for more than half the year. Trees cannot grow in tundras because the winters are so long and cold. The summers are short and cool. Certain plants, however, do live in the tundra. They include mosses, grasses, low shrubs, and grasslike plants called sedges *(SEHJ ihz)*.

There are two kinds of tundras—arctic and alpine. Arctic tundras lie near the Arctic Ocean in Greenland and the northern parts of Asia, Europe, and North America. Most arctic tundras are flat lands with many lakes. But some have mountains.

Few people live in arctic tundras. Inuit people (once called Eskimos) live in many parts of the tundra.

Arctic tundras have many kinds of wildlife. Geese, terns, and other birds live there during the spring and summer. Caribou, grizzly bears, musk oxen, reindeer, and wolves roam the land. Smaller animals include arctic foxes and hares. Polar bears, seals, and walruses are found along the coasts.

Arctic tundras have large amounts of minerals. These minerals include coal, natural gas, and oil as well as iron ore, lead, and zinc.

Alpine tundras are found throughout the world on mountains where it is too high and cold for trees. A variety of wildflowers and other plants may grow on alpine tundras during the summer months.

Other articles to read include: **Biome; Grass; Lichen; Moss; Shrub.**

Turnip

A turnip is a vegetable with a round root and green leaves. Turnip roots grow up to 3 inches (8 centimeters) across. They may be white or light yellow.

Turnips are healthful to eat. Their roots have vitamin C, and their leaves are rich in iron and vitamin A. People boil, mash, and serve turnip roots with sauce. The leaves are used in salads, soups, and stews.

Turnips grow quickly from seeds into plants that are ready for picking. Turnips are grown on farms and in home gardens throughout Europe and North America.

Other articles to read include:
Root; Vegetable.

Turnip plants have thick roots and large leaves that can be eaten.

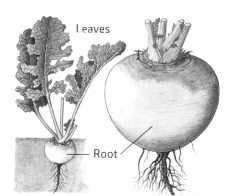

Leaves

Root

Vanilla

Vanilla is a climbing orchid. The plant produces seed pods. The pods of some vanilla plants provide a valuable flavoring. This flavoring also is called vanilla. It is used to flavor ice cream, candies, and other foods.

The vanilla vine has small rootlets. These rootlets attach the plant to trees. Vanilla produces fruit in a pod that measures 5 to 10 inches (13 to 25 centimeters) long. The pod contains an oily black pulp. The pulp contains many tiny black seeds. The pods are gathered when they are yellow-green. They are then dried. Drying shrinks the pod. It turns the pod a rich chocolate-brown color. The pod takes on the familiar flavor and aroma of vanilla. Vanilla is a relatively expensive flavoring. Food scientists have developed artificial vanilla flavors that cost less.

Other articles to read include: **Bean; Orchid.**

Vanilla plants produce long seed pods that provide the flavoring known as vanilla.

Vine

Vines grow along some type of support, such as a stone wall.

A vine is usually a name for a plant with a weak and flexible stem. Vines need some kind of support. Some vines can climb walls, trellises, or other plants. Other vines creep along the ground. Some vines have threadlike parts called *tendrils*. They wind these tendrils around their support. Other vines have disks that cling to the object they are climbing. Some kinds of vines are woody. For example, grapes have woody vines. Sometimes the woody vine can support itself. It is often difficult to tell the difference between such a vine and a shrub. Other vines are not woody. These include cucumbers, garden peas, and beans.

Other articles to read include: **Bean; Cucumber; Grape; Ivy; Liana; Pea; Stem; Wisteria.**

Violet

Violet

The violet is a type of flower known for its blue and purple blossoms. Violet blossoms are considered among the most attractive of all flowers. There are many kinds of violets. Some kinds are white or yellow. Violets grow throughout most of the world. They bloom in groups in early spring. Their leaves partly hide the five-petaled flowers. Each flower grows on a slender stalk.

Purple violets include the common meadow violet, also called the hooded violet, and the bird's-foot violet. The bird's-foot violet is named for its leaves, which are shaped like birds' feet. The dog violet got its name because it lacks a sweet smell. It is different from the dogtooth violet, a kind of lily. The pansy is a kind of violet commonly grown in gardens.

Other articles to read include: **Flower.**

Virus

A virus is a tiny thing that attacks the cells of living things. Ordinarily, viruses can be seen only with a powerful microscope. Viruses are shaped like rods, needles, or balls.

Viruses cause many diseases in plants, including crops. For example, viruses cause mosaic *(moh ZAY ihk)* diseases. These diseases cause leaves to have a speckled appearance. Mosaic diseases affect such crops as beans, blueberries, potatoes, and soybeans, among many others.

By itself, a virus is a lifeless thing. However, inside a living thing, a virus multiplies. The virus takes over a cell. It uses the materials inside the cell to live and make copies of itself. These virus copies spread to other cells. They cause disease by killing or damaging cells.

Many viruses, including mosaic viruses, are spread to plants by insects. When insects eat plants, the viruses get into the plant cells.

Other articles to read include: **Cell; Life.**

Mosaic viruses attack many kinds of plants, damaging the leaves.

Walnut

The walnut is a type of tree valued for its nuts and wood. The nuts are also called walnuts. There are several kinds of walnut trees.

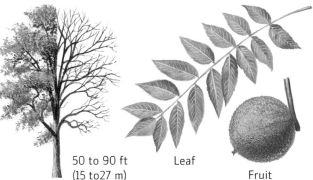 

50 to 90 ft (15 to 27 m)   Leaf   Fruit   Bark

Black walnut

The English walnut tree produces walnuts with the greatest value. It is a large, spreading tree that grows up to 100 feet (30 meters) tall. It has gray bark, large leaflets, and soft wood. The tree bears clusters of small flowers. It produces walnuts after flowering. The nuts have thin shells. They taste mild and sweet. They contain mostly fats and some proteins.

Black walnut trees are highly valued for their dark purplish-brown wood, used in furniture, gunstocks, and interior finishing. The nuts have a distinctive, rich flavor. But their shell, encased in a thick hull, is hard and thick. They are usually shelled before they are sold commercially.

Other articles to read include: **Nut; Tree; Wood.**

Wetland

The Everglades, in southern Florida, is one of the most interesting and unusual wetland areas in the world.

A wetland is a place where there is usually water near or above the surface of the ground. Wetlands are found throughout the world. Many kinds of plants and animals live in them.

There are several kinds of wetlands. They include bogs, fens, marshes, and swamps. Bogs and fens are usually found in cold places. They have large amounts of springy, spongy soil called peat *(peet).* The soil in bogs is high in acid but low in oxygen. Many kinds of mosses grow in bogs and fens. Marshes are flooded with water for most or all of the year. They are common in both warm and cold places. Marshes are found along the shores of lakes, ponds, rivers, and streams. They also are found along coasts where fresh water flows into the sea, such as at the mouths of rivers. Cattails, horsetails, and other plants grow in marshes. Swamps often develop in areas that are flooded only part of the year. Swamps have trees and shrubs.

Wetlands are important in nature. They provide a home for many plants and animals. Wetlands also help control flooding because they hold large amounts of water.

A peat bog in Col de Verde on Corsica, a French island in the Mediterranean Sea. Peat bogs have acidic, spongy soil.

A fen in Norfolk, England. Fens receive some water from the ground and the surface.

A salt marsh is along the coast of County Norfolk in eastern England. Salt marshes lie along coasts where fresh water flows into the sea. Grasses are often the most abundant plants in salt marshes.

A marsh in southern Quebec, Canada. Freshwater marshes develop where the water level is above the surface of the ground for most of the year. Freshwater marshes are usually along the shores of lakes, ponds, rivers, and streams where the water is shallow.

Many wetlands have been destroyed by human activities. Some swamps and marshes have been drained for farmland. Some wetlands have been polluted by industry. Today, many people are working to save the remaining wetlands in the world.

Other articles to read include: **Bog; Conservation; Marsh; Moss; Peat.**

A swamp near the Atchafalaya River in Louisiana in the southern United States. Swamps are usually found in areas where the land becomes flooded for part of the year. Trees and shrubs grow in most swamps.

304 Acknowledgments

The publisher gratefully acknowledges the following sources for photographs. All maps and illustrations unless otherwise noted are the exclusive property of World Book, Inc.

6-7 WORLD BOOK photo
8-11 © Shutterstock
12-13 © Shutterstock; © Thinkstock;
14-15 © Thinkstock; © Shutterstock; © Juergen Rittebach, Alamy; © Thomas Zimmerman, Getty; © David Hughes, Alamy
16-17 © Lon Diehl, Photoedit
18-23 © Shutterstock
14-25 © Shutterstock; © David G. Houser, Corbis
26-27 © Corbis; © Shutterstock
28-29 © Shutterstock; © Thinkstock
30-31 © Thinkstock
32-33 © Shutterstock; © Getty; © Thinkstock
34-35 © Sharon Smith, Bruce Coleman
36-37 © Kim Taylor, Bruce Coleman
38-39 © Ric Ergenbright, Corbis; © Keith Dannemiller, Corbis; © Phillippe Psila, Photo Researchers
40-41 © Animals Animals; © Kevin Schafer, Alamy; © Shutterstock
44-45 © Shutterstock; © Bryan Knox, Corbis
48-49 © Thinkstock; © Shutterstock
50-51 Library of Congress; © Shutterstock
52-53 © Carey, Photo Researchers; © Shutterstock
54-55 © Corbis; © Alamy
56-57 © Shutterstock
58-59 © Shutterstock; © Thinkstock; © Cathy Melloan
60-65 © Shutterstock
66-67 © Shutterstock; © Don Di Sante
68-69 © Thinkstock
70-71 © Alamy; Mark Godfrey, Image Works; © Phil Degginger, Alamy; Grand Canyon National Park
72-73 © Animals Animals; © Kevin Ebi, Alamy; © Ulrich Doering, Alamy
74-75 © Alamy; © Shutterstock
76-77 © Dreamstime; © Shutterstock;
78-79 © Shutterstock; © Corbis
80-81 © Shutterstock
82-83 © Shutterstock; Granger Collection
84-85 © Shutterstock
86-87 © Randy Wells, Corbis; © Gustavo Gilabert, Corbis; © Corbis
88-89 © Steve Bein, Corbis; Ann Hawthorne, Arcticphoto; © Shutterstock
90-91 © Shutterstock; © Simon Colmer, Alamy
92-93 © Michael Willis, Alamy; © Shutterstock
94-95 © Thinkstock
96-97 © Suzanne Long, Alamy; © Alamy
98-99 © Thinkstock; © Shutterstock; © M.I. Walker, Alamy
100-101 © Joseph Sohm, Corbis; © Craig Tuttle, Corbis; © Shutterstock
102-103 © Thinkstock; © Alamy; © Shutterstock; © Larry Lever, Grant Heilman
104-105 © Macduff Everton, Corbis; © Shutterstock; © Konrad Wothe, Minden

106-107 © Gary Kreyer, Grant Heilman; © Getty
108-109 © Thinkstock
110-111 © Stephen Krasemann, Photo Researchers; © Getty; © David Muench, Corbis
112-113 © Andrew Brown, Corbis; © Craig Tuttle, Corbis
114-115 © Julie Houck, Corbis; © Wolfgang Kaehler, Corbis; © Joseph Sohm, Corbis
116-117 © Bob Krist, Corbis; © Shutterstock; © Raymond Gehman, Corbis
118-119 © Shutterstock; © Thinkstock
122-123 © Sidney Moulds, Photo Researchers; © Nigel Cattlin, Photo Researchers; © Michler, Photo Researchers; © Michael Gadomski, Photo Researchers
124-125 © Alamy; © Shutterstock
126-127 © Shutterstock
128-129 © Giuseppe Mazza; © Thinkstock
130-131 © Thinkstock
132-133 © Nigel Cattlin, Photo Researchers
134-135 © Shutterstock
136-137 © Tom Bean, Corbis; © Photo Researchers; © Liu Quanju, Imaginechina; © Corbis; © Walter Edwards, Getty
138-139 © Charles O. Cecil, Alamy
140-143 © Shutterstock
144-145 © Getty
146-147 © Mark Richards, PhotoEdit
148-149 © Thinkstock
150-151 © Russ Merne, Alamy; © Shutterstock
152-153 Arizona Photographic Assoc.; © Andrew McKim, Masterfile; © Alamy
154-155 © Tom Mareschal, Alamy; © Thinkstock
158-159 © Alamy; © Shutterstock
160-161 © Shutterstock; © Thinkstock
162-163 © Shutterstock
164-165 © Shutterstock; © Alamy
168-169 © Thinkstock
170-171 © Getty; © Thinkstock
172-173 National Park Service
174-175 © Thinkstock; © Valerie Giles, Photo Researchers; Image Works
176-177 © Corbis; © S. Fraser, Photo Researchers
178-179 © Shutterstock; © Thinkstock; © David Munns, Photo Researchers
180-181 © Matt Meadows, Peter Arnold; © Cordelia Molloy, Photo Researchers; © Shutterstock; © George Lepp, Corbis
182-183 © Ed Reschke, Peter Arnold; © Alamy; © Thinkstock; © Getty; © Thinkstock
186-187 © Shutterstock
188-189 © Tom Bean, Alamy; © Alamy; © Alex Bartell, Photo Researchers
190-191 © Getty; © Alamy
192-193 © Shutterstock; © Jean-Paul Chassenet, Photo Researchers
194-195 © Loren McIntyre, Woodfin Camp

196-197 © Alamy; © Michael Fogden, Bruce Coleman; © Pascal Alix, Photo Researchers
202-203 © Kit Houghton, Corbis; © Shutterstock
204-205 © Shutterstock
206-207 © Dan Budnik, Woodfin Camp
208-209 © Shutterstock
210-211 © Humberto Cupas, Alamy; © Dreamstime
212-213 © Bruce Coleman
214-215 NFB Phototheque
218-219 © Brent Kent, Animals Animals
220-221 © Shutterstock
222-223 © Alamy; © Nigel Cattlin, Alamy
224-225 © Jerome Wexler, Photo Researchers; © James Robinson, Photo Researchers; © Shutterstock
226-227 © Shutterstock
228-229 © Tom Bean, Corbis; © Eric V. Grave, Photo Researchers; Jerome Wexler, Photo Researchers
230-231 © Kjell B. Sandved, Photo Researchers; © Thinkstock
232-233 © Joanne Lotter, Tom Stack; © Superstock; © Glyn Davies, International Centre for Conservation Education; © Shutterstock
234-235 © Shutterstock; © Alamy; © Sophie De Wilde, Photo Researchers
236-237 © Alamy
238-239 © Shutterstock
242-243 © Shutterstock; © Masterfile; © Harald Theissen, Alamy
244-245 © Shutterstock; © Getty
246-247 © Shutterstock
248-249 © Morton Beebe, Corbis
250-251 © Nigel Cattlin, Photo Researchers
252-253 © Shutterstock; © Charles Winters, Photo Researchers
254-255 © Bilagentur Waldhaeusl, Alamy; © Leigh Smith, Alamy; © Shutterstock
258-259 © Shutterstock; © Thinkstock
260-261 © Robert Pickett, Corbis
262-263 © Hale Observatories; © Alamy; © Marko König, Alamy
264-265 © Shutterstock
266-267 © Joy Spurr, Bruce Coleman; © Alamy; © Shutterstock
268-269 © Simon Fraser, Photo Researchers; © Shutterstock; © Jeremy Horner, Corbis
272-273 © Getty
278-279 © Shutterstock
280-281 © Stephen Kraseman, Photo Researchers; © Galen Rowell, Corbis; © Dreamstime
282-283 © Peter Titmuss, Alamy; © David Sieren, Visuals Unlimited
284-285 © Shutterstock; © Shutterstock; © Alamy
286-287 © Adam Jones, Visuals Unlimited; © Shutterstock
288-289 © Alamy; © G.P. Bowater, Alamy; © Alamy; © Mark Tomalty, IPNstock; © David Hoffman, Alamy; © Robert Francis, Alamy
290-291 © Aaron Ferster, Photo Researchers
292-293 © Shutterstock; WORLD BOOK Photo; © Stanely Flegler, Visuals Unlimited
294-295 © Photo Researchers; © SuperStock
296-297 © Dreamstime